Islam and International Criminal Law and Justice

Tallyn Gray
(editor)

2018
Torkel Opsahl Academic EPublisher
Brussels

This and other publications in TOAEP's *Nuremberg Academy Series* may be openly accessed and downloaded through the web site http://www.toaep.org/ which uses Persistent URLs for all publications it makes available (such PURLs will not be changed). This publication was published on 16 November 2018.

ISBNs: 978-82-8348-188-4 (print) and 978-82-8348-189-1 (e-book).

Dedicated to the memory of M. Cherif Bassiouni,
for his inspiring contributions to international criminal law

FOREWORD BY THE SERIES EDITOR

The *Nuremberg Academy Series* was established in April 2017 by the International Nuremberg Principles Academy, in co-operation with the Centre for International Law Research and Policy, to produce high-quality open access publications on international law published by the Torkel Opsahl Academic EPublisher ('TOAEP'). I have the honour to serve as the Series Editor.

The Series seeks to cover relevant and topical areas that are under-researched or require renewed attention. The Series includes work that is inter- or multi-disciplinary and brings together academics and practitioners focused on practical and innovative applications of international criminal law. Grounded in the legacy of the Nuremberg Principles – the foundation of contemporary international criminal law – it addresses persistent and pressing legal issues and explores the twenty-first century challenges encountered in combating impunity for core international crimes.

The first volume in the Series concerned the deterrent effect of international criminal tribunals. This, the second book in the Series, has emerged from a panel theme and workshop that took place during the Nuremberg Forum, the major annual conference organised by the International Nuremberg Principles Academy, in 2015. It examined the universality of the Nuremberg Principles in a globalised world, concentrating in particular on Islamic perspectives and interrogating the relevancy and applicability of the Nuremberg Principles to notions of justice in the Muslim world. Encouraged by robust debates on multiple themes, indicating a need for further study, the International Nuremberg Principles Academy convened a roundtable of leading experts in 2016, drawn from academia, legal practice, non-governmental organisations, and international organisations. Its brief was to deliberate theoretical and practical concerns related to accountability for core international crimes arising from current conflicts in the Muslim world, with the aim that the event would lead to a significant volume.

The experts discussed questions of legitimacy and acceptance of international criminal justice; the role of local and global institutions intended to ascertain accountability for atrocity crimes; the inter-relationship between Islamic law and international criminal law; and moral, philosophical and political encounters relating to prosecution of these core crimes. Their efforts provide fresh thinking on contemporary issues in a way that is both insightful and practical, especially to gauge cross-cultural consensus on tackling impunity for core international crimes.

It is with great satisfaction that this anthology is published in the Series. The topic 'Islam and International Criminal Law and Justice' has become a major concern in the past years among those committed to the realisation of international justice following mass human rights violations. The book contains valuable chapters by several leading experts. Given its focus on the interplay of theory and practice, the book makes a contribution by assembling a wealth of views and arguments and by opening avenues for constructive dialogue and sustained engagement with different legal traditions. It is hoped that, as an open access publication, this volume will be widely read by scholars, students and practitioners in the coming years, in particular in the Muslim world.

The International Nuremberg Principles Academy takes this opportunity to thank the editor, the contributors and TOAEP for their co-operation.

Dr. Viviane Dittrich
Nuremberg Academy Series Editor
Deputy Director, International Nuremberg Principles Academy

EDITOR'S PREFACE

Thanks first go to the International Nuremberg Principles Academy for advancing this book project. As the project convener, I would like to thank both the former and current directors of the Nuremberg Academy, Bernd Borchardt and Klaus Rackwitz, for giving considerable support. Additionally, my thanks go to the Advisory Council of the Nuremberg Academy for backing this project. I would like to express my gratitude to Dr. Godfrey Musila, former Research Director of the Nuremberg Academy, who was in charge of organising the panel discussion focusing on the universality of the Nuremberg Principles in the Islamic world as a topic during the 2015 Nuremberg Forum. I must thank Dr. Viviane Dittrich, Salim Amin, Jolana Makraiová and Eduardo Toledo at the Nuremberg Academy for their comments and suggestions. Many thanks also to the Torkel Opsahl Academic EPublisher ('TOAEP') for their work.

TOAEP has adopted the Transliteration System approved at the 10th International Congress of Orientalists held in Geneva in 1894, and that has been implemented for Arabic terms in this book (except for a few terms like 'Islam' or 'Islamic' which have a universally recognised spelling in English). The publisher also prefers Professor Arthur John Arberry's classic translation of the *Qur'án*, *The Koran Interpreted*, first published in 1955. It has been used throughout the text except in Chapter 6 and for 2:190 in Chapter 4. Thanks go to Judge Adel Maged, Moojan Momen, Fathi M. Abdel Raouf Ahmed and Fadi Khalil for advice on the Glossary and the transliteration. Sincere thanks also go to TOAEP Editor Manek Minhas for her copy-editing of the volume and Vincent LEE for his editorial assistance.

Furthermore, I also thank the external reviewers, especially Dr. Saira Orakzai for her mapping report and her work on the Glossary. I also extend my deep gratitude to Professor Shaheen Sardar Ali and Professor Mathias Rohe supporting this project as editorial advisors.

While not all of the participants at the conference from which this book has emerged have been able to contribute, I would like to also mention the invaluable conference debates that helped to structure this volume and thank all participants.

Finally, I take this opportunity to show appreciation to the authors of this volume for their dedication, time and patience.

Tallyn Gray
Postdoctoral Fellow, University of Westminster and Universidade de São Paulo Faculty of Law

GLOSSARY

'abd	a slave or servant
'adl	justice
'amdan	intentionally
'ámm	general
'ilm	science
'ilm al-fiqh	science of jurisprudence
'ulama'	jurists, scholars
'urf	customs or recurring practices acceptable to people of sound nature
al-ḍararu yuzál	hardship/harm must be removed
ahl al-Sunnah wa'l-jamá'ah	those who adhere to the *Sunnah* traditions and unite in following it, generally the *Sunnís* (*vis-à-vis Shí'ah*)
al-'áda muḥakkamah	cultural usage shall have the weight of law
al-adillah al-kulliyah	the overall evidence, referring in Islamic *Sharí'ah* to the cherished source of Islamic *Sharí'ah* that leads to respected rulings and opinions
al-aṣl fi'l-ashyáh al-ibáhah	permissibility is the original norm
al-bayyinah 'alá al-mudda'í wa al-yamín 'alá man ankar	the burden of proof is on the claimant and the oath is on the one who denies
al-maṣlaḥah	the interest
al-mashaqqatu tajlib al-taysír	hardship begets ease

al-moṣalaḥah	well-being, conciliation, settlement, peace
al-qawá'id al-fiqhíyyah	legal maxims
al-qawá'id al-fiqhíyyah al-aslíyah	original legal maxims
al-qawá'id al-fiqhíyyah al-kulíyah	overall legal maxims
al-qawá'id al-uṣúlíyyah	fundamental rules on legal/doctrinal methodology
al-umúr bi-maqáṣidhá	acts are judged by their objectives and purposes
al-yaqín lá yazálu bi'l-shak	certainty is not overruled by doubt
amán	tranquility, peacefulness, relief
amr	matter
amr bi al-ma'rúf wa nahy 'an al-munkar	commanding virtue and prevention of vice
asbáb al-nuzúl	circumstances of revelation
áyát	verses of the *Qur'án*
a'ẓam 'inda Alláhi 'azza wa-jalla jurman	the greatest offences as regarded by God
aẓ-ẓulm wa-'l-'udwan	injustice and aggression
baghí	transgression or rebellion against the legitimate leader through the use of force
bayyinah	physical and logical evidence
birr	probity, righteousness, good acts
bugháh	armed rebels/transgressors against the legitimate leader
caliph	ruler of the Muslim nation in medieval Islam
dár al-ḥarb	jurisdictions at war with the Muslim nation

dár al-Islam	jurisdictions under the rule of the Muslim nation
diyah	blood money
diyát	blood money (plural of *diyah*)
fa-'innahu 'udwán	then it is an aggression/enmity
fániyan	frail, mortal
faqíh al-uṣúl	jurist specialised in principles of jurisprudence
fasád	corruption, mischief
fasád fí al-'arḍ	corruption/mischief in the earth, public corruption/mischief
fatwá	expert legal opinion
fiqh	jurisprudence
fitnah	temptation, public uncertainty
fuqahah al-uṣúl	jurists specialised in principles of jurisprudence (plural of *faqíh al-uṣúl*)
furú'	details of jurisprudence
ḥadd	punishment prescribed in the *Qur'án*
ḥadí<u>th</u>	prophetic tradition/narration
ḥajj	pilgrimage to Mecca
Ḥanafí	a *Sunní* school of Islamic law named after Abú Ḥanífa An-Nu'man Ibn Thábit
Ḥanbalí	a *Sunní* school of Islamic law named after Ahmad Ibn Ḥanbal
ḥaqíqí	real, true
ḥarám	forbidden/prohibited by Islam
ḥirábah	highway robbery/banditry

ḥudúd	punishments prescribed in the *Qur'án* (plural of *ḥadd*)
Hijrah	the journey of the Prophet from Mecca to Medina
i'ráḍ	turning away
ijmá'	consensus of opinion
ijtihád	individual/independent legal reasoning
ikráh	duress, coercion
innamá al-a'mál bil-niyyát	acts are valued in accordance with their underlying intentions
iṣmat al-anbiyá	prophetic infallibility
Ismá'ílí	a branch/sect of the *Shí'ah* denomination of Islam
isnád	first part of a *ḥadíth*, in which the chain of transmission of the *ḥadíth* is given
istiḥsán	juristic preference, application of discretion in Islamic law, literally meaning "that which is good or agreeable for all"
istiṣḥáb	presumption of continuity
jáhiliyyah	pre-Islamic period, often has the connotation that this was a historical era before Islam where aberrance and perversity were predominant in the Arab Peninsula
jawámi' al-kalim	conciseness of the Prophet's *ḥadíth*
jihád	any form of struggle in the way of God, particularly just war
jizyah	tax paid by non-Muslims (*vis-à-vis zakah* paid by Muslims)

káfir	unbeliever, infidel
kafálah	akin to foster-care
kuffár	unbelievers, infidels (plural of *káfir*)
kháṣ	specific
Khawárij	an Islamic sect that left the mainstream of Islam, often referred to as those who rebelled against Imám Ali Ibn Abí-Taleb, the Fourth *Rashíd Caliph*
lá ḍarar wá-lá dirár	injury/harm shall not be inflicted or reciprocated
lá yalḥaquhum al-ghawth	helpless and cannot be rescued
lá yujhaz 'alá jaríḥihum	their injured may not be killed
lá yutba' mudbiruhum	not to be followed from their rear (for killing or injuring)
laysa naskhan bal huwa min qism al-mansí	there is no abrogation, but rather, it is part of forgetting
Málikí	a *Sunní* school of law named after Málik Ibn Anas
ma'rúf	that which is good
madháhib	schools of thought in Islamic jurisprudence (plural of *madhhab*)
madhhab	school of thought in Islamic jurisprudence
mafsadah	a cause of *fasád*
majází	metaphorical
man'ah	resistance, force
maqáṣid	purposes, objectives (plural of *maqaṣad*)
maqaṣad	purpose, objectives

maqáṣid al-Sharí'ah	objective and purpose of Islamic *Sharí'ah*
maqṣúd	specific purpose, intention
maṣádir	sources
maṣlaḥah mursalah	unrestricted considerations of public interest (considered a source of *Sharí'ah* in cases where no special provision is made in the *Qur'án* and/or *Sunnah*)
matn	body, text
mu'áhadah	treaty
mu'áhadát	treaties (plural of *mu'áhadah*)
mu'tadilún	moderate (Muslims)
muḥáribún	highway robbers, or literally "those who fight"
mughálabah	combat, verbal quarrel, forcefully
mujtahid	independent reasoner/jurist
munáẓarah	debate
muqbilún	attackers
murtaddún	apostates
mushrikún	polytheists
naṣṣ	text, provision
naskh	abrogation/repeal of a provision
qáḍí	judge
qánún	law
qadhf	slander, defamation, groundless accusation of fornication/adultery
qawá'id	rules
qira'át	readings
qiṣáṣ	retribution

qitál	fighting
qiyás	analogy
Qur'án	the book of God
quṭṭá 'uṭ-ṭaríq	highway robbery, banditry, brigandage
ra'y	opinion
Rabb	Lord
riddah	apostasy
ṣabr	forbearance, patience
ṣafḥ	pardon
ṣaḥábah	companions of the Prophet
salám	peace and submission to God
sariqah	theft
S̲h̲áfi'í	a *Sunní* school of Islamic law named after Al-S̲h̲áfi'í
s̲h̲arb al-k̲h̲amr	drinking alcohol
S̲h̲arí'ah	the path or way, referring to a body of Islamic religious law
s̲h̲awkah	might, power
S̲h̲í'i	followers of the *S̲h̲í'ah* denomination of Islam
s̲h̲íbh 'amd	quasi-intentional
s̲h̲ubhah	doubt
sirah	biography of an exemplary person
siyásah	political expediency/politics
siyásah al-S̲h̲arí'ah	governance exercised in accordance with *S̲h̲arí'ah*
siyar	an early system of Islamic international law

súrah	chapter of the *Qur'án*
Sunnah	prophetic tradition, the sayings and practices of the Prophet Muḥammad
Sunní	follower of the *Sunní* denomination of Islam
ta'áwwun	co-operation
ta'áwwun alá al-birr wa-al-taqwá	co-operation for goodness and righteousness
ta'zír	discretionary punishment
ṭághút	idol/false god/evil
Takfír	excommunication/accusation of unbelief in Islam
taqlíd	imitation
tawḥíd	unity of God
ta'wíl	speculative interpretation
Twelvers (or *al-Ithná 'ashariyyah*)	a branch/sect of the *Shí'ah* denomination of Islam
ummah	community/nation of Muslims
umúr	matters (plural of *amr*)
úṣúl	fundamental guiding principles
úṣúl al-fiqh	fundamental guiding principles of Islamic jurisprudence
wahy	revelation
Wahhábi	follower of the *Wahhábi* denomination of Islam
wa-lá ta'tadú	do not commit aggression
waqf	religious endowment
yufarraqu bayn al-'ilmi baynahu idhá thabata yaqínan	knowledge that is based on mere probability is to be differentiated from knowledge that is based on certainty

yuḥáribún	literally, those who fight or make war (upon God and His Messenger)
ẓahir	manifest
ẓann	opinion (as opposed to fact), uncertainty
zakáh	religious taxes/alms
Zaydí	a branch/sect of the *Shí'ah* denomination of Islam, law named after Zayd ibn 'Alí
ziná'	sexual relations outside marriage
ẓulm	injustice

TABLE OF CONTENTS

Foreword by the Series Editor .... *i*

Editor's Preface .... *iii*

Glossary .... *v*

1. Introduction 1
   By Tallyn Gray
   - 1.1. Origins and Purpose of this Book 1
   - 1.2. Situating this Book 5
   - 1.3. Structure of this Book 9
   - 1.4. Thinking About the Future – Aware of the Past and the Present 14

2. The Principal Sources of Islamic Law 15
   By Onder Bakircioglu
   - 2.1. Introduction 15
   - 2.2. Primary Sources 16
     - 2.2.1. The *Qur'án* 16
     - 2.2.2. The *Sunnah* 25
   - 2.3. Secondary Sources 32
     - 2.3.1. Critical Thinking (*Ijtihád*) 34
     - 2.3.2. Juristic Consensus (*Ijmá'*) 36
     - 2.3.3. The Temporary Ending of Critical Thinking 39
   - 2.4. Conclusion: Re-opening the Door for Critical Thinking 41

3. Islamic Socio-Legal Norms and International Criminal Justice in Context: Advancing an 'Object and Purpose' cum '*Maqáṣid*' Approach 45
   By Mashood A. Baderin
   - 3.1. Introduction 45

3.2. 'Object and Purpose' and '*Maqáṣid*' as Comparable Normative Principles 48
3.3. The Basis of International Criminal Justice in Relation to Islamic Socio-Legal Norms 54
3.3.1. Islamic Socio-Legal Connection with International Humanitarian Law 55
3.3.2. Islamic Socio-Legal Connection with International Human Rights Law 60
3.3.3. Islamic Socio-Legal Connection with International Criminal Law 63
3.4. Advancing a Holistic Perspective of International Criminal Justice in Relation to the 'Object and Purpose' and '*Maqáṣid*' Principles 67
3.4.1. Social Dimension of International Criminal Justice 68
3.4.2. Moral Dimension of International Criminal Justice 73
3.4.3. Political Dimension of International Criminal Justice 75
3.4.4. Legal Dimension of International Criminal Justice 78
3.5. Conclusion 80

4. Islamic Law and the Limits of Military Aggression 83
By Asma Afsaruddin

4.1. Exegeses of *Qur'án* 2:190 84
4.2. Survey of Juridical Works 86
4.2.1. *Máliki* Views on *Jihád* as Contained in *Al-Mudawwana Al-Kubrá* by Málik Ibn Anas 87
4.2.2. *Sháfi'í* Views on *Jihád* 88
4.2.3. *Al-Ḥáwí Al-Kabír* by Abú Al-Ḥasan Al-Máwardí 88
4.3. Modern Scholars and Jurists 90
4.4. Conclusion 98

5. *Jus in Bello* and General Principles Related to Warfare According to Islamic Law 101
By Abdelrahman Afifi

5.1. Introduction 101
5.2. General Definitions 104
5.2.1. Meaning of *Sharí'ah* 104
5.2.2. Primary Sources of Islamic Law 105
5.2.3. 'Legal Maxims' (*Al-Qawá'id Al-Fiqhíyyah*) 105
5.2.4. *Siyásah Al-Sharí'ah* and *Maqáṣid Al-Sharí'ah* 106
5.2.5. *Asbáb Al-Nuzúl* 106
5.3. General Principles Governing Warfare under Islamic Law 107

5.3.1. Non-Aggression 107
5.3.2. Proportionality 109
5.3.3. Justice 109
5.3.4. Amnesty 110
5.4. *Jus in Bello* and Islamic Law 110
5.4.1. Categories of Enemy Non-Combatant Not to be Targeted 111
5.4.2. Further Prohibitions and Rules of Conduct in War 114
5.4.3. 'I Give You Ten Rules': Specific Orders for Conduct in War 117
5.5. Conclusion 118

6. Non-International Armed Conflicts under Islamic Law: The Case of ISIS 121

By Ahmed Al-Dawoody

6.1. Introduction 121
6.2. Fighting Against *Al-Bugháh* 123
6.3. Fighting Against *Al-Khawárij* 130
6.4. Fighting Against *Al-Muḥáribún* 133
6.5. The Case of ISIS 136
6.6. Conclusion 141

7. Arab and Islamic States' Practice: The *Sharí'ah* Clause and its Effects on the Implementation of the Rome Statute of the International Criminal Court 145

By Siraj Khan

7.1. Introduction 145
7.2. The Convergence of the Islamic Legal Horizon with International Law 145
7.3. The *Sharí'ah* Law Clause 154
7.4. Case Studies and Recent Developments 157
7.4.1. Egypt 158
7.4.2. Palestine 162
7.4.3. Tunisia 163
7.4.4. The Maldives 164
7.4.5. Sudan 166
7.5. Conclusion 168

8. What is the Measure of 'Universality'? Critical Reflections on 'Islamic' Criminal Law and Muslim State Practice *vis-à-vis* the Rome Statute and the International Criminal Court 175
By Shaheen Sardar Ali and Satwant Kaur Heer

8.1. Introduction 175
8.2. Islamic Criminal Law: A Brief Contextual Journey 177
8.3. Muslim State Practice in National, International Law and Treaty Formation: Connecting the Dots 183
8.4. Statements of Support from Muslim States for the Draft Rome Statute: Token 'Universality' or Shared Criminal Law Principles? 190
8.5. Protecting National Interests through Principles of Complementarity: A 'Muslim' Ploy or Wider State Practice? ... 191
8.6. Political and Historical Factors Influencing Statements of Participants: Call to Look Beyond Western Legal Systems for Genuine Universality 192
8.7. Limiting the International Criminal Law Menu? The Internal/External Conflict Debate 195
8.8. Claiming Universality through Inclusivity: Some Concluding Remarks 197

9. Is There a Place for Islamic Law within the Applicable Law of the International Criminal Court? 201
By Mohamed Elewa Badar

9.1. Introduction 201
9.2. *Sharí'ah* Introduction to Islamic Law (*Sharí'ah*) 203
9.2.1. The Application of Islamic Law in Muslim-Majority States Today 204
9.2.2. Sources of Islamic Law: *Sharí'ah* and *Fiqh* 206
9.2.3. The Leading Schools of Islamic Jurisprudence (*Madháhib*) 208
9.2.4. Categories of Crimes in Islamic Criminal Law 209
9.3. Core Principles of Islamic Law Corresponding to Core Principles of International Law 213

9.3.1. Islamic Legal Maxims (*Al-Qawá'id Al-Fiqhíyyah*)...... 213
9.3.2. Principle of Legality and Non-Retroactivity 217
9.3.3. Presumption of Innocence 220
9.3.4. *Mens Rea* 223
9.3.5. Standards Used for Determining Intention in Murder Cases 225
9.3.6. Duress and Superior Orders.. 226
9.3.7. Rulers are Not Above the Law: Irrelevance of Official Capacity-Immunity.. 229
9.4. General Remarks and Conclusion 230

Index 233

TOAEP Team 241

Other Volume in the Nuremberg Academy Series 243

1

Introduction

Tallyn Gray*

1.1. Origins and Purpose of this Book

The international community is witness to massive violations of human rights throughout the world, potentially amounting to international crimes. This book focuses its attention on the Muslim world. All those involved in the book's development have been cognisant of the times during which this collection of essays is being published. The situations in Syria, Iraq, Nigeria, Libya, Lebanon, Afghanistan, the allegations of genocide against the Rohingya Muslims in Myanmar, and the atrocities committed by the so-called 'Islamic State' of Iraq and Syria ('ISIS'), to name some serious examples, present the institutions and practitioners of international criminal law with a complex set of potential cases and challenges for future undertakings in tackling impunity and upholding the rule of international criminal law.

These challenges are compounded by the problem that some of these countries – for example, Syria, Iraq, and Myanmar – are not States Parties to the Statute of the International Criminal Court ('ICC Statute').[1] It is in that knowledge that this book has been conceived, aware that today's crisis is tomorrow's reckoning. International criminal law has already been a significant tool for bringing a measure of justice to some Muslim minority groups, who have been targets of genocide and/or mass murder. For example, the International Criminal Tribunal for the former Yugoslavia ('ICTY') and the on-going trials at the Extraordinary Chambers in the Courts of

---

* Dr. **Tallyn Gray** is a post-doctoral fellow at the Faculty of Law, University of São Paulo, Brazil, and a Fellow at the Westminster Law and Theory Centre, University of Westminster, United Kingdom. He is a specialist on transitional justice, international criminal law, genocide studies, legal anthropology, and Buddhist and Islamic studies in the Asia-Pacific region.

1 Julian D. Veintmilla, "Islamic Law and War Crimes Trials: The Possibility and Challenges of a War Crimes Tribunal against the Assad Regime and ISIL", in *Cornell International Law Journal*, 2016, vol. 49, no. 2, p. 512.

Cambodia ('ECCC') demonstrate that international criminal law has offered a conduit to access justice for Muslim peoples, in these cases Muslim Bosniaks and the Cham respectively. Hence, mindful of the alleged and proven core crimes committed within and towards the global community of Muslims (the *ummah*),[2] an exploration of the role of international criminal law in tackling such crimes in the Islamic world is a theme that demands attention.

In undertaking this theme, important considerations emerge: the chief consideration, perhaps, is that Islamic law is employed to varying levels and degrees in many majority Muslim countries. Islamic law is not a single, uniform body of law but is divergent, complex and nuanced with different groupings, theories and practices.[3]

However, regardless of how Islamic law is employed, it is nevertheless one of the world's most utilised 'legal families', central to the lives, laws and ethical structures of huge populations who have experienced mass violence and atrocity. Thus, when discussing international criminal law in relation to the *ummah,* the question of the legitimacy and acceptance of international criminal law in these settings, as well as the aptness and role of local institutions potentially mandated to ascertain accountability and deliver justice after atrocities, becomes evident. Additionally, when discussing accountability for international crimes in the Islamic world, a wider set of moral, philosophical, and political dimensions emerge. Key to these is the relationship between the idea of justice and the practice of law across cultural and legal plurality.

This book has its origins in an international expert conference and ensuing project organised and supported by the International Nuremberg Principles Academy ('Nuremberg Academy'). The Nuremberg Academy is an institution uniquely positioned to facilitate addressing these themes. As a foundation dedicated to the fight against impunity for universally recognised core international crimes (genocide, crimes against humanity, war crimes, and the crime of aggression), the Nuremberg Academy is at the forefront of tackling major debates, questions and challenges emergent

---

2 Transliteration of Arabic terms throughout this volume follows the system approved at the 10th International Congress of Orientalists held in Geneva in 1894.

3 Werner Menski, *Comparative Law in a Global Context: The Legal Systems of Asia and Africa*, 2nd ed., Cambridge University Press, Cambridge, 2006, pp. 20–21.

from the pursuit of sustainable peace through justice and the promotion of international criminal justice and human rights.

The focus of the Nuremberg Academy's Annual Forum in 2015 was 'The Nuremberg Principles 70 Years Later: Contemporary Challenges'. At this forum, both a panel and a workshop addressed the topic of 'Universality of the Nuremberg Principles from an Islamic Perspective'. The debates and discussion at these events raised important issues, which the participants and the Nuremberg Academy opted to explore further in a dedicated project on the subject of 'International Criminal Law and Justice and Islam'.

In October 2016, the Nuremberg Academy convened an expert roundtable on 'Islam and International Criminal Justice'. This roundtable brought together ground-breaking scholars and practitioners to deliberate the theoretical and practical concerns related to accountability for core international crimes arising from conflicts in the Muslim world. The principal aim and accomplishment of this expert meeting was to bring together the leading authors who have published on and worked within the field of Islam and international criminal law, and indeed have been engaging each another's work for years, but had never previously been gathered together in one place or appeared together in the same publication. As such, this gathering was not to dictate the terms of their research, but rather to provide a space and a broad thematic focus for them to discuss their long-established knowledge of the topic from the wide range of traditions and experience from which they originate.

The Nuremberg Academy asked these experts to contemplate in their presentations and contributions certain key questions, including but not limited to the following: What are the sources of Islamic law that deal with issues around war crimes, crimes against humanity, and genocide? Can Islamic jurisprudence and international criminal law communicate in terms of common goals? What is the impact of the plurality of the Islamic legal traditions on Muslim state practice and international criminal law and what are the implications in terms of authority and legitimacy? Is international criminal law truly universal or so rooted in Eurocentrism that claims to universality are unsustainable? What does it mean for the legitimacy of international trials against Muslims? What possibilities and challenges would prosecution of atrocities in recent conflicts in the Islamic world present in the theory and practice of Islamic law and international criminal law? What can be done to increase the number of Muslim States Parties to the ICC Statute?

Several key points emerged from the final discussion of the participants at the roundtable, which feed into the development of this volume. In particular, two powerful and inter-related myths need to be addressed. Firstly, within the Muslim world, the idea that international criminal law is a 'Western' concept – that is, something imposed on Islamic societies by Western interests, rather than a system that complements, enhances, and works in tandem with the ethical traditions of Islamic jurisprudence and philosophy. International criminal law is a body of developing law in which the Muslim world can confidently claim ownership and stakeholder involvement, as much as any other culture and legal tradition. In order to address this, a vital and appropriate response should emanate from Islamic scholars. In this regard, *fiqh* (Islamic jurisprudence) needs to be robustly articulated, demonstrating how international criminal law norms and *fiqh* synergise. Simultaneously, *fiqh* can, and should, be observed within international criminal law as one of the great and important legal traditions.

The second myth, emergent from International Relations theory,[4] is that of a 'clash of civilisations', that is, the idea that Islamic civilisation is inherently incompatible with the concepts of democracy, human rights and, it may be argued by extension, international criminal law. The workshop participants and those who have contributed to this collection reject this premise entirely. Instead, they clearly emphasise the common ground between civilisations, philosophies and legal traditions, and demonstrate the Islamic civilisational synergy with the universalism and legality of international criminal law, which transpires through a process of intercultural dialogue.

The roundtable participants agreed that this was not only a pressing topic, but that the research presentations of the roundtable participants dovetailed well and that a wider audience would benefit from the publication of a serious expert-authored volume on the topic of Islam and international criminal law. The result is the present book.

---

4 Most notably advanced by Samuel P. Huntington, *The Clash of Civilizations and the Remaking of World Order*, Simon & Schuster, New York, 1996.

1.2. Situating this Book

The chapters explore how the Islamic legal family finds common ground with international criminal law, and vice versa, in tackling the core crimes. The interplay of theory and practice is a central focus. While all the authors are legal scholars or practitioners, they are also alert to developments in critical legal studies and to the significance of the interdisciplinary turn in the social sciences. Hence, this collection is not uncritical of either international criminal law or Islamic law in theory and practice. The book affirms a mutual spirit within international criminal law and Islamic legal principles; but it does not shy away from the problems of either. This book is not an exercise to change or challenge the core principles of international criminal law, but an endeavour to clarify a holistic and accepted understanding of international criminal law's core principles across cultural difference and discourses. The chapters present a way to think about law in the context of a globalised world.

Taking a cue from Werner Menski, these chapters are produced in a spirit of awareness that universalised outlooks of modern international criminal law institutions, jurisprudence and the concept of justice itself need to be cognisant of positivistic and Eurocentric preconceptions that potentially inhibit the acceptance of international criminal law in the *ummah*, and therefore its ability to deal with the troubles of a pluralistic world.[5] Similarly, within the Islamic tradition, there is some necessity for self-reflection on legal responses to human rights violations and on the place of Islamic law in the context of increasingly internationalised consolidation around globalising norms. The prolific and widely cited Islamic legal scholar Abdullahi Ahmed An-Na'im made this point in the mid-1980s, arguing that modern Muslims should endeavour towards reform in order to "reconcile the *Sharí'ah* with present day human rights requirements and expectations";[6] he noted that "early [Muslim] jurists […] did an excellent job and succeeded in serving the needs and aspirations of their community for centuries", but that "by the same token […] it should be open to modern Muslim jurists to state and interpret the law for their own

5 Menski, 2006, p. 613, see *supra* note 3.

6 Abdullahi Ahmed An-Na'im, "A Modern Approach to Human Rights in Islam: Foundations and Implications for Africa", in Claude E. Welch and Ronald I. Metzler (eds.), *Human Rights and Development in Africa*, State University of New York Press, Albany, 1984, pp. 76–77.

contemporaries even if such a statement and interpretation were to be in some respects different from the inherited wisdom".[7]

Perhaps the most important foundational work on Islam and international criminal law is that of the late M. Cherif Bassiouni; his *The Shari'a and Islamic Criminal Justice in Time of War and Peace*[8] is the established introduction to Islamic criminal legal concepts and their compatibility with modern international criminal law and international humanitarian law.[9] Bassiouni differentiates modern Muslim jurists into three archetypes: 'traditionalist-fundamentalists' are literalists who apply the letter of the *Qur'án* and seek "to apply the solutions of earlier times to complex contemporary problems";[10] then there are 'traditionalist-reformists' who seek out Qur'ánic-based solutions to modern problems, often requiring that non-scriptural knowledge also be used to an extent in devising solutions for appropriate modern application; finally, 'progressives'[11] make innovative interpretations that do not require a link to past practice and knowledge.[12] These are useful categories to bear in mind whilst reading these chapters – not in order that the reader should classify the authors into these groups, but to create a framework within which to think about some of the examples and case studies that the authors discuss. Bassiouni further contends that the practices of extremist movements such as Al-Qaeda transgress not only international criminal law, but indeed Islamic law itself.[13] The iteration and reiteration of this point is especially important in undermining the validity of claims made by ISIS today. Ahmed Al-Dawoody's chapter on non-international armed conflicts also explores this question.

Farhad Malekian is another significant author on the topic of Islamic international criminal law and justice. Malekian has authored multiple volumes, chapters and articles, which contextualise this book. Indeed, Ma-

---

7 Abdullahi Ahmed An-Na'im, as quoted from Mashood A. Baderin (ed.), *Islam and Human Rights: Selected Essays of Abdullahi An-Na'im*, Routledge, 2017, pp. 27–29.

8 M. Cherif Bassiouni, *The Shari'a and Islamic Criminal Justice in Time of War and Peace*, Cambridge University Press, Cambridge, 2013.

9 *Ibid.*, pp. 16–17.

10 *Ibid.*, p. 72.

11 *Ibid.*, p. 73.

12 *Ibid.*, pp. 71–84.

13 *Ibid.*, p. 200.

lekian's contribution to one of the Nuremberg Academy's previous edited volumes, *The Nuremberg Principles in Non-western Societies: A Reflection on their Universality, Legitimacy and Application*, concluded that there was direct synergy between the Nuremberg Principles and the core principles of Islamic law. He explained:[14]

> [T]here is significant homogeneity between the Nuremberg Principles and Islamic international criminal law […] A comparative approach to the jurisprudence of Nuremberg- Islamic principles demands that we urgently need to strengthen international criminal jurisdiction regarding the enforcement of laws criminalizing war crimes, crimes against humanity, aggression, genocide, torture, discrimination, humiliation, unlawful imprisonment, and rape in peace or in war. The relevant principles of both systems regarding these crimes apply to all nations through their establishment as *jus cogens* norms […] Any realistic international lawyer cannot deny the presence of human rights law in the inner structure of both legal systems.

In his seminal comparative analysis titled *Principles of Islamic International Criminal Law: A Comparative Search*, Malekian provides a complex and detailed comparative study of the substance of 'Islamic international criminal law', a system emergent from *siyar* ("the early system of Islamic international law governing the conduct of sovereigns"[15]) and the modern system of international criminal law, to explain overlap and divergence. Malekian demonstrates that the differences between the two systems are not over core principles, but "ideological, political, procedural and more importantly, the consequence of specific misinterpretations of both legal systems".[16] Malekian's latest work calls directly for an 'Islamic international criminal court' when appropriate (for example in response to ISIS crimes). By this, he does not mean that there should be a new court but rather "a court that maintains and acts under the same ICC principles",

---

14 Farhad Malekian, "Comparative Substantive International Criminal Justice", in Ronald Slye (ed.), *The Nuremberg Principles in Non-Western Societies: A Reflection on their Universality, Legitimacy and Application*, International Nuremberg Principles Academy, Nuremberg, 2016, pp. 47–49.

15 Farhad Malekian, *Principles of Islamic International Criminal Law A Comparative Search*, 2nd ed., Brill, Leiden, 2011, p. 5.

16 *Ibid.*, p. xxiv.

which would work inclusive of Islamic ethics and staffed by jurists knowledgeable of Islamic law, effectively establishing its own "*ad hoc* legal personality".[17]

Whether or not one agrees with their views, the work of Bassiouni and Malekian demonstrates how creative scholarly thinking can provide real options and ways to think about innovative approaches to legal pluralism. They show that legal scholarship across 'legal families' can be a 'two-way street', by which both traditions can be enriched.

This collection is unique, benefiting from the contributions of leading academic experts, in its scope, breadth and focus on the interplay of theory and practice. One of the book's most significant values is that it brings together field-leading experts for the first time in a single volume, one exclusively dedicated to the topic of Islam and international criminal law and international criminal justice. The focus on Islam and international criminal law and justice makes this collection especially significant in that, while there has been considerable work around Islam and international law,[18] and Islam and human rights,[19] work on Islam and international criminal law beyond the works of Bassiouni and Malekian has been considerably developed and advanced by the authors here. The authors represented in this volume have extensively written on Islamic law and on international criminal law and made substantial contributions to and linkages within the field. For example, Onder Bakircioglu's work on Islam and warfare,[20] Mashood A. Baderin's works on the compatibility of international human rights and Islamic law,[21] Asma Afsaruddin's exploration of the historical,

[17] Farhad Malekian, *Corpus Juris of Islamic International Criminal Justice*, Cambridge Scholars Publishing, Cambridge, 2017, p. xx.

[18] Marie-Luisa Frick and Andreas T. Müller (eds.), *Islam and International Law*, Brill, Leiden, 2013.

[19] For example, Mohammad Hashim Kamali, *Freedom, Equality and Justice in Islam*, Islamic Texts Society, Cambridge 2002; Abdullahi Ahmed An-Na'im, *Toward an Islamic Reformation: Civil Liberties, Human Rights, and International Law*, Syracuse University Press, 1996; Abdulaziz A. Sachedina, *Islam and the Challenge of Human Rights*, Oxford University Press, Oxford, 2014.

[20] Onder Bakircioglu, *Islam and Warfare: Context and Compatibility with International Law*, Routledge, New York, 2014.

[21] Mashood A. Baderin, *International Human Rights and Islamic Law*, Oxford University Press, Oxford, 2005.

legal and socio-political concept of *jihád*,[22] Shaheen Sardar Ali's examination of the varied interpretations of Islamic law in the modern world and its influences on daily life,[23] Mohamed Elewa Badar's substantial contributions on international criminal law and his upcoming work on the challenges Islamist groups present to both Islamic law and international criminal law – these are the foundations on which the authors helped to create this volume.[24]

Abdelrahman Afifi, Ahmed Al-Dawoody and Siraj Khan bring a practitioner's perspective from their legal careers in international criminal law, making this volume not simply a scholarly tome, but a work rooted in legal practice, drawing on the experience and wisdom of those at the forefront of international criminal law practice.

1.3. Structure of this Book

This book consists of nine chapters, including the present introduction. The chapters move in a logical sequence, from dealing with core issues of Islamic law, and the challenges the Islamic legal system faces in the context of developments in contemporary international criminal law, to exploring parallels in both classical and modern Islamic legal writings on justification of war and conduct in war, and the development of *jus in bello* and *jus ad bellum* in the twentieth and twenty-first centuries. The final chapters deal with Islamic law in relation to the development of international criminal law in the post-Nuremberg trials era – in particular the Rome Statute – and its interactions with the International Criminal Court ('ICC').

---

22 Asma Afsaruddin, *Striving in the Path of God: Jihad and Martyrdom in Islamic Thought*, Oxford University Press, New York, 2013.

23 Shaheen Sardar Ali, *Modern Challenges to Islamic Law*, Cambridge University Press, Cambridge, 2016.

24 Mohamed Elewa Badar, *The Concept of Mens Rea in International Criminal Law: The Case for a Unified Approach*, Hart Publishing, Portland, 2013; Mohamed Elewa Badar, "The Self-Declared Islamic State and Ius ad Bellum under Islamic International Law", in *Asian Yearbook of Human Rights and Humanitarian Law*, 2017, vol. 1, pp. 35–75; Mohamed Elewa Badar, ElSayed Amin and Noelle Higgins, "The International Criminal Court and the Nigerian Crisis: An Inquiry into the Boko Haram Ideology and Practices from an Islamic Law Perspective", in *International Human Rights Law Review*, vol. 3, 2014, pp. 29–60; Mohamed Elewa Badar, "The Road to Genocide: The Propaganda Machine of the Self-declared Islamic State (IS)", in *International Criminal Law Review*, 2016, vol. 16, no. 3, pp. 361–411.

In Chapter 2, Onder Bakircioglu begins the sequence by examining the main sources of Muslim law, and establishes a basis for readers from which subsequent analysis of Islamic principles and modern international criminal justice can proceed. His chapter sets the tone for the volume, advocating the need to "re-open the door for critical thinking" by historical and contextual re-reading of the main sources of Islamic law and highlighting how reformist-minded thinkers are tackling difficult themes such as science *vis-à-vis* religion, secularism, rule of law, religious freedoms, human rights, and Islamic use of force. Bakircioglu concludes that new modes of critical thinking have the potential to undo the perception that Islam is inherently war-like and obscurantist.

In Chapter 3, Mashood A. Baderin analyses the relationship between Islamic socio-legal norms and international criminal justice. Baderin critically engages with the concept of international criminal justice and how to enhance its acceptance and effectiveness in the Muslim world, highlighting the role of Islamic socio-legal norms in that regard. He notes that conflicts in different parts of the Muslim world such as Iraq, Libya, Syria and Yemen, in which serious atrocities have been committed by both state and non-state actors, beg the question of what role Islamic socio-legal norms can play in ensuring the effective realisation of the objectives of international criminal justice. Baderin proposes that, with reference to the Muslim world, Islamic social-legal norms have positive potential that can and should be explored to deepen the universality and effectiveness of international criminal justice in today's world. The chapter disagrees with the view that Islamic law is irreconcilable with modern international law and international criminal justice. However, it goes beyond comparative narratives and argues the need for a contextual approach for a better appreciation of how the two systems can support one another to fulfil the shared objective of a more humane world. Baderin proposes a holistic perspective of international criminal justice, a perspective that encompasses social justice and addresses the social and moral conscience of humanity to abhor the commission of heinous atrocities in the first place. He argues that international criminal justice should not be restricted to secular legalistic worldviews, but should also be examined within the context of religious and cultural beliefs; he notes that people who commit heinous international crimes often act on certain distorted beliefs and cultural understandings that need to be challenged, by reference to alternative superior internal evidence, in order to morally win minds from committing those atrocities in the first place. The chapter proposes a combined application of the concept of 'object and purpose' under international law and the similar concept of *maqáṣid* under Islamic law, rationalising the relationship between the two systems. Pursuant to the proposed object and purpose approach, the chapter then presents an analysis that encompasses the social, moral, political and legal dimensions of international criminal justice in relation to Islamic socio-legal norms based on the *maqáṣid* principle in order to promote the appreciation and effectiveness of international criminal justice in the Muslim world.

In Chapter 4, Asma Afsaruddin discusses Islamic law of war in relation to both *jus ad bellum* and *jus in bello*. Starting from a historical perspective, Afsaruddin discusses how early Muslim jurists maintained that the Qur'ánic text 2:190 unambiguously forbade the initiation of military hostilities, stating that military activity could be launched defensively, not pre-emptively. It was the concessions made by classical Muslim jurists close to imperial power structures that diluted the *Qur'án*'s absolute prohibition on initiating military aggression by articulating the principle of offensive *jihád*. Going back to the earliest sources, Afsaruddin argues that it is possible to highlight adherence to the Qur'ánic principle of non-aggression and trace the emergence of the legal principle of non-combatant immunity during the course of war. Afsaruddin argues that reclamation of this earlier strand of juridical thinking should spur contemporary Muslim jurists to re-evaluate the classical juridical views on the parameters of combative *jihád*. Modern Muslim jurists increasingly invoke the *Qur'án*'s pronouncements on military ethics to question some of the legal provisions that developed concerning warfare after the first century of Islam. By doing this, a larger area of commonality with contemporary international law on the conduct of war becomes apparent. Significantly, Afsaruddin further notes the continuity between classical and modern jurists on the insistence that civilian life be protected during warfare, categorically placing mass killings and genocide beyond the moral limits of Islamic law. This position establishes a synergy with modern international criminal law and international humanitarian law *jus in bello* principles.

In Chapter 5, Abdelrahman Afifi begins by discussing *jus in bello* specifically; he highlights parallels between international law and Islamic law. Afifi concludes that Islamic law is not in contradiction with international law, and that Islamic law could and should become an essential and effective factor in ensuring the universality of international humanitarian law and international criminal law. Investigating this from the perspective of *siyásah al-Sharí'ah* (*Sharí'ah*-oriented policy) and *maqáṣid al-Sharí'ah* (objectives of *Sharí'ah*), Afifi's study demonstrates the considerable opportunities for adaptation, harmonisation, and integration of international law into Islamic law. Indeed, Afifi argues that Islamic law could easily be read in perfect harmony with international criminal law and that the intellectual tradition of Islam actively encourages legal research and adaptation to geographic and temporal contexts. However, Afifi further argues that political and religious leadership in parts of the Muslim world impede the intellectual dynamism that would allow for such harmonisation; in particular, he identifies in some societies an over-attachment to the concept of imitation, *taqlíd*, which leads to intellectual stasis.

In Chapter 6, Ahmed Al-Dawoody examines the currently understudied topic of non-international armed conflicts under Islamic law. While classical Islamic law books did not categorise international versus non-international armed conflicts, international armed conflicts were treated under the headings of *al-jihád* or *al-siyar*. Due to historical precedents during the first four decades of the Islamic era, these classical texts treated four specific forms of non-international armed conflicts, namely: (1) fighting against *al-murtaddún* (apostates); (2) fighting against *al-bugháh* (armed rebels, separatists); (3) fighting against *al-Khawárij* (roughly, violent religious fanatics); and (4) fighting against *al-muḥáribún* (highway robbers, bandits, pirates, terrorists). The first three forms of conflict fall under the definition of non-international armed conflicts, while the fourth could be also treated as non-international armed conflict under certain conditions. Al-Dawoody studies the characteristics and conditions of rules of engagement with, and the punishment, if any, for those who take part in the last three forms of non-international armed conflicts. In doing so, he aims to explore, first, if the case of the militants of ISIS can be categorised in any of these three forms of conflicts. Second, if the answer to this is positive, he asks if there might be any grounds for prosecuting the ISIS militants in a (hypothetical) *Sharí'ah* court that applies exclusively Islamic law, and what might be the appropriate punishments. This chapter is of particular importance in addressing the question of how far conflicting parties abide by the Islamic restraints on the use of force and how far these classical Islamic rules correspond with modern international humanitarian law. Al-Dawoody further argues that the confusion between the laws of fighting against *al-bughāh* and *al-Khawārij* has been used and abused to criminalise opponents of the state.

The final three chapters discuss the relationship between the modern international criminal law regime, the ICC and Islamic law. In Chapter 7, Siraj Khan discusses how Islamic law and international criminal law interact within Muslim states. He seeks to assess the level of conflict or congruence between Islamic law and international criminal law on the practical level, approaching the topic by focusing on selected states that apply Islamic law, and the relationship between the application of Islamic law in those states and the ratification of, and compliance with, the ICC Statute. Khan sees the relationship between international criminal law and Islamic law as necessarily dynamic and context-specific. This opens up the discussion for the final two chapters, which deal specifically with the evolution of the Nuremberg Principles in a pluralistic world.

In Chapter 8, Shaheen Sardar Ali and Satwant Kaur Heer reflect on conceptual issues informing comparative discourse on international criminal justice and the ICC on the one hand, and Islamic conceptions of justice on the other. Contributions in this collection have explored substantive and procedural aspects of international and Islamic criminal justice and the extent to which these resonate with international criminal law and 'universality'. Ali's and Heer's chapter problematises these concepts by posing the question: What is the measure of universality of principles and norms and is 'formal' acceptability its only measure? Is it only on the basis of lack of ratification and accession to the ICC Statute that it is assumed that Islamic criminal justice and the ICC are incompatible? Ali and Heer advance the argument that, rather than simply seeking to understand why so few Muslim-majority states have ratified the ICC Statute, it would be more useful and fruitful to place state practice in international law at the centre of the debate, rather than Islam and Islamic criminal justice. Using formal acceptance of the ICC Statute, as a 'measure of universality', would imply that all common and civil law jurisdictions that have failed to ratify it are incompatible with 'international' and 'universal' criminal justice principles.

Finally, in Chapter 9, Mohamed Elewa Badar addresses the ways the ICC could recognise the contribution to the knowledge of law and legal systems made by the Islamic world. He contends that, despite being instructed by the ICC Statute to apply general principles of law derived from national laws of legal systems of the world, including the national laws of States that would normally exercise jurisdiction over the crime, the Court has so far relied only on Western inspiration; as a consequence, this could risk its legitimacy in the eyes of the Muslim world in establishing a truly universal system. Badar argues that the principles of Islamic law, for the most part, are consistent with internationally-recognised norms and standards, particularly those enshrined in the ICC Statute, and are on an equal footing with the common and continental legal systems currently employed by the Court in the search for general principles of law. Badar also argues that there is a way of bringing the Islamic legal tradition to the ICC – not so much in terms of filling lacunae in procedural law, as those seem to have been largely dealt with by applying principles from common law and civil law systems, but in terms of symbolic recognition of Islamic law's core principles.

1.4. Thinking About the Future – Aware of the Past and the Present

This book, as an open access publication, is addressed to scholars and practitioners throughout the world to better understand the moral and ethical bonds between the essences of the Islamic and international legal regimes as the global community moves forward in tackling impunity. Whilst this book is a new contribution to the field as a whole, the Nuremberg Academy and the authors have all developed this contribution mindful of the fact that this volume will be read across the Muslim world.

Given the consciously varied nature of the essays, the volume obviously provides no overarching policy recommendations. However, there is a future that urgently needs to be thought about in relation to the on-going situation occurring throughout the *ummah*. The international community needs to think of what might be done at the time when ISIS is defeated, or what will follow the end of the Syrian civil war, or what processes of law and transitional justice could be applied to the Rohingyas. Answers are not presently obvious to these emerging questions. This volume sees its task as contributing to the ways in which jurists, scholars, and policy makers may consider these issues in the future. In doing so, it builds on the work of not only the scholars and practitioners included in this volume, but also on a growing body of work around international criminal law principles and the Islamic world. These essays will become a useful resource for those involved in the on-going global project to ensure accountability for atrocity crimes, and will open up fresh debates that can be taken up by others in legal practice and academic theory at all levels and across both the Muslim and non-Muslim world.

2

The Principal Sources of Islamic Law

Onder Bakircioglu*

2.1. Introduction

Islam carries significant characteristics of an elaborate legal system seeking to regulate broad areas of human conduct in accordance with its ideal paradigm of what constitutes right and wrong. Islamic precepts, which Muslims believe to have been inspired by God, should be followed by believers by means of thought and deed. Classical Islamic jurisprudence rests on a monotheistic outlook that regards God as the ultimate source of law, for He alone is taken to be the ultimate sovereign whose omnipotence over human affairs stems from His status as the creator of the universe. Humankind accordingly needs no further justification to be subordinate to His will. Unsurprisingly, in relation to Lord (*rabb*), Islam characterises humans as servants (*'abd*).[1] The word 'Islam', likewise, derives from the Arabic term *salám*, which has a two-fold meaning: peace and submission (to God).[2] A Muslim, then, is a person who submits to God's will to the exclusion of any other revered entity.

The challenging questions of how Islamic law regulates international affairs in general, as well as just recourse to and just conduct in warfare, along with issues germane to peaceful settlement of disputes and criminal justice,[3] demand a general examination of the origins, development and hierarchy of *Sharí'ah*. This chapter will explore the primary sources of

---

* **Onder Bakircioglu** is an Associate Professor of Law at the University of Leicester, United Kingdom since August 2014. Dr. Bakircioglu's research interests are in the fields of public international law and human rights law. He is particularly interested in the use of force discourse in international and national settings. In 2014, he completed his second monograph, *Islam and Warfare: Context and Compatibility with International Law* (Routledge, 2014).

1 Montgomery W. Watt, *Islam and Christianity Today*, Routledge, London, 1983, p. 125.

2 Bernard Lewis, *The Political Language of Islam*, University of Chicago Press, Chicago, 1988, p. 78.

3 Such issues pertinent to Islamic international law (*siyar*) will be examined in later chapters of the present volume.

Sharí'ah, namely the *Qur'án* and the *Sunnah* (the Prophetic tradition), and the main secondary sources, namely *ijtihád* (independent critical reasoning) and *ijmá'* (consensus of commentators on a controversial point of law). Rejecting literal and narrow hermeneutics, this chapter will highlight the need for a contextual reading of Islamic sources, whose varied interpretation informs most contemporary debates. By providing an overview of the key sources of Islam, this chapter aims at setting the ground for the volume.

2.2. Primary Sources

2.2.1. The *Qur'án*

The *Qur'án* (which literally means recitation or reading) constitutes the most important source of Islam, which is composed of the divine revelations received by the Prophet, who sought to form a moral socio-political order operating in accordance with the sacred messages delivered by God. The *Qur'án* is the primary and most authoritative source of Islamic law. Since the *Qur'án* is believed to contain the literal words of God, it is deemed the most authentic record of Islamic law,[4] incarnating the final, inimitable and infallible injunctions of everlasting validity. God in the *Qur'án* affirms Islam's complete nature, saying: "Today I have perfected your religion for you, and I have completed My blessing upon you, and have approved Islam for your religion".[5] Although the *Qur'án* expresses that "[e]very nation has its Messenger"[6] and that there is no difference between these Prophets,[7] Muḥammad is believed to have closed the line of Messengers[8] by re-introducing the original and unadulterated teaching of God. According to Islam, God's revelations have not been preserved in their pristine forms in earlier scriptures.[9] Muslims thus believe that the

---

4 Farooq A. Hassan, "The Sources of Islamic Law", in *Proceedings of the Annual Meeting (American Society of International Law)*, 1982, vol. 76, p. 66.

5 The *Qur'án* (translation by Arthur J. Arberry), 5:5.

6 *Ibid.*, 10:48.

7 *Ibid.*, 2:130.

8 *Ibid.*, 33:40.

9 Yúsuf Ali, *The Meaning of the Holy Quran*, 11th ed., Amana Publications, Maryland, 2008, p. 56.

Qur'án is God's final effort to reconstruct the undistorted message preached by other Prophets since Abraham.[10]

The *Qur'án*, in other words, presents Islam as the very religion that had been preached by earlier Prophets including Abraham, Noah, Moses, and Jesus[11] who themselves were originally Muslims. Among other Prophets, Muslims ascribe to Abraham a prominent standing, as he is considered a perfect model for the faithful and the harbinger of monotheism.[12] The fact that the Muslim tradition rooted itself within the soil of monotheism rendered the appeal of the *Qur'án* more acceptable to those who were already familiar with the monotheistic conception of the universe. Indeed, the Prophet Muḥammad had never rejected the legacy of his predecessors; he rather saw himself part of a long series of Prophets appointed by God to preach the divine truth. Like Abraham, Muḥammad proclaimed monotheism and advised his followers to comport themselves in a manner of righteousness and piety.[13] As with Christ, he reminded humankind of resurrection, the Day of Judgement, and of the punishments and rewards in the hereafter.

2.2.1.1. The Collection of the *Qur'án*

Islamic tradition holds that the *Qur'án* is revealed to Muḥammad by God through the medium of the angel Gabriel.[14] According to Muslim theology and jurisprudence, the entire corpus of the *Qur'án* sprang from Muḥammad's reception of divine revelations (*wahy*). Muḥammad received revelations in instalments during the Mecca and Medina period, over the course of twenty-two years (AD 610–632) until his demise.[15] The *Qur'án* is revealed in Arabic, containing 114 chapters (*súrahs*), 6,236 verses (*áyát*), and a total number of 77,934 words. The whole body of the

10 *Ibid.*, 2:127–130.

11 Jonathan Berkey, *The Formation of Islam: Religion and Society in the Near East, 600–1800*, Cambridge University Press, Cambridge, 2003, p. 48.

12 John L. Esposito, *The Oxford Dictionary of Islam*, Oxford University Press, Oxford, 2003, p. 7.

13 The *Qur'án*, 2:131–133, see *supra* note 5.

14 *Ibid.*, 53:1–18.

15 Michael Cook, *The Koran: A Very Short Introduction*, Oxford University Press, New York, 2000, p. 5.

Qur'án was completed during the lifetime of the Prophet who called on his scribes to record what had been revealed to him.

The Prophet's recitations were initially written down on whatever material came to hand, including palm leaves, wood pieces, and parchment. Under Muḥammad's supervision, these fragmented pieces were subsequently collected into *súrahs* or chapters. Although the *Qur'án* existed in its full, albeit fragmented, form since the first revelation, the written material was not brought together into a single codex during the Prophet's lifetime. The assembly of the entire Qur'ánic text was a lengthy and arduous task. Most commentators concur that an official codex had been collected under the rule of Uthmán, the third *Caliph*, within the period of 20 years following Muḥammad's death.[16]

Uthmán concerned himself with ascertaining whether the texts he assembled had been directly recited by the Prophet. During this process, the chief Qur'ánic material was the one collated by Muḥammad's chief secretary, Zaid Ibn Thábit. Uthmán is known to have ordered an authorised version of the *Qur'án* to be assembled and copied, and to have commanded his governors to destroy all variant texts.[17] For one of the main challenges lay in the fact that Arabic was the language of desert nomads, and its spoken form was far more sophisticated than its written form at a time when written Arabic lacked vowels or diacritical marks. This led to the acknowledgement of seven variant, but equally authoritative, readings (*qira'át*) of the *Qur'án*, which could have caused significant controversy over the meaning. However, when the *Qur'án* was redacted and an authoritative version was adopted, this put an end to alternative readings. This redacted version, effected by a number of learned *ṣaḥábah* (companions of Prophet Muḥammad), "has since remained unchanged and unchallenged".[18]

[16] John Burton, *The Collection of the Quran*, Cambridge University Press, Cambridge, 1977, p. 139.

[17] Al-Sayyid Abú Al-Qásim Al-Musawi Al-Khu'i, (translated by Abdulaziz A. Sachedina), *Prolegomena to the Quran*, Oxford University Press, New York, 1998, p. 135.

[18] M. Cherif Bassiouni, "Evolving Approaches to Jihad: From Self-Defense to Revolutionary and Regime-Change Political Violence", in *Chicago Journal of International Law*, 2008, vol 8, p. 119.

2.2.1.2. The Substance and Structure of the *Qur'án*

The *Qur'án*, as touched upon earlier, is deemed to embody an authentic record of God's eternal and unalterable word.[19] Incorporating an amalgamation of legal and ethical principles, as well as ritualistic and moral exhortations, the *Qur'án* provides the fundamental substance of the Islamic law (*Sharí'ah*) and imposes a clear set of legal and moral obligations on Muslims. The *Qur'án* covers the basic aspects of mundane and spiritual existence, envisaging guidelines for legitimate and ideal human conduct.[20] Lessons of right behaviour in daily matters, and wisdom in spiritual matters, may thus be sought from the *Qur'án*. In view of the fact that God's ordinance is contained in the *Qur'án*, the ideal life for Muslims is one that is lived in line with the relevant Islamic precepts and injunctions, whether ritualistic, moral or legal in character.[21] The *Qur'án* is thus a system of duties and responsibilities, which if duly performed may not only give a believer an inner satisfaction in the temporal domain, but also assure him a place in Heaven.

Muslim scholars usually distinguish between three main categories of ethico-legal injunctions in the *Qur'án*. The first pertains to the doctrine of belief in God, His messengers and the Day of Judgment; the next is essentially concerned with ethical human conduct; and the third part is associated with practical or daily actions of believers under Islamic law.[22] These categories are then sub-divided into relevant sections, which, among other things, deal with rituals, private and public matters, as well as wide issues of domestic and foreign policy. Whilst the *Qur'án* incorporates a detailed set of practical, legal and moral rules, when its meaning remains obscure or when it is silent on a particular matter, other sources of *Sharí'ah* (which will be explored below) may be drawn on to generate answers for the problem at hand. The *Qur'án*, in this context, may be compared to a constitution that provides the key material on issues of social, political, legal and practical nature. It is then the role of the scholar,

---

19 The *Qur'án*, 10:37, see *supra* note 5.

20 Mohammad Hashim Kamali, *Principles of Islamic Jurisprudence*, Islamic Texts Society, Cambridge, 1989, p. 18.

21 Joseph Schacht, *An Introduction to Islamic Law*, Oxford University Press, Oxford, 1982, p. 11.

22 M. Izzi Dien, *Islamic Law: From Historical Foundations to Contemporary Practice*, Edinburgh University Press, Edinburgh, 2004, p. 37.

jurist, or legislator to explain or flesh out, while remaining loyal to the letter and spirit of the main text, norms to address what is required by concrete circumstances. Naturally, the ever-changing needs of societies require appropriate refinement and elaboration of Qur'ánic norms through human reasoning.

It is worth noting that a notable portion of the *Qur'án*'s contents had essentially been informed by the prevailing socio-political, economic, and religious circumstances of its day; thus, many moral, religious, and social pronouncements of the *Qur'án*, even though divinely inspired and transcendental, answer some of the problems faced at the time of Muḥammad's ministry. As some of the early verses make it clear, the *Qur'án* was primarily concerned with the acute problems of its time, which include such issues as polytheism, idolatry, the exploitation and maltreatment of the poor, malpractices in trade, and the overall injustice affecting society.[23] The practical facet of the *Qur'án* becomes quite evident when considering that a remarkable part of Qur'ánic revelations was handed down to Muḥammad over the course of twenty-two years in response to practical questions. Not surprisingly, therefore, the *Qur'án* contains a rich repository of guidance on real-life situations, with injunctions regulating a vast field, from issues of international relations and matters of war and peace, down to the habits of everyday life such as relations between spouses, child custody, eating, drinking, and personal hygiene.

In addition to containing timeless moral and spiritual injunctions, the *Qur'án*, then, responded to some of the important socio-political issues of its period. However, there is a controversy on whether the *Qur'án* subsumed all previous legislation. Some commentators maintain that Islam invalidated all previous legal systems, because the *Qur'án* provided a comprehensive account of everything.[24] Other scholars, particularly *Ḥanafī* jurists, assert that only those pre-Islamic rules, which had not been expressly abrogated by the divine will could be recognised as valid.[25] Evidence suggests that Islam had not repudiated the validity of all pre-Islamic doctrines; especially during the nascent stages of Islam, there was

---

[23] Fazlur Rahmán, *Islam & Modernity: Transformation of an Intellectual Tradition*, University of Chicago Press, Chicago, 1982, p. 2.

[24] The *Qur'án*, 16:89; 6:28, see *supra* note 5.

[25] Majid Khadduri, *War and Peace in the Law of Islam*, Johns Hopkins Press, Baltimore, 1955, p. 3.

widespread adoption of many legal and administrative institutions and practices of the newly conquered territories. There were "multiple influences on Muslims in places where they have adopted many social and cultural practices of pre-Islamic origin".[26] This was natural as the expansion of the Islamic State necessitated the management of foreign people with their particular traditions, which resulted in the fusion of some raw Islamic legal material with pertinent local customs and traditions. Prominent examples were seen in the law of taxation, religious foundations (*waqf*), and the way in which tolerated (monotheistic) religions were managed. The retention of some pre-Islamic traditions and local institutions was accompanied by the adoption of novel legal concepts, maxims, or methods of reasoning. In this way, as Schacht argues, many rules that had their origin in Roman and Byzantine law, Canon law of Eastern Churches, Rabbinic law, or Sassanian law, became part of the Islamic law.[27] Certainly when integrated within the Islamic law, some of such laws must have assumed a character in tune with the overall tenor of Islam. More importantly, Islam's rejection of idolatry in favour of God's supremacy resulted in the rejection of many pre-Islamic customs and practices that were idolatrous in nature.[28]

It is important to highlight the nexus between certain Islamic injunctions and pre-Islamic customary law because some Islamic norms may be better understood in light of knowledge concerning the pre-Islamic social setting. Hence, when an analyst is confronted with some obscure verse, a detailed evaluation of the relevant socio-historical backdrop must be conducted with a view to contextualising the issue involved. Given that the Qur'ánic material was communicated to the Prophet piecemeal, it is often possible to comprehend any ambiguity through studying the historical setting or specific challenges faced by Muslims.

2.2.1.3. The Elucidation of the *Qur'án*

As with other religio-legal systems, Islamic law has been subjected to interpretation in varying degrees, a process that has taken such modes of hermeneutics as traditional, customary, critical, and innovative. Consider-

26 Mushirul Ḥasan, *Moderate or Militant Images of India's Muslims*, Oxford University Press, Oxford, 2009, p. 102.

27 Schacht, 1982, pp. 18–21, see *supra* note 21.

28 Khadduri, 1955, p. 3, see *supra* note 25.

ing the socio-historical dynamics that shaped the contours of Islamic law, any hermeneutical effort should arguably consider the overall historical context, connected verses and prophetic traditions, as well as the underlying logic, object and the purpose of Islam. As subjectivity constitutes an inevitable element of interpretation, regular revisiting and review of all relevant facts and rereading of relevant sources is also essential. But, notwithstanding the need to keep religious norms responsive to changing conditions, not every aspect of the religion may be subject to reinterpretation; for instance, there is very little scope in reinterpreting most ritualistic rules, or such timeless themes as the unity of God (*tawḥíd*), the profession of faith or affirming Muḥammad's status as the seal of all Prophets.[29]

For the purposes of interpreting the *Qur'án*, the aforementioned contextual method calls for the identification of the general atmosphere within which a verse was revealed, the particular problem (if any) to which the revelation responded, as well as the overall corpus, objective, and spirit of the Islamic legal system. The stress on context-specificity does not, of course, preclude the analyst from deducing general principles from a specific command or injunction, provided that such inferences accord with the fundamental tenets of Islam.

Islamic law is expounded through *úṣúl al-fiqh,* a method of extracting rules (*fiqh*) from primary sources. Hence, it is through the branch of *úṣúl al-fiqh* that secondary norms may be obtained.[30] The elaboration of Islamic norms has often been necessitated by the changing socio-political conditions. While the *Qur'án* states that it explains "everything",[31] and that nothing is "neglected [...] in the Book",[32] this, as Ramadan argues, should refer "to general principles, to essential and immutable rules".[33] The *Qur'án*, in this sense, contains the indispensable elements of legislation and the imperative will of God out of which secondary rules may be deduced.[34]

---

29 The *Qur'án*, 7:158, see *supra* note 5.

30 Kamali, 1989, p. 2, see *supra* note 20.

31 The *Qur'án*, 16:91, see *supra* note 5.

32 *Ibid.*, 6:38.

33 Tariq Ramadan, *Radical Reform: Islamic Ethics and Liberation*, Oxford University Press, Oxford, 2009, p. 24.

34 Dien, 2004, p. 35, see *supra* note 22.

The modalities of interpreting the *Qur'án* present certain challenges on account of its directly revealed character and superiority over other sources. Like other scriptures, the *Qur'án* may not always be straightforward in its message,[35] which raises the challenge of comprehending the real sense of a verse while extracting rulings. This phenomenon resulted in distinct methods of interpretation that emerged within and between various Islamic cultures of different epochs. Evidently, the passage of time significantly affected the manner in which some verses are read, since what had been straightforward during the lifetime of the Prophet may have appeared relatively obscure to the commentator of subsequent ages. During his lifetime, Muḥammad expounded the meaning and implications of opaque passages. In fact, the *Qur'án* notes that it was incumbent upon the Prophet to "make clear to mankind what was sent down to them".[36] But since the prophetic mission could not be bequeathed to succeeding *Caliphs*, both divine legislation and its authoritative interpretation drew to an end. This led to serious complications, particularly when Islam embarked upon expansion outside Arabia. The development of Islamic law would have been much more linear and clear-cut had Muslim rule been confined to Arabia. The newly conquered territories, including Egypt, Syria, Iraq, and Persia, presented unprecedented legal challenges that could not be readily met merely through unelaborated principles. This challenge compelled Muslim jurists to make recourse to the prophetic tradition, personal opinion (*ra'y*) and certain pre-Islamic concepts to supplement the divine legislation and thereby to address the demands of culturally different societies.[37]

The theme of Qur'ánic order of rank and priority features prominently in textual interpretation; for not all verses, albeit all being of divine origin, enjoin the same normative status. Some verses are indeed more imperative than others in the way they impose duties on the believer. Likewise, some verses may be more direct about what they demand of humankind; some may be more explicit, while others may appear implicit in meaning, or they may require to be read in conjunction with other verses.[38] Naturally, the broader context of each era marks out the theoretical

[35] The *Qur'án*, 3:7, see *supra* note 5.

[36] *Ibid.*, 16:45.

[37] Khadduri, 1955, p. 27, see *supra* note 25.

[38] Ismail R. Al-Faruqi, *The Cultural Atlas of Islam*, Macmillan, London, 1986, p. 246.

contours of the analysis, informing the way in which the textual material of the *Qur'án* is understood and applied to real-life situations.

It follows that a commentator may often have a penchant for approaching the Qur'ánic text with a mindset conditioned by the presuppositions, concerns and expectations of his time. Hence, even when the commentator seeks to identify the rationale behind a verse, which may link the cause and consequences of the revelation, he is likely to approach the verse with a frame of mind that searches for its immediate practical implications. This dialectic relation between the text and its analyst is not only inescapable, but necessary to retain the scriptural guidance germane to changing human needs. Such an active engagement with the Qur'ánic material dovetails with the notion that the *Qur'án* incorporates sempiternal guidance for humankind of all ages. Indeed, were the *Qur'án*'s message restricted to the questions faced during the time of its revelation, the 'timeless' tenor of the text could be compromised; or it might have lost its central pertinence to Muslims of various epochs who need tailored solutions to complex problems they confront.

One of the barriers to interpretation is the extent to which elaboration may be carried out. The debate among conservative, liberal, reformist, or revivalist commentators has never actually been about whether there should be interpretation of the primary sources, but rather, about the degree to which this could occur. In their efforts to extract secondary rulings, some scholars, including such canonical figures as Abú Ḥanífah, faced accusations of neglecting the primary sources and disproportionately relying on their own views.[39] The key concern has always been whether commentators remained loyal to the divine legislation while distilling individualised responses. Although, as discussed below, systemic expansion of primary norms was generally interrupted after the age of "classical" theologians, Muslims have developed various schools of thought which sought to contribute to the development of Islamic law.[40]

In their quest to extricate further rules or extrapolate abstract constructions to concrete cases, Muslim jurists developed sophisticated methods of interpretation to reduce the margin of error. These techniques of law-making make use of deductive, inductive, and analogical reasoning,

---

39 Ramadan, 2009, pp. 53–56, see *supra* note 33.

40 John L. Esposito, *The Future of Islam*, Oxford University Press, Oxford, 2010, p. 88.

distinguishing the general principle (*'ámm*) from the specific (*khás*), the manifest (*ẓahir*) from the explicit (*naṣṣ*), or the literal (*ḥaqíqí*) from the metaphorical (*majází*). Jurists mayalso invoke, among others, the doctrine of preference (*istiḥsán*) to respond to a problem in light of such considerations as equity, justice and fairness.[41] To sum up, the main purpose of generating secondary norms is to safeguard the applicability of primary sources to evolving socio-cultural context. Nevertheless, as human subjectivity is unavoidable in hermeneutical efforts, there emerged numerous schools of jurisprudence (with their varying interpretative frameworks) over the course of Islamic history. The following pages will turn to the second most important source of Islamic law.

2.2.2. The *Sunnah*

Loyal observance of the example of the Prophet, along with the commands of God in the *Qur'án*, plays a key role for Muslims in their quest to secure peace in this world and achieve salvation in the hereafter. The prophetic practice, also known as the *Sunnah*, forms the second principal source of *Sharí'ah*. The *Sunnah* includes the anecdotal accounts of Muḥammad's sayings, deeds, views, habits, or tacit (dis)approvals of certain practice. The concept of *Sunnah* is occasionally used to refer to the practice of Muḥammad's companions, too. The written account of these practices is termed the *ḥadíth*,[42] which contains the documented record of what Muḥammad is considered to have uttered or done during his lifetime. While the *Qur'án* embodies the binding law in God's own words, *Sunnah* is taken to be the reflection of God's wisdom with which the Prophet had been inspired.[43] Confirming this point, the *Qur'án* demands believers to follow the model pattern of behaviour exhibited by the Prophet.[44]

For Muslims, the significance of the *Sunnah* lies in the fact that Muḥammad was the final messenger of God, and as such his practice

41 James P. Piscatori, *Islam in a World of Nation-States*, Cambridge University Press, Cambridge, 1986, p. 4; Kamali, 1989, p. 3, see *supra* note 20.

42 Mir Mustansir, "The Sura as a Unity: A Twentieth Century Development in Quran Exegesis", in G.R. Hawting and A.A. Shareef (eds.), *Approaches to the Quran*, Routledge, New York, 1993, p. 218.

43 The *Qur'án*, 3:164, see *supra* note 5; Majid Khadduri, "The Maslaha (Public Interest) and Illa (Cause) in Islamic Law", in *New York University Journal of International Law and Politics*, 1980, vol. 12, p. 213.

44 The *Qur'án*, 33:21, see *supra* note 5.

bears a decisive role for a better appreciation of the *Qur'án*. As Esposito points out, Muḥammad has over the centuries "served as the ideal model for Muslim life, providing the pattern that all believers are to emulate. He is, as some Muslims say, the 'living *Qur'án*'".[45] A connected *Sunní* proposition is that only the Prophet was divinely protected from committing major errors in interpreting the revelations. This moot doctrine is known as the 'Prophetic infallibility' (*iṣmat al-anbiyá*). Having rejected the view that Muḥammad was a fallible being who had been "subject to the same experiences as the rest of men",[46] apologists of the 'infallibility' doctrine posit that while the Prophet could commit minor errors (*ḍalálah*) as a human being, his interpretive infallibility is unquestionable, for he is the "seal of the Prophets" who passed away without an heir of his stature.[47] After him, the argument runs, there remained no intermediary between God and humankind; and the successors (*Caliphs*) lacked the mandate to promulgate, or authoritatively explain, God's law.[48]

Although this is not the place to discuss whether the 'infallibility doctrine' stands on solid grounds, it is certainly true that the death of the Prophet had marked the termination of divine legislation. Remarkably, shortly before his demise in 632, Muḥammad recited what many scholars believe to be the final verse of the *Qur'án*: "Today I have perfected your religion for you". [49] This verse indeed signalled the termination of Muḥammad's prophetic mission, after which no divine law was to be sent down. The law of God was henceforth to be developed through (fallible) human effort, an enterprise whose results had to comply with the basic tenets of Islam. This fact alone made the traditions ascribed to Muḥammad all the more important, for they provided a perfect paradigm for the manner in which divine injunctions must be observed and applied.

45 John L. Esposito, *Islam: The Straight Path*, Oxford University Press, Oxford, 1994, p. 13.

46 Daniel W. Brown, *Rethinking Tradition in Modern Islamic Thought*, Cambridge University Press, Cambridge, 1996, p. 66.

47 Jackson Sherman, *Islam and the Black American: Looking Toward the Third Resurrection*, Oxford University Press, New York, 2011, p. 4.

48 Albert Hourani, *A History of the Arab Peoples*, Faber and Faber, London, 2005, p. 22.

49 The *Qur'án*, 5:5, see *supra* note 5.

2.2.2.1. The Structure and Role of the *Ḥadíths*

A *ḥadíth* is a narration containing a report of what the Prophet said or did in a certain form as transmitted one of his companions, who in his turn would relate it to someone belonging to the following generation.[50] Every *ḥadíth* has two parts. The first part (*isnád*) comprises a list of narrators that handed down accounts of the actions, sayings, teachings, decisions, overt or tacit views of Muḥammad or his immediate companions. This chain traces the sources through which the Prophetic practice had been reported with a view to attesting the historical authenticity of a particular *ḥadíth*. *Isnád* employs a classical formula along these lines: "It has been related to me by A on the authority of B on the authority of C on the authority of D that Muḥammad said […]". The second part, on the other hand, contains the actual content or text (*matn*) of the *ḥadíth* that communicates what the Prophet had reportedly said or done.[51] The report's main function is to shed light on a wide array of important matters in Islam.[52]

Roughly since the second century of Islam, Muḥammad's well-attested manner of behaviour has been considered to constitute a normative rule of conduct for Muslims. The phenomenon of precedent or normative custom, however, is not entirely foreign to the pre-Islamic period; Arabs have felt bound by tradition or precedent since time immemorial. The conventional wisdom dictated that the precedent of ancestors was to be revered and imitated. Adherence to ancient traditions often left no noteworthy room for new experiments and innovations that could alter the status quo. Entrenched customs thus presented a significant obstacle to innovation, so much so that in order to discredit an idea, it was generally sufficient to label it an 'innovation'.[53] The emergence of Islam, in this sense, proved to be the most radical innovation in Arabia at the time. Yet once Islam successfully prevailed over the Arabian Peninsula, the conven-

50 Annemarie Schimmel, *And Muhammad is His Messenger: The Veneration of the Prophet in Islamic Piety*, University of North Carolina Press, London, 1985, p. 26.

51 Israr A. Khan, *Authentication of Hadith: Redefining the Criteria*, International Institute of Islamic Thought, London, 2010, p. 28.

52 John Burton, *An Introduction to the Hadith Tradition*, Edinburgh University Press, Edinburgh, 1994, p. 19.

53 Majid Khadduri and Herbert J. Lienbesny, *Law in the Middle East*, The Lawbook Exchange, New Jersey, 2008, p. 34.

tional adherence to customs reasserted itself in the form of following the dictates of the new religious system.[54]

Concerning the role of the traditions, jurists reached a consensus that secondary norms had to be derived from the primary sources (as opposed to mere speculative reasoning). To be sure, this necessitated a much greater emphasis on the documentation of genuine (*sahih*) traditions.[55] Muslim scholars, among whom Al-Sháfi'í played a prominent role, sought to ensure the authenticity of transmitted *ḥadíths* so that legal certainty and predictability could be achieved. Rejecting the thesis that the authority of the Prophet had been that of an individual who had been better placed than any other human person to interpret the *Qur'án*, Al-Sháfi'í defended the position that the Prophet's overall practice was divinely inspired. This thinking, he reasoned, was the inexorable consequence of the Qur'ánic injunctions to obey God and His Messenger.[56] The eventual prevalence of Al-Sháfi'í's proposition that the acts or sayings of the Prophet reflected the divine will meant that accepted traditions could no longer be rebutted through content analysis of the narrations.[57] It followed that the veracity of a *ḥadíth* became generally dependent on the reliability of the chain of narrators transmitting the tradition. The wide acceptance of this position eventually raised controversy on the extent to which the reported traditions could be trusted.

2.2.2.2. Credibility of the *Ḥadíth* Literature

As alluded to earlier, the *Sunnah* has hitherto been employed to contextualise and understand the Qur'ánic material, as well as to enrich extant rules, customs and principles. Yet, the veracity of certain *ḥadíths* came to be questioned on the grounds that some of them might well have been fabricated to consolidate a given religio-political stance – as a certain position or attitude could be deemed correct, if a reliable chain of transmission testified to a corresponding practice of the Prophet.

---

[54] Schacht, 1982, p. 17, see *supra* note 21.

[55] Dien, 2004, p. 35, see *supra* note 22.

[56] The *Qur'án*, 8:20; 4:59, see *supra* note 5; Andrew Rippin, *Muslims: Their Religious Beliefs and Practices*, Routledge, New York, 2005, p. 223.

[57] Noel J. Coulson, *A History of Islamic Law*, Edinburgh University Press, Edinburgh, 1964, p. 56.

The possibility of producing seemingly authentic *ḥadíth* was indeed not an unlikely risk, which loomed larger when spatial and temporal distance grew from the source of a reported tradition. Certainly, one of the most significant factors leading certain jurists to doubt the authenticity of some *ḥadíths* was that traditions had only been collected and recorded in the second and third centuries of Islam. This mindfulness explains why only such authoritative records of *Sunnah* as those of Al-Bukhari (d. 870) and Muslim Ibn Al-Hajjaj (d. 874) have been considered credible by the majority of scholars.[58] Such reliable transmitters related traditions through a chain of trustworthy authorities, who handed down the relevant piece of information from generation to generation. The companions of Muḥammad, who witnessed the practice or heard the sayings of the Prophet, were undoubtedly best positioned to convey a tradition. After the passing of the Prophet's contemporaries, the following generations had to be content with the information handed down from the earlier generations.[59]

One notable source of distrust rose out of occasional inconsistency and variability found among the relevant traditions attributed to Muḥammad. This led such scholars as Mu'tazila (d. 748), Sayyid Ahmad Khan (d. 1898), and Ghulam Ahmad Parwez (d. 1986) to doubt the authenticity of some traditions. But the number of Muslim critics has hitherto been small, since the majority of scholars recognise the authority of varied *ḥadíths* on the basis that there was nothing wrong with the Prophet having changed tactics in responding to the circumstances.[60] While it may be accepted that flexibility and prudent statesmanship has served the cause of God and made Islam responsive to the particular challenges it has faced, the danger of cherry-picking certain traditions (and Qur'ánic verses, often by divesting them of their context) in a bid to further a cause has always plagued the Muslim world.

Although the criticism of the *ḥadíth* literature originated within Muslim circles, some Western scholars, including Goldziher, Alfred Guillame, and Joseph Schacht, took issue with the very foundation and validi-

58 Abdullahi Ahmed An-Na'im, "The Rights of Women and International Law in the Muslim Context", in *Whittier Law Review*, 1988. vol. 9, p. 49.

59 Ignác Goldziher, *Introduction to Islamic Theology and Law*, Princeton University Press, Princeton, 1981, p. 37.

60 Piscatori, 1986, p. 4, see *supra* note 41.

ty of prophetic traditions as a source of Islamic jurisprudence.[61] The main arguments for their critical position are essentially built upon these premises: (1) the *ḥadíth* literature relies on oral transmissions, which significantly grew larger than those contained in earlier anthologies; (2) *ḥadíths* transmitted by the younger companions of the Prophet surprisingly exceed those reported by the older ones; (3) the transmission system was applied in such an arbitrary fashion that the genuineness of the traditions could not be proved; (4) there are many contradicting *ḥadíths* that are equally deemed valid, since Muslim scholars concerned themselves solely with the validity of the chain of transmission, and not with the content of the *ḥadíth*.[62] Ignác Goldziher, one of the most prominent critics of the *ḥadíth* literature, went as far as to argue that:[63]

> each point of view, each party, each proponent of a doctrine gave the form of *ḥadíth* to his theses, and that consequently the most contradictory tenets had come to wear the garb of such documentation. There is no school in the areas of ritual, theology, or jurisprudence, there is not even any party to political contention, that would lack a *ḥadíth* or a whole family of *ḥadíths* in its favour, exhibiting all the external signs of correct transmission.

Schacht similarly challenged the credibility of the transmission system, positing that it lacked historical value, being largely invented by those who sought to authenticate their doctrines. Hardly any legal tradition of the Prophet could therefore be considered accurate, according to such sceptics.[64] Nonetheless, well before such Orientalists, concerns about the authenticity of traditions had been raised by Muslim scholars who eventually developed a rigorous method of sifting credible traditions from apocryphal ones whenever contradictions, vagueness or doubtfulness surfaced. This method divided the *ḥadíths* into three categories: those trans-

---

61 Shaheen S. Ali, "The Twain Doth Meet! A Preliminary Exploration of the Theory and Practice of As-Siyar and International Law in the Contemporary World", in Javaid Rehman and Susan Breau (eds.), *Religion, Human Rights and International Law*, Martinus Nijhoff Publishers, Leiden, 2007, p. 86.

62 Muhammad Siddiqi, *Hadith Literature: Its Origin, Development & Special Features*, Islamic Texts Society, Cambridge, 2008, p. 125.

63 Goldziher, 1981, p. 37, see *supra* note 59.

64 Muhamad Al-Azami, *On Schacht's Origins of Muhammadan Jurisprudence*, Oxford Centre for Islamic Studies, Oxford, 1996, p. 2.

mitted by virtuous people of high religious knowledge; those reported by people of lesser knowledge, but virtuous in character; and, finally, those suspected reports that did not fit within the overall matrix of Islam.[65] Authoritative traditionalists, such as Al-Bukhari and Muslim, invoked the said method and applied stringent criteria to collect merely the most authentic traditions. Bukhari is reported to have interviewed more than one thousand scholars of *ḥadíth* during his lifetime (810–869), and looked for transmitters of exemplary character possessing literary qualities. Bukhari sought evidence to confirm that the transmitters in question had actually met in real life and learned from one another – a method which differed from that of Muslims who opined that if two transmitters lived in the same locale, one could safely assume that they learned from each other. Bukhari's relentless search for solid evidence for a real encounter elicited wider recognition.[66]

Viewed from this perspective, it seems to be an over-generalisation to claim that the majority of the traditions emerged from suspect transmitters who, whether directly or indirectly, served the purpose of supporting a political agenda through forged *ḥadíths*. True, there exist traditions that are misleadingly, or with an ulterior motive, attributed to the Prophet, among which some contravene key Islamic principles, while some others, albeit fabricated, are yet congruent with Islam's ethical values including justice, equality and fairness.[67] Moreover, as Coulson notes, there were also such reporters who were "in the *bona fide* belief" that the Prophet would have so acted had he dealt with the same issue.[68] While there is no room in this chapter to discuss this matter extensively, suffice it to note that some Western scholars are also critical of Goldziher's and Schacht's sweeping dismissal of the *ḥadíth* literature. These scholars claim that oral and written transmissions go hand in hand, and that the majority of the traditions had been scrupulously scrutinised, particularly by such chroniclers as Muslim and Al-Bukhari.[69] A reasonable solution to the difficulty

65 Goldziher, 1981, p. 39, see *supra* note 59; Esposito, 2003, p. 217, see *supra* note 12.

66 Abdullah Saeed, *Islamic Thought: An Introduction*, Routledge, New York, 2006, p. 42.

67 The *Qur'án*, 16.90; 4:135; 2:178; 7:56, see *supra* note 5.

68 Coulson, 1964, p. 42, see *supra* note 57.

69 Siddiqi, 2008, p. 131, see *supra* note 62.

of distinguishing authentic *ḥadíths* from counterfeit ones arguably lies in the following saying attributed to the Prophet:[70]

> [C]ompare what I am reported to have said or done with the Book of God. If it agrees, I did actually say it; if it disagrees, I did not say it.

It follows that if a *ḥadíth* plainly negates the spirit of the *Qur'án*, it should not be taken seriously.

2.3. Secondary Sources

As stated earlier, Muḥammad has metaphorically been described as the corporeal scripture. Having contributed to establishing a blueprint for a moral life, his demise imposed a disquieting task on Muslims to keep the Islamic law responsive to unprecedented challenges. Despite the absence of continuous prophetic guidance, the companions of Muḥammad eventually managed to develop the raw legal material by devising new juristic tools to meet the demands of a rapidly changing social milieu.

These tools, known as the 'non-revealed' sources on account of their non-divine origin, mainly include: (1) *ijmá'*: the general consensus of commentators on a moot point of law; (2) *qiyás:* the method of analogical reasoning;[71] and (3) *ijtihád:* the application of critical personal reasoning in the interpretation of Islamic law.[72] These sources, particularly the *ijmá'* and *ijtihád,* proved to be crucial in providing answers to questions of law when primary sources were silent. As alluded to earlier, norms springing from the primary sources cannot be altered, whilst they may be subject to interpretation – whether through *ijmá'* or *ijtihád* all of which involve derivative legal reasoning.[73] Of course, novel principles

---

70 Burton, 1977, p. 54, see *supra* note 16.

71 This chapter, for lack of space, will not focus on such supplementary law-making processes as *qiyás*, which designate the analogical assimilation and application of a principle established in one case to subsequent cases involving similar issues. *Qiyás* is, therefore, not about bringing about a new ruling, but about the implementation of an extant injunction (or precedent) to a new case. It is, to put it simply, a tool used by jurists to compare cases and achieve a ruling by resorting to analogical methodology (see further, Dien, 2004, pp. 50–56, *supra* note 22).

72 Kamali Hashim, "Methodological Issues in Islamic Jurisprudence", in *Arab Law Quarterly*, 1996, vol. 11, p. 3; Noor Mohammed, "Principles of Islamic Contract Law", in *Journal of Law and Religion*, 1988, vol. 6, p. 115.

73 Hassan, 1982, p. 67, see *supra* note 4.

whose roots are not strictly embedded within primary sources may also be crafted, provided that the results fit the overall Islamic framework.

Secondary sources have thus provided a degree of flexibility to the development of law. In fact, although Islamic law owes its origins to the primary sources, it has overwhelmingly flourished due to juridical activity,[74] which was particularly intense during the classical period of Islamic civilisation. Classical jurists were keen to harmonise non-peremptory and derivative principles with socio-political dynamics. Al-Qarafi (d. 1285), in this context, wrote that "holding to rulings that have been deduced on the basis of custom, even after this custom has changed, is a violation of unanimous consensus and an open display of ignorance of the religion".[75]

When deriving secondary rulings, however, Muslim jurists have been restricted relative to their secular counterparts. Non-religious jurists are certainly restrained with such concerns as the hierarchy of the norms and principles of equity, but they may rely on their own resources while making law. The Muslim jurist, on the other hand, must lay bare the will of God reflected in the *Qur'án* and credible traditions, rather than proclaim the dictates of his own judgement. But this hardly prevented Muslim scholars from expanding on positive law without being cramped in blind literalism, though they were much more cautious about immutable principles.[76] Putting it otherwise, early scholars employed personal or collective reasoning to devise solutions for the immediate challenges, while trying to remain loyal to the objective, rationale and spirit of primary sources. As discussed below, it was only in the aftermath of this classical period that Islamic scholarship assumed a more constrained, text-oriented approach in disregard of evolving social and human context.

Whilst the supremacy of the holy sources is beyond dispute in Islamic law, equally important is the fact that this body of law is by no means bestowed upon humans as a panacea for all the troubles afflicting them. Contribution to the development of the law in keeping with the shifts of life is hence encouraged, if not ordained, by Islam. One of the

---

74 Schacht, 1982, p. 5, see *supra* note 21.

75 Al-Qarafi, cited in Sherman A. Jackson, "Jihad and the Modern World", in *Journal of Islamic Law and Culture*, 2002, vol. 7, p. 9.

76 Bernard G. Weiss, "Interpretation in Islamic Law: The Theory of Ijtihad", in *American Journal of Comparative Law*, 1978, vol. 26, p. 201; Ramadan, 2009, p. 39, see *supra* note 33.

principal requirements of Islamic belief is that the individual must attain a level of consciousness whereby he perceives the world not in an unquestioning way, but through the eyes of his heart and intellect. Reason in this sense must be put in the service of comprehending the world and understanding the signs of divine presence.[77] Indeed, the *Qur'án* invites and demands believers to reflect upon the real meaning of messages delivered to them, and when necessary to elaborate on divine rules.[78] As Weiss notes, very few rules of the divine legal corpus are "precisely spelled out for man's convenience", thus "man has the duty to *derive*" more detailed principles "from their sources" – a task which calls for "human involvement".[79]

It is in such an effort to keep pace with changing times that Muslim jurists crafted very many fresh principles and doctrines. But Islamic hermeneutics was bound to be derivative in nature, contingent on the absolute authority of God. This meant that there was no automatic validity accorded to the declarations of the jurist, who could only assert that what he formulated flowed from the divine law.[80] This explains why Muslim scholarship insists that the outcome of the derivative process constitutes mere opinions (*ẓann*), as opposed to definitive knowledge (*'ilm*).[81] Regardless of how rigorous the reasoning behind the construction of *ẓann* could be, the juridical outcome is indeed indefinite knowledge. The following pages turn in more detail to two most significant secondary sources: *ijtihád* and *ijmá'*.

2.3.1. Critical Thinking (*Ijtihád*)

The term *ijtihád* literally means 'striving' or 'self-exertion'. In legal usage, it is commonly defined as the endeavour of a jurist (*mujtahid*) to infer, by exerting himself to the best of his ability and on the basis of evidence found in the primary sources, a rule of Islamic law. *Ijtihád* thus incorporates an intellectual effort undertaken by qualified jurists to derive sec-

---

77 Colin Turner, *Islam: The Basics*, Routledge, New York, 2006, p. 72.

78 The *Qur'án*, 10:24; 30:8; 30:21; 34:46; 39:42; 59:21; 3:191, see *supra* note 5.

79 Weiss, 1978, p. 199, see *supra* note 76.

80 *Ibid.*, p. 203.

81 Jean J. Waardenburg, "The Early Period: 610–650", in Jean J. Waardenburg (ed.), *Muslim Perceptions of Other Religions: A Historical Survey*, Oxford University Press, New York, 1999, p. 4.

ondary norms.[82] Such independent reasoning is, then, exercised to provide answers to questions when the *Qur'án* and *Sunnah* are silent.

Reportedly, the permissibility of deducing secondary rulings through critical thinking had been encouraged by the Prophet himself. Tradition has it that when Muḥammad appointed Muadh Ibn Jabal as a judge in Yemen, he questioned the latter concerning the legitimate dynamics of decision-making: "Through which will you judge?", asked the Prophet. "Through the book of God", answered Muadh. "And if you find nothing in the Book of God?", returned Muḥammad. "I shall judge according to the tradition of God's Messenger", said Muadh. "And if you find nothing in the Messenger's tradition?", asked again the Prophet. "I shall not fail to make an effort [*ajtahidu*] to reach an opinion". It is reported that this response pleased the Prophet.[83] Nonetheless, *ijtihád* by qualified jurists is not only about deriving norms when the primary sources are silent; it is also about elucidating the divinely inspired material, particularly when the latter contained general or imprecise injunctions. The main role of independent reasoning has thus been to complement, expound and flesh out the primary norms in a bid to bridge the theory and practice of Islamic law.[84]

Ijtihád is often dubbed as independent or critical reasoning, because its use requires analytical thinking, and not the blind emulation (*taqlíd*) of past judgements of authoritative jurists. *Ijtihád* may hence be said to be the most significant source of Islamic law after the *Qur'án* and *Sunnah*; for while divine legislation had discontinued after the demise of Muḥammad, *ijtihád* retains its role for relating divine rulings to the human context. The theory of *ijtihád* clearly acknowledges the import of critical reasoning in contextualising the law, a process, which requires a dialectical engagement with relevant texts and ever-changing life. Weiss is thus right in emphasising that "the Law of God is empirically available [mainly] […] in the formulations of jurists".[85]

---

82 Vincent J. Cornell, *Voices of Islam: Voices of Tradition*, Praeger Publishers, Westport, 2007, p. 155; Schacht, 1982, p. 69, see *supra* note 21.

83 Tariq Ramadan, *The Messenger: The Meanings of the Life of Muhammad*, Penguin Books, London, 2007, p. 199.

84 Abdullahi Ahmed An-Na'im, *Toward an Islamic Reformation: Civil Liberties, Human Rights, and International Law*, Syracuse University Press, Syracuse, 1996, p. 27.

85 Weiss, 1978, p. 200, see *supra* note 76.

It must, however, be stressed that adherence to the letter of texts has enjoyed pride of place within orthodox Muslim scholarship. The supremacy of the textualist approach, particularly with regard to peremptory rulings, is evident in most Sunní scholars' attempts to steer clear of all appearances of formulating new rules independent of the divinely ordained norms.[86] In actual fact, the success of any critical thinking has essentially been judged by the extent to which consonance is achieved between the primary legislation and secondary law-making process. In Kamali's language, "since *ijtihád* derives its validity from divine revelation, its propriety is measured by its harmony with the *Qur'án* and the *Sunnah*".[87] The doctrine of *ijtihád*, then, does not presuppose a full measure of novelty, as the interpreter is charged with the duty to elucidate God's transcendent will for humans living in various ages and contexts.

This thinking, in other words, presupposes that a Muslim jurist does not *invent* rules, but midwifes norms and principles that are already present, albeit in a concealed or gnomic form, in sacred texts. However, it should be reiterated that opinions forged through *ijtihád* are deemed conjectural (*ẓann*). This means that a Muslim jurist is not bound by the rulings of other jurists exercising *ijtihád*, unless such an opinion is formed by a judge in a case constituting precedent. But, as illustrated below, when an individual opinion is so widely recognised as to generate a consensus opinion (*ijmá'*), it may become binding.

2.3.2. Juristic Consensus (*Ijmá'*)

The concept of juristic consensus (*ijmá'*) as an authoritative, binding source of Islamic law was originally conceived through the exercise of *ijtihád* undertaken by the Prophet's companions and learned scholars of the classical period,[88] a phenomenon that highlights the dialectical relationship between these two secondary sources. While a theological basis of *ijmá'* may not be found in the Qur'ánic text, it is said to have been based on a tradition attributed to the Prophet: "My community will not

---

86 Bernard G. Weiss, *The Spirit of Islamic Law*, University of Georgia Press, London, 2006, p. 86.

87 Kamali, 1989, p. 468, see *supra* note 20.

88 An-Na'im, 1996, p. 27, see *supra* note 84.

agree on error".[89] This is generally read to mean that after the Prophet, the Muslim community could concur with man-formulated doctrines and practices that were not expressed in the *Qur'án* and *Sunnah*. Absent prophetic guidance, Muḥammad's companions (*ṣaḥábah*) hence invoked the method of general consensus (*ijmá'*) to enrich the Islamic law. New norms extracted through this method formed a substantial portion of Islamic law, supplementing the primary sources.

The deduction of laws through *ijmá'* enabled jurists to formulate widely shared principles. But as the creation of new norms had been a collective effort drawing upon the sacred sources, the prevailing assumption was that novel principles forged through consensus could not be deemed ordinary in nature; rather, they formed part and parcel of the sacred law. This conclusion was borne out by the aforesaid tradition that the Muslim community was safeguarded against error. Accordingly, the process of *ijmá'* came to assume an "aura of holiness", the repudiation of whose outputs "became sinful in the eyes of some",[90] even though the law obtained via consensus remained derivative in character.

Ijmá' generally involved lengthy debates conducted by jurists over legal, moral, and practical matters. When such learned scholars reached an agreement on a controversial point, *ijmá'* was declared to have transpired, settling the matter conclusively – or at least until revoked by further *ijmá'*. The norm created through this process was considered binding.[91] Therein lay the principal difference between *ijtihád* and *ijmá'*, although they are interlaced: while the former could engender conflicting views over a moot point, the latter produced an authoritative response thereto. Consensus of opinion thus had the advantage of achieving definitive knowledge until a new, invalidating consensus crystallised to replace the former. As Esposito puts it, "the relationship between *ijtihád* and

---

89 Iysa A. Bello, *The Medieval Islamic Controversy Between Philosophy and Orthodoxy: Ijma and Tawil in the Conflict between Al-Ghazali and Ibn Rushd*, Brill, Leiden, 1989, p. 35.

90 Ali Khan, "The Reopening of the Islamic Code: The Second Era of Ijtihad", in *University of St. Thomas Law Journal*, 2003, vol. 1, p. 365.

91 Hassan, 1982, p. 65, see *supra* note 4.

ijmá' was an on-going process, moving from individual opinion to community approval to accepted practice to difference".[92]

Certainly, in the absence of consensus opinion, alternative views were considered equally valid. When there had been competing viewpoints advanced by recognised schools of thought, these were correspondingly deemed authoritative. In the absence of unanimity, there was no basis to require Muslims of various schools to adhere to a single view – each school could justify their reading of the authoritative sources.

The doctrine of consensus in this sense tacitly recognised difference over moral and legal issues as inevitable. By the mid-tenth century, jurisprudential schools had generally demarcated their intellectual territories through their distinguishing doctrines, expanding upon a sizeable corpus of politico-legal literature. Among these schools, only the principal ones managed to survive into contemporary times. These are the *Ḥanafí* school, founded by Abú Ḥanífah (d. 767); the *Máliki* school, established by Málik Ibn Anas (d. 795); the *S͟háfi'í* school, based on the teachings of Idris Al-S͟háfi'í (d. 820); the *Ḥanbalí* school, set up by Ahmed Ibn Ḥanbal (d. 855); and the *Ja'farí* school, a *S͟hí'ah* school of jurisprudence, following the teachings of Abú Jafar Muḥammad Al-Baqir (d. 731) and Jafar Sadiq (d. 765).[93] Through scholarly consensus, a notable body of judicial speculations were rendered into categorical rulings,[94] giving substance to many tentative positions.

Over time, *ijmá'* had not only reinforced the authority of learned jurists (*'ulama'*), but also largely standardised the legal position on thorny issues. Arguably, the most damaging consequence of consensus-based doctrines was that disagreeing jurists had effectively been deterred from re-examining established judgements. What is more, particularly from the tenth century onwards, *Sunní* scholars came to think that since classical jurists of the calibre of Ḥanífah, Málik, Ḥanbal and S͟háfi'í had ceased to thrive, jurists of established schools would henceforth dominate the intel-

92 John L. Esposito, *Women in Muslim Family Law*, Syracuse University Press, New York, 2001, p. 148.

93 Slim Laghmani, "Les Écoles Juridiques du Sunnisme", in *Pouvoirs*, 2003, vol. 104, p. 25.

94 Wael B. Hallaq, "On the Authoritativeness of Sunní Consensus", in *International Journal of Middle East Studies*, 1986, vol. 18, p. 428.

lectual scene of the Muslim jurisprudence.[95] Over time, Muslim jurists had been urged against challenging entrenched doctrines, a stance which paved the way to orthodoxy where more liberal thinking was replaced by analogical reasoning and crude modelling on precedents.

2.3.3. The Temporary Ending of Critical Thinking

It was stressed above that, by the turn of the ninth century, independent reasoning and consensus-based doctrines led to the growth of a sizeable corpus of rulings and precedents. From this point onwards, however, most scholars, generally representing the *Sunní* tradition, came to claim that all key questions of law had been resolved by major schools, and hence personal interpretation of Islamic law was no longer necessary.[96] The early signs of legal rigidity had already become visible due to the purported infallibility of the consensus method. Scholars of this age posited that since all crucial questions had been exhaustively settled, the future activity of the jurist needed to be confined to the clarification of the law or doctrine as had already been laid down. The task of the jurist was simply to emulate (*taqlíd*), follow or expound the existent precedent or principle.[97]

This policy finally assumed an official character by the declaration of the Iraqi jurists to "close the door" for the exercise of *ijtihád*,[98] which confined independent reasoning chiefly to applying precedents, and to drawing straight conclusions from the recognised handbooks. This signified that legal norms could no longer be extracted directly from the primary sources, but from the textbooks of recognised schools, and hence any juristic attempt to breach the confines of endorsed doctrines could give rise to claims of heresy.

---

[95] Wael B. Hallaq, "On the Origins of the Controversy about the Existence of Mujtahids and the Gate of Ijtihad", in *Studia Islamica*, 1986, vol. 63, p. 136; Bernard Lewis, *The Middle East: 2000 Years of History from the Rise of Christianity to the Present Day*, Phoenix Press, London, 2000, p. 225.

[96] Esposito, 1994, p. 195, see *supra* note 45.

[97] Bernard Lewis and Buntzie Ellis Churchill, *Islam: The Religion and the People*, Wharton School Publishing, New Jersey, 2008, p. 29; Karima Bennoune, "*As-Salámu Alaykum*? Humanitarian Law in Islamic Jurisprudence", in *Michigan Journal of International Law*, 1994, vol. 15, p. 613.

[98] Irshad Abdal-Haqq, "Islamic Law: An Overview of its Origins and Elements", in Hisham M. Ramadan (ed.), *Understanding Islamic Law: From Classical to Contemporary*, AltaMira Press, Oxford, 2006, p. 21; Wael B. Hallaq, "Was the Gate of *Ijtihád* Closed?", in *International Journal of Middle East Studies*, 1984, vol. 16, p. 5.

Arguably, in addition to the propensity of dominant circles to maintain the politico-legal status quo, a key contributor to the discontinuation of *ijtihád* had been the concern to standardise the legal tradition in an empire whose borders stretched far and wide. Muslim rulers and orthodox scholars alike dreaded the possibility of divisive impact of critical thinking and independent reasoning over the unity of Islamic jurisprudence-which was already splintered into numerous schools. Standardisation of the tradition through imitation and strict analogy could initially have prevented the intrusion of anomalous concepts, ideas, or traditions. However, casting the law into rigid formulas and black-letter analyses, and divesting the tradition of its dynamism eventually took its toll on the progress and adaptability of Islamic law.

Certainly, Muslim jurists had not altogether abandoned the practice of independent reasoning.[99] For instance, the eminent philosopher and jurist Al-Ghazálí (d. 1111) argued that critical thinking based on wider analogy, as opposed to narrow syllogism, and on the general purposes of law was permissible.[100] Ibn Taymiyya (d. 1328) likewise advocated the indispensability of *ijtihád* so that Islamic thought could be saved from stagnation.[101] Nonetheless, the tide of relying on orthodox interpretation of extant sources progressively rose, and over the centuries far fewer jurists claimed to possess the required qualifications to formulate novel ideas. Hence, whilst the doors of *ijtihád* remained ajar, Muslim jurists ceased to widely exercise it to resolve new problems. As Hashmi observes, the fact that some of the most canonical source books on Islamic law, like Al-Shaybání's work on Islamic law of nations (*Kitáb Al-Siyar Al-Kabír*), remain centuries old demonstrates the extent to which Islamic thought stagnated.[102] A mental straightjacket of this sort indeed stunted the Muslim law for nearly a millennium. Be that as it may, there is no hard-and-

---

99 Abdulaziz A. Sachedina, *The Just Ruler in Shi'ite Islam: The Comprehensive Authority of the Jurist in Imámite Jurisprudence*, Oxford University Press, Oxford, 1988, p. 159.

100 Imran A. K. Nyazee, *Theories of Islamic Law: The Methodology of Ijtihád*, The Other Press, Islamabad, 1994, p. 195.

101 Bernard Haykel, "On the Nature of Salafi Thought and Action", in Roel Meijer (ed.), *Global Salafism: Islam's New Religious Movement*, Columbia University Press, New York, 2009, p. 43.

102 Sohail H. Hashmi, "Islamic Ethics in International Society", in Sohail H. Hashmi (ed.), *Islamic Political Ethics: Civil Society, Pluralism, and Conflict*, Princeton University Press, Princeton, 2002, p. 151.

fast rule in Islam to prevent contemporary scholars from resorting to *ijtihád* to invigorate the law and make it more responsive to current realities.

2.4. Conclusion: Re-opening the Door for Critical Thinking

There is little doubt that blind adherence to orthodox doctrines up until modern times has, in large measure, been responsible for the decline of Muslim thought in almost all intellectual realms. The artificial shackles placed on Islam's inherent dynamism further paved the way for Western domination and colonialism in all its forms and manifestations over large parts of the Muslim-majority world. This eventually sparked considerable debate over the ways in which such hegemony could be countered and the once-glorious Islamic culture could be resurrected. By the end of the eighteenth century, it became unmistakably clear that the key institutions of the Muslim world were in steep decline, as judged against Western standards and progress in most areas that were defining the socio-political and economic contours of the modern period.[103]

Western domination eventually compelled Muslim thinkers to reflect on the precarious balance between entrenched religious standards and the changing demands of modern exigencies. The pressures exerted by such material and conceptual novelties, paired with the colonial enterprise over Muslim countries, eventually divided Muslim intellectuals as to whether essential modern concepts, ideas and institutions needed to be integrated or rejected-whether wholly or in part.[104] As Esposito puts it, Muslim reactions to Western power and domination ranged from rejection to adaptation, from a policy of cultural isolation and non-cooperation to acculturation and reform.[105]

By the late nineteenth century, reformist movements incrementally gained momentum within Muslim intelligentsia, advocating an overhaul of politico-legal, economic, military and cultural institutions.[106] Irrespective of their intellectual backgrounds, almost all reformist thinkers chal-

[103] Harry F. Hinsley, *Power and the Pursuit of Peace: Theory and Practice in the History of Relations between States*, Cambridge University Press, Cambridge, 1963, p. 153.

[104] Fazlur Rahmán, *Islam & Modernity: Transformation of an Intellectual Tradition*, University of Chicago Press, Chicago, 1982, p. 4.

[105] John L. Esposito, *Islam and Politics*, Syracuse University Press, Syracuse, 1987, p. 43.

[106] Khaled Fahmy, *All the Pasha's Men: Mehmed Ali, His Army and the Making of Modern Egypt*, The American University in Cairo, Cairo, 1997, p. 253.

lenged the *status quo ante* in a quest for ways to transform their societies by, among other things, criticising dogmatic religious premises and advocating progress to reverse the tide of decline. Islam, they essentially maintained, had to undergo a process of reformation and reinvigoration in respect of "mutable principles"[107] so that Muslims could awaken from their debilitating slumber that rendered Islamic thought bankrupt of any viable intellectual remedy responsive to modernity.

Reformers saw the restrictions on innovative thinking as hampering the progress of Muslims, positing that each generation of Muslims must be permitted to resolve the particular problems of their age through critical deliberation. For only in this way would the deleterious effects of unquestioned emulation be averted and the richness of Islamic thinking be saved from rigid dogmas. Reformist thinking hence highlighted the imperative for substantial reinterpretation and reconstruction of many basic concepts and principles via free discussion, open-mindedness, and rigorous scholarship.[108]

The impact of such reformist calls has hitherto been notable across the Muslim world, which, particularly since the nineteenth century onwards, has gone through dramatic transformations, including the phenomena of modernity in all spheres of life, socio-political liberalisation, and independence from colonial subjugation. In an effort to allow Islamic law to meet the growing challenges of faith and contemporary exigencies, many reformist-minded thinkers have rightly championed the revival of independent, critical thinking. Among the most pressing problems constituting battlegrounds for reformists have been such controversial themes as science *vis-à-vis* religion, secularism, rule of law, religious freedoms, human rights, and Islamic use of force.[109] Having drawn on the overall Islamic ethical framework, which places significant emphasis on such notions as justice, equity, non-discrimination and reciprocity, Muslim schol-

---

[107] John L. Esposito, "Trailblazers of the Islamic Resurgence", in Yvonne Yazbeck Haddad, John Obert Voll and John L. Esposito (eds.), *The Contemporary Islamic Revival: A Critical Survey and Bibliography*, Greenwood Publishing, Westport, 1991, p. 53; Beverly M. Edwards, *Islamic Fundamentalism since 1945*, Routledge, London, 2005, p. 20.

[108] Olivier Roy, *Secularism Confronts Islam*, Columbia University Press, New York, 2009, p. 45.

[109] Abdullahi Ahmed An-Na'im, *Islam and the Secular State: Negotiating the Future of Shari'a*, Harvard University Press, Massachusetts, 2008, p. 111; Ramadan, 2009, p. 207, see *supra* note 33; Esposito, 2010, p. 86, see *supra* note 40.

ars still seek to address these thorny problems that require radical rethinking.

One critical consequence of this change in perspective is that *non-eternal* rulings may now be understood against the backdrop of their politico-cultural setting and context that provided the rationale thereof. Consequently, such a contextualised method of hermeneutics requires the abandonment of outdated doctrines, except for timeless principles, in favour of developing new modes of thinking. This will in all likelihood also enable Muslims to undercut the generally ideological and biased portrayal of Islam as an inherently war-like and obscurantist faith. Finally, reopening the door widely for critical thinking has the potential to demonstrate the complexity of religious attitude towards issues of warfare, peace and criminal justice – themes to which the remainder of this edited collection will devote attention.

3

Islamic Socio-Legal Norms and International Criminal Justice in Context: Advancing an 'Object and Purpose' cum '*Maqáṣid*' Approach

Mashood A. Baderin*

3.1. Introduction

The idea of international criminal justice is underpinned by the need for international *responsiveness* (as opposed to mere reaction) to "the most serious crimes of concern to the international community as a whole".[1] Such crimes are committed mostly during armed conflicts without the perpetrators being brought to justice by the states in whose jurisdiction they are committed, thus prompting the need for international responsiveness. Past and ongoing conflicts in different parts of the Muslim world such as Iraq, Libya, Syria, and Yemen, in which atrocious crimes have been committed by both state and non-state actors, beg the question of what role can Islamic norms play in ensuring the effective realisation of the objectives of international criminal justice, particularly in the Muslim world? Do Islamic social norms generally have anything to contribute to the effectiveness of modern international criminal justice? Is Islamic law, as some have argued,[2] so radically different and unsupportive of interna-

---

* **Mashood A. Baderin** is a Professor of Laws at the School of Oriental and African Studies (SOAS), University of London, United Kingdom. He teaches and researches in the areas of Islamic law, international law, human rights law, and law and development in Africa, with particular interest in the interaction between human rights law and Islamic law in Muslim-majority states. He served as the UN Independent Expert on the Situation of Human Rights in the Sudan from May 2012 to November 2014.

1 Statute of the International Criminal Court, 17 July 1998, in force 1 July 2001 ('ICC Statute'), Article 5 (http://www.legal-tools.org/doc/7b9af9/).

2 See, for example, David A. Westbrook, "Islamic International Law and Public International Law: Separate Expressions of World Order", in *Virginia Journal of International Law*, 1993, vol. 33, p. 819; Christopher A. Ford, "Siyar-ization and Its Discontents: International Law and Islam's Constitutional Crisis", in *Texas International Law Journal*, 1995, vol. 30, p. 499.

tional criminal justice, or can it contribute to the effective implementation of international criminal justice in the modern world?[3] These questions have become more pertinent due to the increasing influence of Islamic socio-legal norms in many Muslim-majority states today and also the status of Islamic law as a recognised legal system in the modern world, with growing propositions for the recognition of its principles by international tribunals such as the International Court of Justice ('ICJ'), pursuant to Article 38(b) of the ICJ Statute,[4] and the International Criminal Court ('ICC') pursuant to Article 22(1)(c) of the ICC Statute.[5]

Like other questions of international law, questions of international criminal justice are often addressed monolithically from Western secular legal perspectives without much consideration of contributions that other worldviews, such as Islam, can make to strengthen its universal acceptance. With reference to the Muslim world, this chapter proposes that Islamic socio-legal norms (broadly defined) have positive potential, which can and should be explored to deepen the universal effectiveness of international criminal justice in today's world. The chapter disagrees with the view that Islamic law is irreconcilable with the concept of international criminal justice, and provides a contextual analysis of how the two systems can complementarily effect the shared objective of a more humane world. Also, international criminal justice is often perceived restrictively, as a form of punitive justice that is applicable only after the commission of heinous crimes that shock the human conscience globally. Much of the traditional literature on the subject focuses mainly on punitive justice "in the form of international war crimes trials"[6] to punish perpetrators of in-

3 Michael J. Kelly, "Islam and International Criminal Law: A Brief (In)compatibility Study", in *Pace International Law Review Online Companion*, 2010, vol. 8, pp. 2–31.

4 Clark Lombardi, "Islamic Law in the Jurisprudence of the International Court of Justice: An Analysis", in *Chicago Journal of International Law*, 2007, vol. 1, pp. 85–118; Mashood A. Baderin, "Religion and International Law: Friends or Foes?", in *European Human Rights Law Review*, 2009, pp. 655–57. See also Statute of the International Court of Justice, 26 June 1945, Article 38(b) (http://www.legal-tools.org/doc/fdd2d2/).

5 See Mohamed Badar, "Islamic Law (Shari'a) and the Jurisdiction of the International Criminal Court", in *Leiden Journal of International Law*, 2011, vol. 24, no. 2, pp. 411–33. See also ICC Statute, Article 22(1)(c), *supra* note 1 (http://www.legal-tools.org/doc/7b9af9/).

6 Gideon Boas, "What is International Criminal Justice", in Gideon Boas, William A. Schabas and Michael P. Scharf (eds.), *International Criminal Justice: Legitimacy and Coherence*, Edward Elgar Publishing Ltd., Cheltenham, 2012, p. 1.

ternational crimes, with the hope that such punishment would serve as a legal deterrent against future crimes.[7] In view of the debate about whether international criminal trials have really succeeded in serving as a deterrent against future atrocities,[8] this chapter advances a holistic view of international criminal justice, not perceived restrictively as a post-conflict punitive concept, but also understood and promoted as a pre-conflict humane concept that addresses the social and moral conscience of humanity to detest the commission of such heinous crimes in the first place. It advances a holistic conceptualisation of international criminal justice covering its social, moral, political and legal elements in relation to Islamic socio-legal norms and how that can be explored for enhancing international criminal justice, particularly in the Muslim world.

In addressing the question "What is international criminal justice?", Gideon Boas states:[9]

> International criminal justice is about more than responses. How do we learn from history or sometimes fail to do so? Can we use our understanding of human psychology to respond better to mass atrocity, or to prevent or address it sooner? What of the sociological elements that are infused in our response to heinous international crimes; how do these affect our understanding of international criminal justice?

He then notes that "while as international lawyers we have raised important questions about legitimacy and coherence, we do not always open ourselves to a genuinely multidisciplinary approach to international criminal justice".[10] Relatedly, the need has also been identified for "considering international criminal justice as a critical [universalist] project", particularly with reference to alternative perspectives that question its Euro-

7 Cf. Mark Findlay and Ralph Henham (eds.), *Beyond Punishment: Achieving International Criminal Justice*, Palgrave Macmillan, Basingstoke, 2010.

8 Chris Jenks and Guido Acquaviva, "Debate: The Role of International Criminal Justice in Fostering Compliance with International Humanitarian Law", in *International Review of the Red Cross*, 2014, vol. 96, pp. 775–94; Jennifer Schense and Linda Carter, *Two Steps Forward One Step Back: The Deterrent Effect of International Criminal Tribunals*, International Nuremberg Principles Academy, Nuremberg, 2016.

9 Boas, 2012, p. 1, see *supra* note 6.

10 *Ibid.*

centrism and promote its universal legitimacy.[11] Thus, this chapter proposes the need for an inclusive approach to international criminal justice that involves learning from our collective human history and accommodating social, moral, political, and legal understandings of relevant norms from different civilisations, with specific reference to Islamic socio-legal norms, to enhance international responsiveness to heinous crimes that shock the conscience of the international community as a whole.

The social and moral perspectives ask the question 'why?' relating to the normative foundations of international criminal justice, while the political and legal perspectives ask the question 'what?' relating to its institutional constructions. This reflects the necessary linkage between the socio-moral and politico-legal dimensions of international criminal justice. International responsiveness to heinous crimes should thus not be restricted to secular legalistic worldviews, but should also be examined within the context of religious and cultural beliefs. People who commit international crimes often act on certain distorted beliefs and understandings, which need to be challenged by reference to alternative convincing internal evidence, to win and dissuade minds from committing those atrocities in the first place. To effectively dissuade the commission of international crimes during armed conflicts in the Muslim world, it is necessary to promote a holistic and complementary understanding of the relationship between international criminal justice and Islamic socio-legal norms. In doing so, this chapter advances a combined application of the 'object and purpose' principle under international law and the '*maqâṣid*' principle under Islamic law to rationalise the complementary relationship between the two systems.

3.2. 'Object and Purpose' and '*Maqâṣid*' as Comparable Normative Principles

Basically, the concepts of 'object and purpose' and '*maqâṣid*' are comparable normative principles of international law and Islamic law respectively. The object and purpose principle is an international law concept applicable to the law of treaties for ensuring adherence to the primary objective of a treaty. The relevancy of this principle lies in the fact that treaties are a fundamental basis of international criminal justice and also the most im-

[11] Julien Pieret and Marie-Laurence Hébert-Dolbec, "International Criminal Justice as a Critical Project: Introduction", in *Champ Pénal/Penal Field*, 2016, vol. XIII.

portant source of international law generally. The effect of the object and purpose principle is reflected in eight different articles of the 1969 Vienna Convention on the Law of Treaties.[12] It is obvious from the provisions cited that the object and purpose is the nucleus of a treaty, which the substantive provisions are aimed to achieve.

There is some debate about how the object and purpose is to be determined where not specifically stated by the treaty. Nevertheless, there is established judicial and academic understanding that the object and purpose can be deduced from a treaty's historical context or its preamble. Hulme notes that "preambles are more frequently cited as sources or evidence of a treaty's 'object and purpose'".[13] The preamble normally provides insight into the context, philosophy and morals underlying a treaty's adoption. Ironically, not much attention is paid to the object and purpose of treaties to enhance their moral strength and effectiveness. Hulme further argues: "In light of treaties' longstanding structure [...] it is surpris-

---

12 Vienna Convention on the Law of Treaties ('VCLT'), 23 May 1969, in force 27 January 1980 (http://www.legal-tools.org/doc/6bfcd4/). In ascending order, Article 18 of the VCLT obligates states "to refrain from acts that would defeat the object and purpose of a treaty"; Article 19(c) prohibits states from entering any reservation that "is incompatible with the object and purpose of [a] treaty"; Article 20(2) provides that a reservation to a treaty will require the acceptance by all parties to the treaty, when it appears from the object and purpose of the treaty that the application of the treaty in its entirety between all the parties is an essential condition for each one to be bound by the treaty; Article 31(3) provides that a treaty shall be interpreted in good faith "in the light of its object and purpose"; Article 33(4) provides that the object and purpose of a treaty shall be a reference point in resolving any differences of meaning in different authentic texts of the treaty; Article 41(1)(b)(ii) provides that two or more parties to a multi-lateral treaty may only agree to modify the treaty as between themselves alone if the modification in question is, *inter alia*, not incompatible with the effective execution of the object and purpose of the treaty as a whole; Article 58(1)(b)(ii) provides that two or more parties to a multi-lateral treaty may only agree to suspend the application of provisions of the treaty temporarily as between themselves if the suspension in question "is not incompatible with the object and purpose of the treaty"; and Article 60(3)(b) provides that "violation of a provision essential to the accomplishment of the object and purpose of [a] treaty" constitutes a material breach of the treaty.

13 Max H. Hulme, "Preambles in Treaty Interpretation", in *University of Pennsylvania Law Review*, 2016, vol. 164, p. 1300. For an earlier judicial position, see the dissenting opinion of Judge Anzilotti in the Permanent Court of International Justice ('PCIJ'), Advisory Opinion in Interpretation of the Convention of 1919 Concerning Employment of Women During the Night, (1932) PCIJ, Series A/B, No. 50, pp. 383–89 (http://www.legal-tools.org/doc/1839b9/). See also Isabelle Buffard and Karl Zemanek, "The 'Object and Purpose' of a Treaty: An Enigma?", in *Australian Review of International and European Law*, 1998, vol. 3, pp. 311–43.

ing that the ubiquitous preamble has received so little attention".[14] Attention is often placed mainly on the substantive provisions of a treaty to the detriment of the preamble, which is usually considered as having no binding effect.[15] Although its binding nature is debatable, the moral value of the preamble as repository of a treaty's object and purpose is settled. Thus, the moral justification of a treaty is in its object and purpose, which should be evoked to advance universal acceptance of the international norm conveyed by the treaty.

As the object and purpose principle applies generally to international treaties, it is applicable to all treaties relating to international criminal justice such as international humanitarian law, international human rights law and international criminal law, as will be analysed later. We can aim to identify the object and purpose of each of these specific areas of international law from the respective treaty preambles and their historical contexts. This provides an objective and common moral yardstick for reconciling the norms of international criminal justice with relevant Islamic norms. As academic efforts to reconcile Islamic norms with international norms are sometimes misconceived as questionable attempts to simply subjugate Islamic norms to international norms, identifying and advancing the object and purpose of the respective international norm provides an objective moral justificatory basis of complementarity between the two systems.

Similarly, the concept of *maqáṣid* is also a normative principle of Islamic law formulated by classical Islamic jurists to promote a contextual understanding of *Sharí'ah* provisions. The full Arabic terminology for the principle is '*maqáṣid al-Sharí'ah*', which has been translated variously in the English language as "objects and purposes of the *Sharí'ah*",[16] "aims and intentions of the law",[17] "existential purpose of the law",[18] "higher

[14] Hulme, 2016, p. 1283, see *supra* note 13.

[15] *Ibid.*, p. 1285.

[16] Mashood A. Baderin, *International Human Rights and Islamic Law*, Oxford University Press, Oxford, 2003, p. 40.

[17] Wael B. Hallaq, *A History of Islamic Legal Theories*, Cambridge University Press, Cambridge, 1997, p. 167

[18] *Ibid.*, p. 168.

objectives of Islamic law",[19] "higher intents of Islamic law"[20] "goals and purposes of the *Sharí'ah*",[21] "the goals and objectives of Islamic law"[22] and "philosophy of Islamic law".[23] It is similar in many ways to the object and purpose principle under international law. For Muslims, the *Sharí'ah* (consisting of the *Qur'án* and the *Sunnah*) is the fundamental source from which all Islamic norms draw validity. The *Qur'án* contains the divine and immutable injunctions of God while the *Sunnah* depicts the practices of Prophet Muḥammad as reported in authentic *aḥádíth* (Traditions). The provisions of both sources are, however, subject to human speculative interpretations, which can be either literal or contextual. Literal interpretations can often lead to out-of-context and reductionist understandings of the *Sharí'ah*. Thus, the classical Islamic jurists formulated the concept of *maqáṣid* to ensure that the provisions of the *Sharí'ah* are not interpreted contrary to its intended objectives.

Based on Qur'ánic verses such as "God desires ease for you, and desires not hardship for you",[24] "God does not desire to make any impediment for you",[25] "[God] has laid on you no impediment in your religion",[26] "We have not sent thee [Muḥammad], save as a mercy unto all beings",[27] "Now there has come to you a Messenger from among yourselves, grievous to him is your suffering";[28] and authentic Traditions of the Prophet such as "Verily the religion is easy, and no one overstretches himself in the religion except that it crushes him, so be moderate and try

[19] Ahmad Al-Raysuni (translated by Nancy Roberts), *Imam Shatibi's Theory of the Higher Objectives and Intents of Islamic Law*, The International Institute of Islamic Thought, Washington, 2005, p. xxi.

[20] Gamal Eldin Attia, *Towards Realization of the Higher Intents of Islamic Law*, The International Institute of Islamic Thought, Washington, D.C., 2007.

[21] M. Cherif Bassiouni, *The Shari'a and Islamic Criminal Justice in Time of War and Peace*, Cambridge University Press, Cambridge, 2014, p. 68.

[22] Mohammad Hashim Kamali, "*Maqáṣid Al-Sharí'ah*: The Objectives of Islamic Law", in *Islamic Studies*, 1999, vol. 38, no. 2, pp. 193–208.

[23] Jasser Auda, *Maqasid Al-Shariah as Philosophy of Islamic Law: A Systems Approach*, International Institute of Islamic Thought, London, 2007.

[24] The *Qur'án* (translation by Arthur J. Arberry), 2:184.

[25] *Ibid.*, 5:6.

[26] *Ibid.*, 22:78.

[27] *Ibid.*, 21:107.

[28] *Ibid.*, 9:128.

to be near perfection and take glad tidings",[29] "The best of your religion is that which is easiest, the best of your religion is that which is easiest",[30] and "Make things easy and do not make things difficult, give glad tidings and do not put people off";[31] the classical Islamic jurists identified the general *maqáṣid* of the *Sharí'ah* as the promotion of human well-being (*al-moṣalaḥah*) and prevention of harm (*mafsadah*), often referred to collectively as *al-moṣalaḥah.* This concept of *al-moṣalaḥah* may be perceived narrowly as promoting only the well-being of the Muslim community (*ummah*) specifically or broadly as promoting the well-being of humanity generally. Obviously, perceiving it broadly as the well-being of humanity generally is more consistent with international norms. The primary Islamic jurisprudential position is that the *maqáṣid* of the *Sharí'ah* is to promote the well-being of humanity generally, which also incorporates the well-being of the Muslim *ummah.* This is evidenced by the *Qur'án*'s description of God as "[t]he Lord of men",[32] "[t]he Lord of all Being"[33] and of the Prophet as "a mercy unto all beings".[34] However, where the well-being of the Muslim *ummah* is endangered, then the *maqáṣid* would, justifiably, revolve to protecting the well-being of the Muslim *ummah* specifically. Thus, similar to the object and purpose principle under international law, the *maqáṣid* principle is for ensuring adherence to the objectives of the *Sharí'ah,* deducible from the *Qur'án* and the *Sunnah* as promoting human well-being generally.

Although the notion of *maqáṣid al-Sharí'ah* had been in use informally much earlier,[35] the fourteenth century Andalusian Islamic jurist Abú Isháq Al-Shátibí is considered generally to be its formal initiator owing to his contribution to its formal recognition as we know it today. In his renowned Islamic jurisprudential work, *Al-Muwáfaqát fí Usúl al-Shari'ah,*

---

29 Reported by Al-Bukhári, Book 2, *ḥadíth* 39.

30 Reported by Musnad Ahmad (3/479).

31 Reported by Al-Bukhári, Book 3, *ḥadíth* 69.

32 The *Qur'án*, 114:1, see *supra* note 24. The verse is "*rabb al-Nás*" in Arabic. While the term "*al-Nás*" is often translated as 'men' in English, as in Arberry's translation here, this should not be misconstrued genderwise as meaning the plural of 'man' and thus excluding women, but construed as meaning 'mankind' or humans generally, and thus '*rabb al-Nás*' should be contextually understood as meaning "[t]he Lord of all mankind".

33 *Ibid.*, 1:1.

34 *Ibid.*, 21:107.

35 Kamali, 1999, p. 2, see *supra* note 22.

Al-Shátibí noted that the original intention of God in revealing the *Sharí'ah* is to protect human well-being and thus in interpreting any verse of the *Qur'án* or Tradition of the Prophet, care must be taken not to contradict the general objective of the *Sharí'ah* which is *maṣlaḥah*. He considered the *maqáṣid* as a necessary principle for proper jurisprudential reasoning (*ijtihád*) in Islamic law.[36] Today, the *maqáṣid* principle is acknowledged by most contemporary Islamic scholars and jurists as the necessary jurisprudential tool for reconciling Islamic law with different contemporary issues such as human rights and humanitarian law generally. For example, Kamali has observed that the *maqáṣid* principle is an evidently important theme of the *Sharí'ah* and that "the *Sharí'ah* generally is predicated on benefits to the individual and the community, and its laws are designed so as to protect these benefits and to facilitate the improvement and perfection of the conditions of human life on earth".[37] Thus, the *maqáṣid* principle provides a proper contextual approach for advancing the benevolent scope of Islamic law.

Apart from the general *maqáṣid* of the *Sharí'ah*, there is also recognition that each specific area of Islamic law, such as Islamic family law, Islamic humanitarian law and Islamic international law, has its respective objective (*maqṣúd*) within the context of the general *maqáṣid*. Thus, the *maqáṣid* principle will be employed to explore the role of Islamic socio-legal norms in enhancing international criminal justice, particularly in the Muslim world, by reference to relevant provisions of the *Qur'án* and the *Sunnah* in relation to both the general *maqáṣid* of the *Sharí'ah* and the specific *maqṣúd* of identified areas of Islamic law relevant to international criminal justice.

From the above analysis of these two comparable normative principles, it is obvious that both international law and Islamic law are not instituted or meant to be applied *in abstracto*. Rather, both systems were instituted to achieve identifiable objectives, the appreciation of which is necessary for establishing an objective relationship between the two systems. Generally, these two respective principles of international law and Islamic law provides the basis for a common objective of attaining a more hu-

36 Ibrahim Al-Shatibi (translated by Imran Ahsan Khan Nyazee), *The Reconciliation of the Fundamentals of Islamic Law*, Al-Muwáfaqát fí Úṣúl Al-Sharí'a, vols. 1 and 2, Garnet Publishing Ltd., 2012, p. 229.

37 Kamali, 1999, p. 229, see *supra* note 22.

mane world, which can be evoked for promoting a complementary relationship between the two systems.

3.3. The Basis of International Criminal Justice in Relation to Islamic Socio-Legal Norms

Today, certain acts are considered international crimes for which perpetrators must be brought to justice, based "largely on the notion that some crimes are so heinous that they offend the interest of all humanity, and, indeed, imperil civilization itself".[38] Thus, international criminal justice is essentially linked to international humanitarian law, which regulates and puts constraints on the conduct of warfare; international human rights law, which promotes the protection of human dignity; and international criminal law, which prohibits and prescribes punishments for certain core crimes under international law. These three specialised areas of international law may be described as the three pillars of the international criminal justice system, as they together provide the substantive basis for which international criminal justice applies. For example, 'war crimes' and 'genocide' are two of the substantive crimes punishable under international criminal law, with the former being a consequence of the violation of core norms of international humanitarian law and the latter being a consequence of the violation of the norms of international human rights law. Thus, an appreciation of international humanitarian law, international human rights law and international criminal law as the basis of international criminal justice is essential for an effective preventive international criminal justice system. For example, it is when the rules of international humanitarian law are violated that the need to punish war crimes arises under international criminal justice. Thus, promoting adherence to international humanitarian law is essential to preventing the occurrence of war crimes in the first place. Similarly, respect for international human rights law would prevent the occurrence of atrocities such as genocide, while respect for international criminal law would automatically ensure a preventive international criminal justice system.

While international humanitarian law, international human rights law and international criminal law are all international legal regimes, they

---

38 Leila Nadya Sadat, "Competing and Overlapping Jurisdiction", in M. Cherif Bassiouni (ed.), *International Criminal Law*, vol. 2, 3rd ed., Martinus Nijhoff Publishers, Leiden, 2008, p. 207.

are evidently motivated by morals and humaneness, which are important factors for promoting adherence to them. In relation to the Muslim world, linking the morals underlying international humanitarian law, international human rights law, and international criminal law to Islamic socio-legal norms can go a long way to ensure adherence to these international normative regimes. Thus, a better contextual understanding of the relationship between Islamic socio-legal norms and international criminal justice first requires an Islamic socio-legal connection with each one of international humanitarian law, international human rights law and international criminal law as the basis of international criminal justice.

3.3.1. Islamic Socio-Legal Connection with International Humanitarian Law

Bassiouni traced the history of warfare back to the biblical account of Cain's murder of his brother Abel, which also has an Islamic account in the *Qur'án*,[39] noting that what started with brother against brother subsequently "turned to family against family, tribe against tribe, and nation against nation",[40] as is witnessed today. He observed that "between 1945 and 2008 there were an estimated 313 conflicts, which collectively resulted in the killing of an estimated one hundred million persons, excluding other human and material harm".[41] The numbers have escalated greatly since 2008. The morality of such human annihilation and harm is difficult to justify from both an Islamic or secular point of view. Wars have been traditionally fought with brutality aimed at total destruction of the enemy and resulting in the commission of heinous atrocities, devastation and great human suffering. In light of the difficulty in preventing warfare completely, the realistic option, from ancient times, was to aim at regulating the conduct of warfare to limit, on humanitarian grounds, the devastation of war. This was first achieved through customary rules and subsequently through formal treaty law in modern times.[42] The regulation of

[39] The Islamic account of this incident is in the *Qur'án*, 5:12–31, which rounds up with two important verses proscribing arbitrary killing and mischief on Earth at 5:32–33.

[40] M. Cherif Bassiouni, "Perspectives on International Criminal Justice", in *Virginia Journal of International Law*, 2010, vol. 50, no. 2, pp. 278–79.

[41] *Ibid.*, p. 280.

[42] See, for example, Michael Howard, George Andreopoulos and Mark R. Shulman (eds.), *The Laws of War: Constraints of Warfare in the Western World*, Yale University Press, Yale,

warfare in ancient times was not limited to one civilisation, nor is it solely a Western concern in modern times. Alexander has succinctly observed:[43]

> Laws of war have always existed to limit the destruction of war. The ancients, the knights of the middle ages, the jurists of the early modern period all testify to the record of this concern. Nor is it just a Western concern. Other cultures, such as China, Japan, India and the Islamic world, have their own traditions of rules of warfare. Yet, despite this universal concern, the attempt to limit war has suffered various setbacks. It was not until the 19th century that a movement to codify the laws of war began and modern international humanitarian law was born.

The historical context of international humanitarian law[44] and the preambles of relevant international humanitarian law instruments[45] clearly indicate that the general object and purpose of international humanitarian law is to diminish the evils of war, promote humanitarianism in war and lessen the horrors, evils and unnecessary human suffering in warfare, through international political and legal co-operation. For example, the preamble of the second Hague Convention with Respect to the Laws and Customs of War on Land of 1899 states, *inter alia*, that its provisions had "been inspired by the desire to diminish the evils of war so far as military necessities permit".[46] Similarly, the Preamble of the third Hague Convention for the Adaptation to Maritime Warfare of 1899 states that the Plenipotentiaries were "animated by the desire to diminish, as far as depends on them the evils inseparable from warfare".[47] Also, the Preamble of the Geneva Convention (IV) of 1949 states that its purpose is for the protec-

---

1997; Leslie C. Green, *The Contemporary Law of Armed Conflict*, 3rd ed., Manchester University Press, Manchester, 2008, Chapter 2.

43 Amanda Alexander, "A Short History of International Humanitarian Law", in *European Journal of International Law*, 2015, vol. 26, no. 1, pp. 111–12.

44 See, for example, Henry Dunant, *A Memory of Solferino*, International Committee of the Red Cross, Geneva, 1939; Frits Kalshoven and Liesbeth Zegveld, *Constraints on the Waging of War: An Introduction*, 4th ed., Cambridge University Press, Cambridge, 2011.

45 See, generally, the ICC Legal Tools Database for all these instruments.

46 Hague Convention (II) with Respect to the Laws and Customs of War on Land, 29 July 1899, Preamble (http://www.legal-tools.org/doc/7879ac/).

47 Hague Convention (III) for the Adaptation to Maritime Warfare of the Principles of the Geneva Convention of 22 August 1864, 18 October 1907, Preamble (http://www.legal-tools.org/doc/7465fa/).

tion of civilian persons in times of war.[48] This object and purpose of international humanitarian law is based on morals and humaneness acknowledgeable universally, including under Islamic socio-legal norms.

Evidently, the concept of international humanitarian law is consistent with Islamic socio-legal norms. Its object and purpose as identified above is in consonance with the general *maqáṣid* of the *Sharí'ah* and the specific *maqṣúd* of humanitarian law in Islamic jurisprudence.[49] Islam recognised the need for constraint in warfare as early as the time of Prophet Muḥammad in the seventh century, as evidenced by his consistent instructions to the Muslim army urging restraint and humanitarianism in war. Bassiouni has noted that these early instructions of the Prophet later formed the basis of the traditional rules of armed conflict under Islamic law of nations (*al-siyar*) later "codified in the eighth century CE by Al-Shaybáni (d. 189/804) in his famous book *Al-Siyar* [which] [...] constituted the most developed articulation of international humanitarian law until the twentieth century CE, when the foundations of modern customary and conventional international humanitarian laws were laid".[50] Similar to modern international humanitarian law, Islamic law prohibits mutilations, unnecessary destructions, unnecessary bloodshed, unnecessary human suffering, and excesses in warfare.[51] These regulations were derived from the *Sharí'ah*, the practices of the early *Caliphs*, and from treaty obligations. The general tone for constraint in warfare under Islamic law is set in the Qur'ánic text 2:190, prohibiting excesses in the conduct of war: "Fight in the cause of God those who fight you *but do not exceed limits; for God does not love those who exceed limits*". This Qur'ánic provision clearly indicates that there are limits in warfare that should not be exceeded under Islamic law. The details of these limits are found in the recorded traditions of Prophet Muḥammad and the practices of the orthodox *Caliphs* after him. It is recorded that during his lifetime, whenever the Prophet

48 Geneva Convention (IV) relative to the Protection of Civilian Persons in Time of War, 12 August 1949, in force 21 October 1950, Preamble (http://www.legal-tools.org/doc/d5e260/).

49 Karima Bennoune, "*As-Salámu Alaykum?*: Humanitarian Law in Islamic Jurisprudence", in *Michigan Journal of International Law*, 1994, vol. 15, no 4. pp. 605–43.

50 Bassiouni, 2014, p. 162, see *supra* note 21.

51 See, for example, Muḥammad Hamidullah, *The Muslim Conduct of State*, 7th ed., Sh. Muḥammad Ashraf Kashmir Bazar, Lahore, 1977; Syed Imad-ud-Din Asad, "Islamic Humanitarian Law", in *Dawn*, 24 February 2006.

Muḥammad appointed a commander for warfare, he enjoined him with God-consciousness and gave orders for restraint in warfare, for example, as follows:[52]

> [N]ever commit breach of trust nor treachery nor mutilate anybody nor kill any minor or woman. This is the pact of God and the conduct of His Messenger for your guidance […] In avenging the injuries inflicted upon us molest not the harmless inmates of domestic seclusion; spare the weakness of the female sex; injure not the infants at the breast or those who are ill in bed. Refrain from demolishing the houses of unresisting inhabitants; destroy neither the means of subsistence, nor their fruit-trees and touch not the palm […] and do not kill children.

This practice was sustained and followed by the four orthodox *Caliphs* after the Prophet and by subsequent Muslim leaders after them. It is reported that the first *Caliph*, Abú Bakr, also instructed the Muslim army, for example, as follows:[53]

> When you meet your enemies in the fight, behave yourself as befits a good Muslim […] If [God] gives you victory, do not abuse your advantages and beware not to stain your swords with the blood of the one who yields, neither you touch the children, the women, nor the infirm men whom you may find among your enemies. In your march through enemy territory, do not cut down the palm, or other fruit-trees, destroy not the products of the earth, ravage no fields, burn no houses […] Let no destruction be made without necessity […] Do not disturb the quiet of the monks and the hermits, and destroy not their abodes.

Similar orders were issued by the other three orthodox *Caliphs* Umar, Uthmán and Alí, respectively.[54] Based on classical Islamic sources, Hamidullah has identified that acts prohibited in warfare under Islamic law include unnecessary cruel and tortuous ways of killing, killing non-combatants, decapitation of prisoners of war, mutilation of humans or beasts, treachery and perfidy, devastation, destruction of harvests and unnecessary cutting of trees, excess and wickedness, adultery and fornica-

---

52 Bennoune, 1994, p. 624, see *supra* note 49.

53 *Ibid.*, p. 626.

54 *Ibid.*, p. 627; Hamidullah, 1977, pp. 299–311, see *supra* note 51.

tion even with captive women, killing enemy hostages, severing the head of fallen enemies, massacre, burning captured humans or animals to death, using poisonous arrows, and acts forbidden under treaties.[55] Thus, all such atrocities committed, purportedly in the name of Islam, by extremist groups such as ISIS in Iraq and Syria, Boko Ḥarám in Nigeria, and Al-Shabáb in Somalia and Kenya, are not only contrary to international humanitarian law but also violate the rules of warfare under Islamic law, and are therefore punishable under both systems of law.

Similar to the object and purpose of international humanitarian law, the *maqáṣid* of the constraints on warfare under Islamic law is principally to promote humanitarianism in war and lessen the horrors, evils and unnecessary human suffering in warfare. General observance of these rules and reciprocity from the enemy can only be achieved through international political and legal co-operation as recognised under the principle of 'co-operation for goodness and righteousness' (*ta'áwwun alá al-birr wa-al-taqwá*) enjoined on Muslims in the Qur'ánic text 5:2: "Help one another to piety and godfearing; do not help each other to sin and enmity". Such international co-operation is pertinent through ratification of treaties, as is reflected in relevant verses of the *Qur'án*, the Traditions of the Prophet and practices of the *Caliphs* after him. For example, the Qur'ánic text 8:58 refers to the sanctity of treaties and permissibility of reciprocity in breach of a treaty: "And if thou fearest treachery any way at the hands of a people [with whom you have entered a treaty], dissolve it [their treaty] with them equally; surely God loves not the treacherous". The Prophet is also reported to have stated in a Tradition: "Whoever has a treaty of peace with a people should not loosen or tighten it [beyond its terms] until the treaty reaches its appointed term. Otherwise, he should declare the treaty null and void so that they are both on equal terms".[56]

Similar to international humanitarian law treaties, it is interesting to note that the *Qur'án* does not attach specific sanctions to the violations of the specified humanitarian rules by soldiers during warfare. Often, the belief in God's reward for complying with the injunctions and possibility of punishment in the hereafter for its violation provided religious and conscientious incentives and deterrents respectively for compliance by

---

55 Hamidullah, 1977, pp. 205–08, see *supra* note 51.

56 Reported by Abú Dáwúd, taken from Shayka Safiur-Raḥmán Al Mubarakpuri *et al.* (eds.), *Tassir Ibn Kathir (abridged)*, Darussalam, London, 2003, p. 343.

Muslim soldiers in warfare. However, where the violation of the rules of warfare amounted to one of the *ḥudúd* offences under Islamic law, the prescribed *ḥadd* punishment will be applicable. Otherwise, the State can impose discretionary (*ta'zír*) punishments for violations of the rules of warfare either through national law or international humanitarian law treaties ratified by the State pursuant to international co-operation in punishing such atrocities. The State is morally and legally bound to comply with such treaty obligations as enjoined in the Qur'ánic text 5:1: "O Believers, fulfil your bonds", which is considered to be the basis for fulfilling international treaty obligations under Islamic law.[57]

The common objective between international humanitarian law and Islamic law, as established above, provides a strong basis for universal condemnation and punishment of the violations of the common rules of warfare by extremist groups who purport to act in the name of Islam in different parts of the Muslim world today.

3.3.2. Islamic Socio-Legal Connection with International Human Rights Law

international human rights law is another basis for international criminal justice. The Preamble of the Universal Declaration of Human Rights ('UDHR') states that "disregard and contempt for human rights have resulted in barbarous acts which have outraged the conscience of mankind".[58] Where international human rights law is respected, most of the concerns of international criminal justice would be automatically resolved. From its historical context and the preambular statements of the UDHR and other international human rights treaties, it is obvious that the general object and purpose of international human rights law is to compel all states to recognise, promote and protect respect for the inherent dignity of all human beings without discrimination. This is an essential foundation of freedom, justice, and world peace.

Respect for human dignity is among the common norms of humanity, and falls within the concept of '*al-ma'rúf*' (common good) in Islamic socio-legal terms, the promotion of which the *Sharí'ah* enjoins under the

[57] See, for example, Labeeb Ahmed Bsoul, *International Treaties (Mu'áhadát) in Islam*, University Press of America, Lanham, 2008, p. 126.

[58] Universal Declaration of Human Rights, 10 December 1948, preambular paragraph 2 (http://www.legal-tools.org/doc/de5d83/).

doctrine '*amr bi al-ma'rúf wa nahy 'an al-munkar*' (enjoining the right or honourable and forbidding the wrong or dishonourable).[59] Each international human rights treaty also has its specific object and purpose. For example, it is acknowledged that the specific object and purpose of the International Covenant on Civil and Political Rights is to create legally binding standards for the guarantee of the civil and political rights of all individuals by states,[60] which is also justifiable in Islamic law under the principle of *ta'áwwun* (co-operation) as discussed earlier above.

From an Islamic perspective, the general object and purpose of international human rights law is in consonance with the *maqáṣid* of the *Sharí'ah*, which is promotion of human well-being as already analysed above. The basic Qur'ánic provision that expresses the general *maqáṣid* of upholding human dignity in relation to the promotion and protection of human rights is the Qur'ánic text 17:70, which states clearly that God has bestowed innate honour and dignity on every human being, which must be respected:

> We have honoured the children of Adam [that is, human beings], and carried them on land and sea, and provided them with good things, and preferred them greatly over many of those We created.

This is, essentially, a reminder of the sacred nature of human dignity, which the State has a duty under Islamic law to uphold and establish insti-

---

59 This phrase is "[u]sed in the Quran nine times, referring to the collective duty of the Muslim community to encourage righteous behaviour and discourage immorality, as recognized by reason and the Islamic moral and legal system. Aims to remove oppression from society and instead establish justice. Applied to moral, social, political, and economic facests of life. It is, ideally, the distinguishing trait of the Muslim nation", see John L. Esposito (ed.), *The Oxford Dictionary of Islam*, Oxford University Press, Oxford, 2003, p. 19. For a discussion of the rules on the application of this doctrine under Islamic law and its misapplication by the defendant in the Al-Mahdi case before the ICC, see Mohamed Elewa Badar and Noelle Higgins, "Discussion Interrupted: The Destruction and Protection of Cultural Property under International Law and Islamic Law – The Case of *Prosecutor v Al-Mahdi*", in *International Criminal Law Review*, 2017, vol. 17, no. 3, pp. 494–95. See also, Michael Cook, *Commanding Right and Forbidding Wrong in Islamic Thought*, Cambridge University Press, Cambridge, 2000.

60 See, for example, United Nations Human Rights Committee, CCPR General Comment No. 24: Issues Relating to Reservations Made upon Ratification or Accession to the Covenant or the Optional Protocols thereto, or in Relation to Declarations under Article 41 of the Covenant, UN Doc. CCPR/C/21/Rev.1/Add.6, 4 November 1994, para. 7 (https://www.legal-tools.org/doc/4acd3b/).

tutions to protect. This could be either through national law or relevant treaties ratified by the State pursuant to international co-operation. The Preamble of the Cairo Declaration on Human Rights in Islam declares the wish of Muslim-majority states "to contribute to the efforts of mankind to assert human rights, to protect man from exploitation and persecution, and to affirm his freedom and right to a dignified life in accordance with the Islamic *Sharí'ah*".[61] It further states that the fundamental rights and universal freedoms are an integral part of Islam and are binding divine commandments, which no one has the right to suspend, violate or ignore. There is also a vast contemporary literature aimed at establishing the concept of human rights from within Islamic classical jurisprudence and identifying a common moral ground and linkage between the general object and purpose of international human rights law and the general *maqáṣid* of the *Sharí'ah*.[62]

Today, it is well acknowledged that international human rights law is applicable both in peacetime and wartime and gross violations of human rights in warfare could lead to committing international crimes. The former United Nations ('UN') Secretary-General, Kofi Annan, observed in his 2004 report on the rule of law and transitional justice in conflict and post-conflict societies that one of the UN's main objectives in establishing criminal tribunals is to bring to justice to "those responsible for serious violations of human rights and humanitarian law, [and] putting an end to such violations and preventing their recurrence, securing justice and dignity for victims".[63] The active promotion of respect for human rights can be an important means of ensuring preventive international criminal justice that discourages the commission of war crimes and genocide during armed conflicts. Atrocities, such as the Bosnia-Herzegovina and Rwanda

61 Organisation of the Islamic Conference, Cairo Declaration on Human Rights in Islam, 5 August 1990, preambular paragraph 2, available on the Refworld web site.

62 See, for example, Mashood A. Baderin, *International Human Rights and Islamic Law*, Oxford University Press, Oxford, 2003; Abdulaziz A. Sachedina, *Islam and the Challenge of Human Rights*, Oxford University Press, Oxford, 2009; Mohammad Hashim Kamal, *The Dignity of Man: An Islamic Perspective*, Islamic Texts Society, Cambridge, 2002; Recep Şentürk, "Adamiyyah and Ismah: The Contested Relationship between Humanity and Human Rights in Classical Islamic Law", in *Islam Arastirmalari Dergisi*, 2002, vol. 8, pp. 39–69; Bassiouni, 2014, pp. 88–117, see *supra* note 21.

63 United Nations Security Council, Report of the Secretary-General, The Rule of Law and Transitional Justice in Conflict and Post-Conflict Societies, UN Doc. S/2004/616, 23 August 2004, para. 38 (http://www.legal-tools.org/doc/77bebf/).

genocides, have shown that actions that lead to war crimes and genocide often start with extreme dehumanisation of the 'other' by distorting an opponent's image and projecting them as less human or not human at all, which then validates brutalities against them. With regard to the Muslim world, promoting international human rights law as an important pillar of international criminal justice through emphasising its general object and purpose with reference to relevant Islamic socio-legal norms and the *maqáṣid* of the *Sharí'ah,* will enhance its acceptability and effectiveness.

3.3.3. Islamic Socio-Legal Connection with International Criminal Law

The normative foundation of international criminal law is to criminalise and punish violations of some core norms of international humanitarian law and international human rights law. However, regulation of crime is traditionally a domestic responsibility rather than an international one. Crimes are based on some notion of social wrong as recognised within particular societies, which thus creates divergence as to what constitutes crimes from one domestic system to the other. Criminalisation evinces social control, whereby certain acts are identified as morally and socially unacceptable within a particular society and punishment is legally ascribed for committing such acts to reflect some sense of justice in society. Thus, the concept of international criminal law reflects some element of global social control based on a universal notion of social wrongs acceptable by all. This was initially confronted with both substantive and procedural challenges. First, there was the challenge of creating an international agreement on social wrongs that would be accepted as crimes universally and, second, the challenge of international agreement about the procedure for trying and punishing such international crimes. In his 2010 article "Some Objections to the International Criminal Court", Rubin observed that the creation of the ICC "assumes that there is such a thing as international criminal law. But what is its substance? Who exercises law-making authority for the international legal community? Who has the legal authority to interpret the law once supposedly found?".[64] This, he argues, arises from the fact that criminal law is different from civil claims, with the traditional position being that crimes are "not […]

64 Alfred P. Rubin, "Some Objections to the International Criminal Court", in *Peace Review*, 2000, vol. 12, no. 1, p. 45.

defined by international law as such" but rather "by the municipal laws of many states and in a few cases by international tribunals set up by victor states in an exercise of positive law making" with the tribunal's new rules being "accepted under one rationale or another, by the states in which the accused were nationals". One rationale was that "if all or nearly all 'civilised' states define particular acts as violating their municipal criminal laws, then those acts violate 'international law'". Another rationale was that some acts violate "general principles of law recognised by civilised states", and thus violate general international law.[65] The rationale of international criminal law is thus very much tied to its acceptance in divergent municipal orders based on shared human values.

Certainly, there are acts that would be considered morally and socially unacceptable within the international community, either due to their negative impact on international relations or the indignation they cause to the conscience of the international community as a whole, and thus the need to socially control such acts directly or indirectly through international law. One old example is the crime of piracy. As observed by Hyde, piracy "derives its internationally illegal character from the will of the international society".[66] Although not categorised as an international crime *stricto sensu*, piracy has long been considered the grandfather of transnational crimes, conferred with universal jurisdiction as early as the eighteenth century because of the recognisable threat it poses to the maritime interests of all states both individually and collectively. Pirates could thus be prosecuted and punished by any state that caught them, even though they committed their crime elsewhere.

Over time, the concept of international criminal law as the basis for international criminal justice has become legally solidified, first through customary international law and then through treaty law.[67] Today, genocide, war crimes, crimes against humanity and the crime of aggression are considered as the core crimes under international criminal law, obviously due to the indignation they cause to the conscience of the international community as a whole. It is unlikely that there is any state or society to-

---

65 *Ibid.*

66 Charles C. Hyde, *International Law, Chiefly as Interpreted and Applied by the United States*, rev. ed., Little, Brown and Company, Massachusetts, 1945, pp. 768–70.

67 However, see Rubin's argument in *ibid.*, pp. 45–48, which, in the context of the International Criminal Court, tended to disagree on this.

day that would consider these crimes socially or morally acceptable. Thus, similar to piracy, they derive their internationally illegal character from the will of the international society, including the Muslim world, either through customary law or treaty law.[68] The Nuremberg and Tokyo trials after the Second World War in 1945 and 1946 respectively are, usually, the starting point of modern international criminal law. Novak notes that these "were the first attempts to criminalise aggressive war and abuses against civilian populations".[69] The Charter of the International Military Tribunal at Nuremberg[70] is the first formal legal basis for offences considered prohibited under international criminal law, listing crimes against peace, war crimes and crimes against humanity and complicity in committing them as crimes punishable under international law, and defining each one of them in relation to situations of war. The Nuremberg trials were followed in 1993 by the establishment of the International Criminal Tribunal for the former Yugoslavia ('ICTY'), through UN Security Council Resolution 827 of 1993, to prosecute persons responsible for war crimes committed during the conflicts in the Balkans in the 1990s,[71] and the International Criminal Tribunal for Rwanda ('ICTR') established through UN Security Council Resolution 955 of 1994 to prosecute persons responsible for genocide and other serious violations of international humanitarian law committed in Rwanda and neighbouring states between 1 January 1994 and 31 December 1994,[72] and ultimately the establishment of the ICC through the ICC Statute[73] adopted in 1998. While both the ICTY and ICTR were established under Chapter VII of the UN Charter on behalf of the international community, the ICC Statute was established by a multilateral treaty adopted through international co-operation. While

68 See, for example, the Convention on the Prevention and Punishment of the Crime of Genocide, 9 December 1948, in force 12 January 1951 (http://www.legal-tools.org/doc/498c38/).

69 Andrew Novak, *The International Criminal Court: An Introduction*, Springer, New York, 2015, p. 8.

70 Charter of the International Military Tribunal, 8 August 1945 (http://www.legal-tools.org/doc/64ffdd/).

71 United Nations Security Council Resolution 827 (1993), UN Doc. S/RES/827(1993), 25 May 1993 (http://www.legal-tools.org/doc/dc079b/).

72 United Nations Security Council Resolution 955 (1994), UN Doc. S/RES/955(1994), 8 November 1994 (http://www.legal-tools.org/doc/f5ef47/).

73 See ICC Statute, *supra* note 1 (http://www.legal-tools.org/doc/7b9af9/).

Muslim-majority states may not have had much input into the Security Council resolutions establishing the ICTY and ICTR, a sizable number of them, as well as the Organisation of Islamic Cooperation ('OIC'), participated and contributed to the debates and adoption of the ICC Statute.[74] The ICTY had jurisdiction for genocide, war crimes, and crimes against humanity, while the statute of the ICTR also provided for genocide, crimes against humanity and violations of Article 3 common to the Geneva Conventions and the Additional Protocol II.[75] The ICC Statute also recognises genocide, crimes against humanity, war crimes and the crime of aggression as the most serious crimes of concern to the international community as a whole, and punishable under international law.

Evidently, genocide, war crimes, crimes against humanity and the crime of aggression as defined in the statutes of these international tribunals are actions that are equally abhorred under Islamic socio-legal norms. These acts come under the general concept of '*fasád*' (corruption or atrocities), prohibited in the Qur'ánic text 7:56: "Do not [cause] corruption in the land, after it has been set right". These acts are also specifically prohibited under Islamic socio-legal norms regulating warfare, as discussed above. Malekian has comparatively identified that these core international crimes are equally recognised and punishable under Islamic law.[76]

Considering the historical context of international criminal law and looking at the preambles of the Charter of the International Military Tribunal at Nuremberg and the Statutes of the ICTY, ICTR, and the ICC, it is obvious that the object and purpose of international criminal law is to ensure that perpetrators of war crimes are appropriately brought to justice.[77] While bringing the perpetrators of war crimes to justice under international criminal law is mainly perceived in terms of punishing the perpetrators to serve as deterrent for future offenders, other theoretical

[74] See Coalition for the International Criminal Court, "Factsheet: The ICC and the Arab World" (http://www.legal-tools.org/doc/c315d6/).

[75] Statute of the International Tribunal for Rwanda, 8 November 1994, Articles 1–3 (http://www.legal-tools.org/doc/8732d6/).

[76] Farhad Malekian, *Principles of Islamic International Criminal Law: A Comparative Search*, Brill, Leiden, 2011, p. 165. See also Bassiouni, 2014, pp. 88–117, see *supra* note 21.

[77] See the preambular statements of the Agreement for the Prosecution and Punishment of the Major War Criminals of the European Axis, 8 August 1945 (http://www.legal-tools.org/doc/844f64/).

basis of punishment in international criminal law has been proffered by scholars on the subject.[78] Goldstone has noted that prosecution is not the only form of justice, nor necessarily the most appropriate form in every case, which highlights the need for a more holistic approach to international criminal justice. In that regard, it is important to note that the Preamble of the ICC Statute reflects the social, moral, political and legal origins of international criminal law as a basis of international criminal justice as will be analysed later below in relation to the object and purpose and the *maqáṣid* principles respectively.

It is apparent from the above analysis that there is certainly a common social, moral and legal objective for international humanitarian law, international human rights law and international criminal law under both international law and Islamic law respectively, as pillars of international criminal justice. This common objective is important to prevent a perception of moral and legal superiority of one civilisation over the rest, and ensure the promotion of international criminal justice through the collective moral and legal conviction of all civilisations, including Islam.

3.4. Advancing a Holistic Perspective of International Criminal Justice in Relation to the 'Object and Purpose' and '*Maqáṣid*' Principles

The foregoing analyses establish that, while international criminal law judgments are an important aspect of international criminal justice, they are not the only basis for it. As Malekian observed:[79]

> [w]hen we talk of the principles of international criminal justice, we do not necessarily mean only the judgements that may be delivered by international criminal courts, but also the living structures of international criminal law as it exists in the international relations of states.

International criminal justice therefore requires a holistic perspective that combines the objects and purposes of international humanitarian law, international human rights law and international criminal law, making not

[78] See, generally, Farooq Ḥasan, "The Theoretical Basis of Punishment in International Criminal Law", in *Case Western Reserve Journal of International Law*, 1983, vol. 15, no. 1, pp. 39–60.

[79] Farhad Malekian, *Jurisprudence of International Criminal Justice*, Cambridge Scholars Publishing, Newcastle upon Tyne, 2014, p. 1.

only its legal but also its social, moral and political features evident to encourage its universal acceptance, especially in the Muslim world in relation to Islamic socio-legal norms. Such a holistic perspective will link its punitive aspect with its preventive aspect to make the system more effective. The need for such complementation was well articulated by the former UN Secretary-General, Kofi Annan, in his report to the Security Council in 2004:[80]

> [I]n matters of justice and the rule of law, *an ounce of prevention is worth significantly more than a pound of cure.* While United Nations efforts have been tailored […] to address the grave injustices of war, the root causes of conflict have often been left unaddressed. Yet, it is in addressing the causes of conflict, through legitimate and just ways, that the international community can help prevent a return to conflict in the future […] *Viewed this way, prevention is the first imperative of justice.* (emphasis added)

Thus, international criminal justice must be seen as "the fruit of transcultural morality, co-operation, assistance, reciprocity, mutual and multilateral tolerances and a combination of different political necessities".[81] This requires engagement with its social, moral, political, and legal dimensions. Each of these dimensions is reflected in the Preamble of the ICC Statute. Pursuant to the object and purpose approach proposed in this chapter, relevant provisions of the preamble will be referred to in analysing each one of them in relation to Islamic socio-legal norms based on the *maqáṣid* principle to promote international criminal justice in the Muslim world.

3.4.1. Social Dimension of International Criminal Justice

The social dimension of international criminal justice relates to its societal linkages and acceptance. Kennedy observed that international lawyers "are constantly searching for better methods to 'enforce' their norms in international society and feel the need to defend international law when enforcement seems unlikely".[82] This can be addressed through a better

---

80 Report of the Secretary-General, 23 August 2004, para. 4, see *supra* note 63 (http://www.legal-tools.org/doc/77bebf/).

81 Malekian, 2014, p. 1, see *supra* note 79.

82 David Kennedy, "New Approaches to Comparative Law: Comparativism and International Governance", in *Utah Law Review*, 1997, vol. 2, pp. 545–638.

appreciation of the social dimension of relevant areas of international law. As noted earlier, international criminal justice involves some element of global social control, which can be resisted in different societies due to different social and cultural variables.[83] Such resistance can be conciliated through promoting a proper appreciation of the social dimension of international criminal justice. International criminal justice cannot operate simply by imposition, but must be understood in the relevant social context for its acceptability in all societies, including the Muslim world.

The effectiveness of the social dimension of international criminal justice requires two mediations. The first relates to understanding societies, what they aspire to, what is their conception of justice, and whether they perceive that the international criminal justice system can fulfil their aspirations of social justice equitably. Bantekas has noted the absence of a thorough examination of the social and cultural context within which relevant international criminal justice actors operate.[84] The need to understand the social and cultural context that leads to atrocities amounting to international crimes cannot be overemphasised. For example, historical facts show that genocidal acts are often a consequence of built-up hatred of the 'other' due to ethnic supremacism and social injustices, while atrocities amounting to war crimes in armed conflicts are often a consequence of nationalist supremacism deriving from loyalty to the nation-state above respect for human equality, human dignity and universal humanitarianism. As noted by Gat: "War has a reputation for being the ultimate expression of national affinity and solidarity, of the sharp division between 'us' and 'them'",[85] and "studies show that the main cause of the post-1815 wars has been ethnic-nationalist".[86] This leads to the second mediation, which relates to promoting non-territorial common bonds of humanity reflected in values of human equality, human dignity, humaneness and social cohe-

83 See generally, Martti Koskenniemi, *From Apology to Utopia: The Structure of International Legal Argument*, Finnish Lawyers' Publishing Company, 1989; *ibid.*

84 Ilias Bantekas, "The Anthropological Dimension of International Crimes and International Criminal Justice", in Ilias Bantekas and Emmanouela Mylonaki (eds.), *Criminological Approaches to International Criminal Law*, Cambridge University Press, Cambridge, 2014, p. 240.

85 Azar Gat, *Nations: The Long History and Deep Roots of Political Ethnicity and Nationalism*, Cambridge University Press, Cambridge, 2013, p. 313.

86 *Ibid.*, p. 315.

sion within all societies, as important foundations for international criminal justice.

The promotion of non-territorial common bonds of humanity is reflected in the first preambular paragraph of the ICC Statute, which states that it is "[c]onscious that all peoples are united by common bonds, their cultures pieced together in a shared heritage, and concerned that this delicate mosaic may be shattered at any time". The consciousness that "all peoples are united by common bonds" and the concern that this "may be shattered at any time" in the first paragraph of the Preamble emphasises the importance of human equality and social justice, nationally and internationally, as an important first step to achieving a preventive international criminal justice system. This is where the link between international human rights law and international criminal justice is best reflected. The common bonds must be promoted internally through state policy and externally through international co-operation. Although international crimes are committed by individuals during armed conflict, Article 6 of the Charter of the International Military Tribunal at Nuremberg acknowledged that persons to be tried and punished by the tribunal would have been "acting in the interest of the European Axis countries",[87] reflecting the complicit role of states either by commission or omission. States therefore have an important role to play both domestically and internationally in ensuring the advancement of social and cultural norms that promote the common bonds of humanity for the effectiveness of the social element of international criminal justice. The promotion of international human rights and good governance in all societies and equal concern for their violations thereof should be taken seriously by the international community as part of the international criminal justice system. As Boas argues:

> Natural law conceptions of humanity and protection of communities are infused in the dialogue of what constitutes international criminal justice; these require a sense of an 'international community' acting 'collectively' against certain opprobrious behavior. In this way, international criminal justice is an expression of global community.

In relation to the Muslim world, it is first necessary to have a proper social understanding of Muslim societies, with reference to how Islamic

---

[87] Charter of the International Military Tribunal, 8 August 1945, Article 6 (http://www.legal-tools.org/doc/64ffdd/).

social norms are germane to promoting the "common bonds of humanity" expressed in the preamble of the ICC Statute and the perception of "international criminal justice [as] an expression of global community" highlighted by Boas. Both the "common bonds of humanity" and the idea of "global community" form part of the ends of the general *maqáṣid* of the *Sharí'ah* as reflected in the Qur'ánic text 49:13, which is a clear global wake-up call for a much-needed functional global community:

> O mankind, We have created you male and female, and appointed you races and tribes, that you may know one another [not that you may despise one another]. Surely the noblest among you in the sight of God is the most godfearing of you. God is All-knowing, All-aware.

This Qur'ánic provision is the fundamental basis of Islamic social norms in respect of human co-existence, reflecting the common bonds of humanity by reference to our common human ancestry and equality of birth. Ethnicity is acknowledged as a natural phenomenon that should be positively appreciated and not negatively exploited to discriminate against or despise one another. Prior to Islam, ethnic resentment was rife in Arabia, leading to constant tribal wars. With the revelation of this verse, Prophet Muḥammad is reported to have pronounced: "Oh people! God has removed the evils and arrogance of the pre-Islamic period (*jáhiliyyah*) from you".[88] There is consensus among both classical and contemporary Qur'ánic exegetes that this verse established the prohibition of racial or ethnic resentment and discrimination in Islam as early as the seventh century. For example, the thirteenth century Qur'ánic exegete, Al-Bayḍáwí, stated that the verse establishes the fact that all human beings are equal and there is no basis for superiority on grounds of ethnicity or lineage.[89] Also, Qutb stated in his commentary to this verse that God's purpose of creating humanity into nations, races, and tribes is not to "stir up conflict and enmity [but] for the purpose of getting to know one another and living

[88] Reported by Al-Tirmidhí and Al-Bayháqí. For reference, see Mashood A. Baderin, "Islamic Law and International Protection of Minority Rights", in Marie Luisa Frick *et al.* (eds.), *Islam and International Law: Engaging Self-Centrism from a Plurality of Perspective*, Martinus Nijhoff Publishers, Leiden, 2013, p. 320.

[89] Abd Alla Al-Bayḍáwí, "Anwár at-tanzíl wa-asrár at-ta'wíl", in Heinrich O. Fleischer (ed.), *Commentarius in Coranium*, 1846, vol. 2, p. 276.

peacefully together".[90] Similarly, Mawdúdí observed that in this verse "the whole of mankind has been addressed to reform it of the great evil that has been causing universal disruption in the world, that is, the prejudices due to race, colour, language, country and nationality",[91] and according to Sháfi' this verse "proceeds to set down the basis of an all-comprehensive and all-pervading principle of human equality [and] has firmly laid the axe at the false and foolish notions of superiority, born of racial arrogance or national conceit".[92] Prophet Muḥammad is reported to have re-emphasised this in his last major sermon, stating, *inter alia*:[93]

> O People! Be aware that your God is One. An Arab has no superiority over a non-Arab and a non-Arab has no superiority over an Arab, and no white person has any superiority over a black person, and no black person has any superiority over a white person, except on the basis of righteousness. The most honourable among you in the sight of God is the most righteous [...] Let those who are present convey this to those who are absent.

These Islamic injunctions establish strong social norms that can be used to promote the effectiveness of the social element of international criminal justice as analysed above, not only in the Muslim world but also globally. The *maqáṣid* approach requires that any contrary interpretation of the *Sharí'ah* that promotes resentment, discrimination, and enmity amongst humanity is rejected on grounds of contradicting the *maqáṣid* of the *Sharí'ah*. Modern Muslim-majority states, especially those that constitutionally recognise Islam or Islamic law as part of their social order, have an obligation to engrain this Islamic norm into their respective social orders to enhance the spirit of the common bonds of humanity as part of the general object and purpose of international criminal justice and the general *maqáṣid* of the *Sharí'ah*. There is nothing in international law that prohibits the use of these Islamic injunctions as a universal mantra for promoting the "common bonds of humanity" so important to socially encouraging a preventive international criminal justice system globally.

---

90 Sayyid Qutb (translated by M. Adil Salah and Ashur A. Shais), *In the Shade of the Qur'án*, The Islamic Foundation, Leicester, 2009, vol. XVI, p. 97.

91 Sayyid Abul A'lá Mawdúdí, *The Meaning of the Qur'án*, Kazi Publications Inc., Chicago, 1999.

92 Mufti Sháfi' Usmani, *Ma'ariful Qur'án*, vol. 8, p. 143.

93 Muḥammad's Final Sermon, reported by Al-Bayháqí.

3.4.2. Moral Dimension of International Criminal Justice

The moral dimension of international criminal justice relates to its ethical linkages. Morals play a higher justificatory role in international law than in domestic law. International law acquires its general legitimacy mostly from moral justifications to make it acceptable as law in most societies. Generally, morals constitute one of the material sources of international law; history is another one, especially in respect of the international norms underlying international human rights law, international humanitarian law and international criminal law. In all these specific areas of international law, morals provide the material substance that is formally cloaked with the nature and force of law.[94] While law relates to the question 'what?', morals relate to the question 'why?', which is mostly asked in relation to international law norms. The challenge to international norms in most societies is not simply 'What is the law?', but the more complex question: 'Why should the norm be complied with?'. That complex question is not always sufficiently answered by merely saying: 'Because that is the law'. Practically, most international norms, including those of international criminal justice, are more sustainable on moral justifications than strictly legal arguments in most societies, including the Muslim world. In analysing the role of morals in international law, Boldizar and Korhonen refer, for example, to Koskenniemi's argument regarding the prohibition of nuclear weapons[95] that "the prohibition of the 'Killing of the Innocent' is not to be subjected to legal argumentation, even in the mode of justification, because this prohibition is *a priori* already stronger and clearer [morally] than any, however, ingenious, legal argument".[96] This is not to underestimate the importance of legal argumentation, but to highlight the need to also appreciate the importance of the moral argument for the promotion of the concept of international criminal justice as a universal norm. Thus, the moral dimension of international criminal justice requires looking beyond its formal source (the

94 This is by reference to the classification of the sources of law into 'material sources' and 'formal sources', with the former being what the latter gives the force of law. See John Salmond, *Jurisprudence*, 7th ed., Sweet and Maxwell, London, 1924, p. 139.

95 Martti Koskenniemi, "Faith, Identity and the Killing of the Innocent: International Lawyers and Nuclear Weapons", in *Leiden Journal of International Law*, 1997, vol. 10, pp. 137–62.

96 Alexander Boldizar and Outi Korhonen, "Ethics, Morals and International Law", in *European Journal of International Law*, 1999, vol. 10, no. 2, p. 283.

law) to its material source (morals), which forms its normative foundation. Although the ideal in terms of morals is difficult to agree on in most cases, the morals underlying international criminal justice can be generally sustained within most moral systems, especially within Islamic moral norms, as is argued herein.

The atrocities prohibited under international criminal law are: genocide,[97] crimes against humanity,[98] war crimes,[99] and the crime of aggression.[100] There is no doubt that all these crimes and their detailed definitions are underpinned by strong moral justifications. The general object and purpose in prohibiting them is reflected in the second and third preambular paragraphs of the ICC Statute, which state: "[m]indful that during this century millions of children, women and men have been victims of unimaginable atrocities that deeply shock the conscience of humanity" and "[r]ecognizing that such grave crimes threaten the peace, security and well-being of the world". These are, obviously, an appeal to human moral sentiments to justify the prohibition of those atrocious crimes.

With regard to Islam, the role of morals is well established in all its social-legal norms. Both the *Qur'án* and the Prophet's Traditions are replete with moral admonitions as the fundamental basis of devotion, law and social interactions. The Prophet Muḥammad is specifically exalted in the Qur'ánic text 68:4 as having excellent morals, which according to the Qur'ánic text 33:21 Muslims are expected to emulate. The generic Qur'ánic term for morals is '*birr*', translated as righteousness. The importance of morals as a cornerstone of all actions, including law, in Islam is reflected in the Qur'ánic text 2:177, which states that righteousness is not merely turning one's face either to the East or West in devotion to God, but rather to accompany this with different elements of excellent morals in the service of humanity. Similarly, the Qur'ánic text 16:90 provides that "God bids to justice and good-doing [to all] and giving to kinsmen; and

---

97 For the full definition of this crime, see ICC Statute, Article 6, *supra* note 1 (http://www.legal-tools.org/doc/7b9af9/).

98 For the full definition of this crime, see ICC Statute, Article 7, *ibid.* (http://www.legal-tools.org/doc/7b9af9/).

99 For the full definition of this crime, see ICC Statute, Article 8, *ibid.* (http://www.legal-tools.org/doc/7b9af9/).

100 For the full definition of this crime, see ICC Statute, Article 5(2), *ibid.* (http://www.legal-tools.org/doc/7b9af9/); Assembly of States Parties Resolution, Review Conference, Resolution 6, RC/11, 11 June 2010 (http://www.legal-tools.org/doc/de6c31/).

He forbids indecency, dishonour and insolence". The Prophet is also reported to have stated in a Tradition that "I have been sent [by God] to perfect good morals".[101] Thus, the morality of prohibiting those atrocities under international criminal justice is certainly very justifiable under Islamic socio-legal norms and in conformity with the *maqáṣid* of the *Sharí'ah*. As already identified above, a correlative aspect of the *maqáṣid* is the general prohibition of atrocities (*mafsadah*) on earth, clearly evidenced in the Qur'ánic text 7:56: "Do not [cause] corruption in the land, after it has been set right".

In relation to the general object and purpose of international criminal justice to prevent atrocities, as indicated in the preamble of the ICC Statute, reference can also be made to the Qur'ánic text 4:75, which establishes the Islamic moral obligation of assisting the oppressed who cry out for rescue and help, and also to the Prophetic Tradition: "Let there be no harm and no reciprocation of harm".[102] All these Islamic divine injunctions can serve as reference points for promoting the moral dimension of international criminal justice in the Muslim world in relation to the general object and purpose of international criminal justice. Emphasising this moral dimension can encourage a change in attitude and gradually diminish the urge to commit the prohibited atrocities globally, especially in the Muslim world.

3.4.3. Political Dimension of International Criminal Justice

The political dimension of international criminal justice relates to authority and power relations amongst states and "the real question is how that relationship is managed and to what end".[103] A notable hurdle for international criminal justice in that regard is the perceived selectivity and double standards within the international system.[104] This affects the political legitimacy of international criminal justice adversely, as impartiality is essential for its effectiveness. Concerns are often raised by developing countries, including Muslim-majority states, about the apparent political

[101] Reported by Ibn Májah, no. 47, *ḥadíth* 8.

[102] Reported by Ibn Májah, *ḥadíth* 32.

[103] Gideon Boas and Pascale Chifflet, *International Criminal Justice*, Edward Elgar Publishing Ltd, Cheltenham, 2017, Chapter 3.

[104] See, for example, Ramesh Thakur, "Law, Legitimacy and the United Nations", in *Melbourne Journal of International Law*, 2010, vol. 11, no. 1, pp. 14–17.

inequality within the international system, as reflected in Article 27(3) of the UN Charter since 1945,[105] giving a veto power advantage to the five permanent members of UN Security Council on all substantive matters. This political inequality is indirectly incorporated into the ICC Statute through Articles 13(b) and 16, which grant the UN Security Council power of political interference in referring matters of international criminal justice to the ICC,[106] despite unsuccessful agitation for the past two decades for a reformed and better-balanced Security Council. There is apparent concern among states of the Global South about the Security Council's selective use of its referral powers under the ICC Statute based on political expediency to favour the permanent members' political interests. Most developing states, including Muslim-majority states, perceive that the powerful states can use their political advantage to manipulate the international system to make themselves immune from liability under the international criminal justice system. Thakur bluntly argues that the "initiative of international criminal justice meant to protect vulnerable people from brutal national rulers has been subverted into an instrument of powerful against vulnerable countries" for political expediency.[107] The former UN High Commissioner for Human Rights, Louise Arbour, also highlighted that "there would be little hope for the promotion of the rule of law internationally if the most powerful international body makes it subservient to the rule of political expediency".[108]

International criminal justice can only be effectively sustained through equitable international political co-operation. In relating this to the object and purpose of international criminal justice, the fourth preambular paragraph of the ICC Statute affirms that "the most serious crimes of concern to the international community as a whole must not go unpunished and that their effective prosecution must be ensured by taking measures at the national level and by *enhancing international cooperation*", while the fifth preambular paragraph indicates a determination to collectively "put an end to impunity for the perpetrators of these crimes

---

105 Charter of the United Nations, 26 June 1945, in force 24 October 1945, Article 27(3) (http://www.legal-tools.org/doc/6b3cd5/).

106 ICC Statute, Articles 13(b) and 16, see *supra* note 1 (http://www.legal-tools.org/doc/7b9af9/).

107 Thakur, 2010, p. 15, see *supra* note 105.

108 Louise Arbour, "Justice v. Politics", in *International Herald Tribune*, 16 September 2008.

and thus to contribute to the prevention of such crimes".[109] Both the enhancement of international co-operation and determination to put an end to impunity can only be achieved through an equitable international political relationship that transcends the narrow interest of any one or group of states to the detriment of the international criminal justice system. The need for international politics of equality and co-operation must be strongly promoted to enhance international criminal justice globally, particularly in the Muslim world.

From the perspective of *maqáṣid*, Islam enjoins international co-operation based on equity, justice and spirit of solidarity in dealing with international political problems. This is inspired by the Qur'ánic text 49:9–10, which enjoins collective action based on equity, justice and solidarity:

> If two parties of the believers fight, put things right between them; then, if one of them is insolent against the other, fight the insolent one till it reverts to God's commandment. If it reverts, set things right between them *equitably* and *be just*. Surely *God loves the just*. The believers indeed are *brothers*; so set things right between your two [contending] brothers and fear God; haply so you will find mercy' (emphasis added).

Hamidullah describes this Qur'ánic provision as a fundamental objective of Islamic international law.[110] The provision emphasises the importance of equity, justice and solidarity as essential factors of international co-operation and collective action. Many other Qur'ánic provisions corroborate this, including the Qur'ánic text 5:2: "[L]et not [your] detestation for a people, who barred you from the Holy Mosque move you to commit aggression. Help one another to piety and godfearing; do not help each other to sin and enmity"; and the Qur'ánic text 5:8: "[Let not [your] detestation for a people move you not to be equitable [towards them] – that is nearer to godfearing", specifically enjoins Muslims not to act inequitably even against a hostile people or nation. Based on both the object and purpose of international criminal justice and the *maqásid* of the *Sharí'ah*, it is essential to imbibe this Islamic injunction of equity and solidarity into the political dimension of international criminal justice to remedy

[109] ICC Statute, Preamble, see *supra* note 1 (http://www.legal-tools.org/doc/7b9af9/).

[110] Hamidullah, 1977, p. 178, see *supra* note 51.

the political double-standards, and make it more appealing particularly to the Muslim-majority states, which tend to perceive the system as having equitable deficits in its political dimension. Doing so would serve as a big boost for enhancing international criminal justice globally, but particularly in the Muslim world.

3.4.4. Legal Dimension of International Criminal Justice

The legal dimension of international criminal justice relates to the application of its principles through the courts. This climaxed in the creation of the ICC as the main and permanent international court for bringing violators of core international crimes to trial. The general object and purpose of the legal dimension of international criminal justice is reflected in the ninth and eleventh preambular paragraphs of the ICC Statute which state that, in the determination to meet the social, moral and political ends of international criminal justice "for the sake of present and future generations", the ICC is established to exercise legal jurisdiction "over the most serious crimes of concern to the international community as a whole", based on the resolve "to guarantee lasting respect for the enforcement of international justice". However, the ICC may only exercise jurisdiction where national legal systems fail do so or where a state is unwilling or has no capability to prosecute international criminal offenders.[111] States, as members of the international community, have the primary responsibility to bring violators of serious crimes of concern to the international community to justice under their respective domestic legal systems. The system envisages all states supporting the legality of international criminal justice and prosecuting offenders when necessary. This requires states to have effective domestic legal systems that ensure fair trial and due process leading to substantive justice and affording alleged offenders adequate opportunity to defend themselves.

Currently, several Muslim-majority states are parties and signatories to the ICC Statute.[112] This raises the question of whether Muslim-majority states whose domestic legal systems are based on or influenced by the *Sharí'ah* can provide the requisite criminal justice system for the effective

[111] See ICC Statute, tenth preambular paragraph and Article 1, *supra* note 1 (http://www.legal-tools.org/doc/7b9af9/).

[112] International Criminal Court, "The State Parties to the Rome Statute", available on the web site of the Assembly of States Parties.

enforcement of international criminal law domestically. There is a perception, particularly in the West, that legal systems based on the *Sharí'ah* cannot generally provide adequate criminal justice of international standard. While it is true that some of the criminal punishments prescribed by the *Sharí'ah* are contrary to international human rights law, the *Sharí'ah* generally enjoins justice, fairness and due process in criminal trials that are perfectly commensurate with international standards. Many verses in the *Qur'án* and Prophetic Traditions emphasise the maintenance of justice and equity in legal proceedings. For example, the Qur'ánic text 4:135 enjoins that justice be maintained "even though it be against yourselves, or your parents and kinsmen, whether the man be rich or poor", and the Qur'ánic text 16:90 instructs: "Surely God bids to justice and good-doing [...] and you have made God your surety; surely God knows the things you do". Doing justice is considered a duty to God, from which emanate the rights to equality and fairness for all without regard to status, race, gender or religion. The notion that the Crown or King can do no wrong has no place under Islamic law and thus presidents and heads of state are not immune from facing justice (with the opportunity to legally defend themselves) for alleged international crimes. However, the creation of necessary institutions and procedural rules for upholding justice as prescribed by the *Sharí'ah* is the responsibility of respective Muslim-majority states. The need to prosecute offenders and violators of both domestic and international law is well recognised under Islamic law as the *Qur'án* provides specific punishment for *ḥudúd* and *qiṣáṣ* offences, while the provision in the Qur'ánic text 4:16, "[a]nd when two of you commit indecency, punish them both", is understood as authority for the State to prescribe punishments for all other offences known as *ta'zír*. Thus, Muslim-majority states have a duty under Islamic law to establish judicial institutions with adequate fair trial and due processes for criminal trials that meet international standards. Both the object and purpose of the legal dimension of international criminal justice and the specific *maqṣúd* of punishing crimes under the *Sharí'ah* justifies the need for Muslim-majority states to bring offenders of heinous international crimes to justice under their domestic legal systems.

With reference to armed conflicts, regular combatants of Muslim-majority states that apply Islamic law are generally expected to comply with the rules of warfare as prescribed by both Islamic law and international humanitarian law, and any crimes committed in violation of international criminal justice can be prosecuted under the domestic laws of the State; failing this, they may be subject to the jurisdiction of the ICC. However, there is one area of apparent legal conflict between aspects of classical Islamic jurisprudence and international humanitarian law in respect of atrocities being committed by rebellious groups such as ISIS, Al-Shabáb and Boko Ḥarám in different parts of the Muslim world today. Traditionally, there is an established jurisprudential view under classical Islamic international law (*al-siyar*) that rebellious groups with established authority, some territorial control and sustained resistance (*man'ah*) against the main political authority based on some speculative interpretation (*ta'wíl*) of Islamic sources, would not be punishable by the main political authority for actions they committed within the territory they controlled during the conflict. For example, Al-Shaybání expressed the view that "when such rebels repent and accept the authority of the government, they should not be punished for the damage they caused during their rebellion". Contextually, this rule is perceived to offer incentives to rebels for complying with the laws of war, thereby reducing the sufferings of civilians and ordinary citizens. However, this rule is neither absolute nor a licence for rebellious groups to commit heinous crimes with impunity. Based on the *maqáṣid* principle, where such rebels violate the established laws of war with impunity, they would be liable for all atrocities they committed during the rebellion even if they had established authority and some territorial control, and sought to justify their atrocities by reference to some speculative interpretations of the law.[113] Thus, with regard to the legal dimension of international criminal justice, it is submitted, particularly with reference to the object and purpose and *maqáṣid* principles, that members of ISIS, Al-Shabáb and Boko Ḥarám would be liable to face justice and, where convicted, liable to be punished for all the atrocities committed by them in violation of the rules of warfare under both contemporary international humanitarian law and Islamic humanitarian law.

3.5. Conclusion

Essentially, international law cannot operate in a vacuum, but must unavoidably interact with domestic legal systems and cultures for its imple-

[113] See, generally, Sadia Tabassum, "Combatants, Not Bandits: The Status of Rebels in Islamic Law", in *International Review of the Red Cross*, 2011, vol. 93, no. 881, pp. 1–19. See also Bassiouni, 2014, p. 139, *supra* note 21.

mentation. Thus, international law is structured to be implemented primarily by states within their domestic legal systems, with international tribunals stepping in only when domestic implementation fails. This is reflected, for example, in the general requirement to exhaust all available domestic remedies before international human rights tribunals can have jurisdiction for human rights trials and also in the complementarity rule, which gives the ICC jurisdiction to try international crimes only when states fail to or have no capacity to do so. This highlights the need to promote synergy between international law generally and relevant domestic systems of the world. The greater the synergy, the greater would be the prospects of acceptance and effective implementation of international norms within domestic systems. It is in that context that this chapter has critically engaged with the concept of international criminal justice and analysed how to enhance its acceptance and effectiveness in the Muslim world, highlighting the role of Islamic socio-legal norms (broadly defined as social, moral, political and legal norms) in that regard. In doing so, the chapter not only contributes to, but changes, the traditional debate in two important aspects that will hopefully deepen the discourse on the relationship between international criminal justice and Islamic socio-legal norms beyond bare legal formalism.

The first aspect is that, in promoting international criminal justice, the traditional approach has been to focus mainly on the substantive legal provisions of relevant treaties, without much attention to the object and purpose behind the legal provisions or the moral justifications that sustain the concept of international criminal justice. While that approach may impose a compulsive legal obligation on States Parties to the relevant treaties, which they may or may not fulfil in practice, its persuasive and justificatory effect in attracting compliance is very limited universally. In challenging that approach, this chapter has advanced a more holistic approach to international criminal justice, involving its social, moral, political and legal dimensions underpinned by the reference to the object and purpose principle of international law. Similarly, the second aspect is that, in engaging Islamic socio-legal norms with the application of international criminal justice within the domestic systems of Muslim-majority states, the traditional approach has been to focus mainly on the substantive injunctions of the *Sharí'ah* without much attention to the *maqáṣid* behind those injunctions. That approach also does not absorb the benevolent nature of the *Sharí'ah* and conceals the common grounds it shares with the objectives of international criminal justice. The chapter has also challenged that approach by advancing the *maqáṣid* principle of Islamic law.

In conclusion, the arguments herein pierce the legal veil of both international criminal justice and Islamic law by moving the discourse of their relationship beyond strict engagement with legal formalism to include consideration and appreciation of the social, moral and political norms that constitute the justification behind the legal provisions. It is submitted that this approach can be significantly persuasive and could consequently facilitate better acceptance and effective application of international criminal justice in the Muslim world.

4

Islamic Law and the Limits of Military Aggression

Asma Afsaruddin*

When discussing Islamic perspectives on warfare, most scholars will refer to the *siyar* literature, which constitutes a distinctive genre within the voluminous Islamic legal corpus. *Siyar* refers to the law of nations[1] or international law. As an integral part of Islamic law, *siyar* deals with the military *jihád* as one of the obligations of the Muslim ruler and his Muslim subjects in the context of external relations with non-Muslim polities and communities. Because Islamic law is conflated with *Sharí'ah* and the *Sharí'ah* is understood to be of divine provenance, it is frequently assumed that *siyar* regulations must of necessity be derived exclusively from the *Qur'án* and the *Sunnah* (the practices of the Prophet Muḥammad).

This chapter, however, demonstrates the reverse: that rules governing armed combat as explicated in the *siyar* literature in fact frequently deviated from certain fundamental principles articulated particularly in the *Qur'án* about legitimate warfare. Nowhere is this deviation more pro-

* **Asma Afsaruddin** is a Professor of Near Eastern Languages and Cultures in the School of Global and International Studies at Indiana University, Bloomington. She is the author and editor of seven books, including *Contemporary Issues in Islam* (Edinburgh University Press, 2015); the award-winning *Striving in the Path of God: Jihád and Martyrdom in Islamic Thought* (Oxford University Press, 2013); and *The First Muslims: History and Memory* (OneWorld Publications, 2008), which has been translated into Turkish and Malay. Her research has been funded by grants awarded, among others, by the Harry Frank Guggenheim Foundation and the Carnegie Corporation of New York, which named her a Carnegie Scholar in 2005. She lectures extensively in the United States, Europe and the Middle East, and was previously the Kramer Middle East Distinguished Scholar-in-Residence at the College of William and Mary (2012) and advisor to the Pew Research Center's Forum on Religion and Public Life.

1 A general definition of 'law of nations' is offered in Lassa Oppenheim, *International Law: A Treatise*, vol. 1, Longmans, London, 1955, pp. 4–5: "Law of nations or international law is the name for the body of customary or treaty rules which are considered legally binding by States in their intercourse with each other".

found than in the area of *jus ad bellum*, that is, justifications for going to war.

To illustrate this point, this chapter will primarily focus on how the principle of non-aggression unambiguously stated in the *Qur'án* was progressively compromised by classical Muslim jurists in their formulation of international law. The Qur'ánic text 2:190, which articulates the principle of non-aggression, will provide a point of departure for us. To illustrate the chasm between early exegetical understandings of this critical verse (and related verses) and juridical invocations of such verses, I begin by discussing first how early and late *Qur'án* commentators interpreted this verse. I then proceed to discuss how two prominent classical jurists in their articulation of the *siyar* laws pertaining to the military *jihád* engaged and eventually undermined the principle of non-aggression stated in the *Qur'án*, while at the same time upholding the principle of non-combatant immunity as a remnant of the Qur'ánic principle of non-aggression. The principle of non-combatant immunity is a particular strength of premodern Islamic law, which militated against the kind of indiscriminate mass killings that have become an all-too common feature of modern warfare, as will become evident below.

The next section provides an overview of some of the critiques that have been levelled at the classical jurists by modern Muslim jurists in their revisitation of *siyar* law. A primary ingredient of their critique is that classical Islamic law on warfare mostly turned its back on the Qur'ánic principle of non-aggression by using a variety of hermeneutical stratagems, notably the stratagem of *naskh* or textual abrogation. In the conclusion, I briefly reflect on how these developments point the way forward for recuperating the original élan of Muslim legal-ethical deliberations on the legitimacy of warfare and their ramifications for a revised approach to the *siyar* literature.

4.1. Exegeses of *Qur'án* 2:190

This verse states: "Fight in the way of God those who fight you and do not commit aggression, for God does not love aggressors". Our earliest scholars understand the interdiction in the Qur'ánic text 2:190 ("do not commit aggression, for God does not love aggressors") as a clear and general prohibition against initiating hostilities under any circumstance. Thus, the well-known early *Qur'án* exegete Mujáhid Ibn Jabr (d. 104/722) commented that, according to this verse, one should not fight until the other side commences fighting.[2] According to another early scholar Muqátil Ibn Sulaymán (d. 150/767), this verse is specifically a denunciation of the Meccans who had commenced hostilities at Al-Ḥudaybiyya, leading to a repeal of the prohibition imposed upon Muslims against fighting near the Ka'ba. Therefore, "Do not commit aggression" and "God does not love aggressors" wereunderstood by him to be a categorical indictment of the Meccans who began to fight during the sacred month in the sacred sanctuary, which was a clear act of aggression (*fa-'innahu 'udwán*). The following verse, the Qur'ánic text 2:191,[3] subsequently gives permission to believers to slay the polytheists wherever one may find them on account of their aggression and expel them from Mecca (from where the Muslims were expelled); for *fitnah*, glossed by Muqátil as 'polytheism' is a greater offence in the sight of God (*a'ẓam 'inda Alláhi 'azza wa-jalla jurman*) than killing, as affirmed also in the Qur'ánic text 9:49. Permission to engage the pagan Meccans in fighting was clearly contingent, according to Muqátil, upon their having initiated hostilities, which abrogates the earlier, complete prohibition against fighting in the Sanctuary.[4]

In the commentary of the famous exegete Al-Ṭabarí (d. 310/923), we find that a new construal of the non-aggression clause now emerges: that of the immunity of non-combatants. The famed Companion Ibn 'Abbás is quoted by Al-Ṭabarí as having said: "You should not kill women, children, the elderly, and the one who offers peaceful greetings and restrains his hand. If you do so, you have resorted to aggression". Furthermore, the pious Umayyad ruler 'Umar Ibn 'Abd Al-'Azíz (d.101/720) is said to have written to one of his military commanders, and interpreted this verse as: "Do not fight those who do not fight you; that is, women, children, and monks".[5]

On the basis of such evidence, Al-Ṭabarí proceeded to offer his own exegesis of the critical commandment "Do not commit aggression" in the

---

2 Muḥammad Al-Sháfi'í and Al-Risála, (eds.), *'Abd al-Latíf al-Hamím and Máhir Yásín al-Fahl*, Dár Al-Kutub Al-'Ilmiyya, Beirut, 2005, p. 23.

3 The *Qur'án* (translation by Arthur J. Arberry), 2:191.

4 Muḥammad Al-Sháfi'í, *Kitáb Al-Umm*, Dár Al-Kutub Al-'Ilmiyya, Beirut, 2002, vol. 1, pp. 167–68.

5 Tafsír Al-Ṭabarí, *Jámi' al-Bayán fi Tafsír al-Qur'án*, Dár Al-Kutub Al-'Ilmiyya, Beirut, 1997, vol. 2, p. 196.

Qur'ánic text 2:190. He said that this categorical prohibition means that one should not kill children or women or those who pay the *jizyah* or poll-tax from among the People of the Book and the Zoroastrians. Those who transgress these limits and hold licit what God has clearly forbidden regarding these groups of people are those who are indicated in the verse "Indeed God does not love those who transgress".[6] Exceeding these limits constitutes aggression.

It should be noted that Al-Ṭabarí's re-construal of the aggression clause in particular became quite influential and pervasive after him. This interpretation became reflected in the classical laws of war and peace formulated by jurists, who also came to understand the non-aggression clause in this verse as primarily setting up a prohibition against fighting non-combatants, and not a categorical prohibition against initiating fighting under any circumstance, as was clearly the view of the earlier exegetes Mujáhid and Muqátil referenced above.

Other exegetes after the time of Al-Ṭabarí, however, continued to uphold the defensive nature of fighting. Thus, the famous scholar and commentator Fakhr Al-Dín Al-Rází (d. 606/1210) maintained categorically that the divine imperative in the Qur'áṇic text 2:190 is directed at actual, not potential, combatants, meaning that the verse allows fighting only against those who have actually commenced fighting, and not against those who are able and prepared to fight but have not yet resorted to violence.[7]

4.2. Survey of Juridical Works

The Qur'ánic principle of non-aggression in verse 2:190 underwent considerable modification and transformation in juridical works which dealt with *siyar* law. A survey of two key juridical treatises from the *Máliki* and *Sháfi'í* schools of law confirms certain trends, as will now become evident. We begin with a scrutiny of *Al-Mudawwana Al-Kubrá* by Málik Ibn Anas, followed by a look at *Al-Ḥáwí Al-Kabír* by Abú Al-Ḥasan Al-Máwardí, both influential legal treatises that continue to be studied today.

---

6 *Ibid.*, vol. 2, pp. 196–97.

7 Fakhr Al-Dín Al-Rází (or Fakhruddín Rází in Farsi), *At-Tafsír al-Kabír*, Dár Iḥyá' Al-Turáth Al-'Arabí, Beirut, 1999, vol. 2, p. 288. For a fuller discussion of these verses, see Asma Afsaruddin, *Striving in the Path of God: Jihad and Martyrdom in Islamic Thought*, Oxford University Press, Oxford, 2013, pp. 43–58.

4.2.1. *Máliki* Views on *Jihád* as Contained in *Al-Mudawwana Al-Kubrá* by Málik Ibn Anas

This early legal compendium of the *Máliki* school contains the juridical teachings of the early Medinan jurist Málik Ibn Anas (d. 179/795), as transmitted by the Qayrawání jurist ʻAbd Al-Salám Ibn Saʻíd Ibn Ḥabíb Al-Tanukhí (d. 240/855), nicknamed 'Saḥnún', from the Egyptian jurist ʻAbd Al-Raḥmán Ibn Al-Qásim Al-ʻAtaká (d. 191/806), who was a prominent disciple of Málik.

The *Kitáb Al-Jihád* ("The Book of *Jihád*") section of this treatise begins with an emphasis on the importance of issuing a summons to Islam before commencing fighting. According to ʻAbd Al-Raḥmán Ibn Al-Qásim, Málik was of the opinion that polytheists (*al-mushrikún*) could not be fought until they had been summoned, regardless of which side initiated hostilities. Although Málik himself had not specified how this summons should be formulated, Ibn Al-Qásim said customarily "we would invite them to God and His Messenger, so that they may either accept Islam or offer *jizyah*".[8] This, he affirmed, was based on prophetic precedent and on the established practice of early Muslims like ʻUmar Ibn ʻAbd Al-ʻAzíz.[9]

With regard to non-combatants, Málik, according to Ibn Al-Qásim, prohibited the killing of women, children, elderly men, and monks and hermits in their cells. Málik further counselled that the property of monks and hermits be left intact, since that was their sole means of livelihood. Here the *ḥadíth* in which the Prophet forbids his troops to commit treachery and mutilation is cited. Other reports similarly proscribing the killing of non-combatants, particularly women and children, are recorded.[10] Abú Bakr's detailed report in which he forbids the killing of various non-combatants and of animals, the cutting down of trees and destruction of

[8] This is a reference to the *Qur'án*, 9:29; for a discussion of this verse and its exegeses, see Afsaruddin, 2013, pp. 75–79, see *supra* note 7. This verse is often deployed in juridical works along with the *Qur'án*, 9:5 to make the case that non-Muslims can be fought *qua* non-Muslims; see discussion of the contested exegeses of this verse in Afsaruddin, 2013, pp. 71–75, see *supra* note 7.

[9] Saḥnún Ibn Saʻíd Ibn Ḥabíb Al-Tanukhí, *Al-Mudawwana Al-Kubrá*, Maktaba Al-ʻAsriyya, Beirut, 1999, vol. 2, pp. 581–82.

[10] *Ibid.*; see also Abú Jaʻfar Muḥammad Ibn Jarír Al-Ṭabarí, *Ikhtiláf Al-Fuqahá'*, Brill, Leiden, 1933, pp. 6–12.

property is cited, as is the report from 'Umar Ibn Al-Khaṭṭáb in which he forbids the killing of the weak and elderly, women, and children.[11]

4.2.2. *Sháfi'í* Views on *Jihád*

It is clear, therefore, that the Qur'ánic principle of non-aggression leaves its imprint in the legal literature of the third/ninth century primarily in the form of upholding non-combatant immunity and prohibition against the wanton destruction of property and other instances of humane conduct during the waging of armed combat (*jus in bello*). It is also clear from a survey of the most prominent legal works like *Al-Mudawwana Al-Kubrá* (and others discussed below) that exegetes and jurists from after the second/eighth century increasingly began to incline to the view that the refusal of non-Muslims to embrace Islam when invited to do so constituted an act of wrong-doing *in itself* and could merit an attack by the Muslim ruler; in the case of non-scriptuaries (primarily those who were not Jews or Christians), this was expected to lead to their submission to Islam. If this did not occur, fighting is to be continued until submission or death of the non-scriptuaries. In the case of scriptuaries, the payment of *jizyah* was required in the absence of conversion. This position is articulated by Al-Sháfi'í in his legal treatise titled *Umm*.[12] In his other major treatise *Al-Risála*, Al-Sháfi'í describes offensive *jihád* of this sort as a collective duty and not an individual obligation. [13] With regard to the conduct of war, Al-Sháfi'í stipulates that women, children and young boys may not be put to death.[14] He also forbids the torture or mutilation of enemy combatants in accordance with the Prophet's prohibition against the gouging of eyes or amputation of limbs and proscribed the killing of birds and higher animals on the basis of a *ḥadíth*.[15]

4.2.3. *Al-Ḥáwí Al-Kabír* by Abú Al-Ḥasan Al-Máwardí

The principle of the offensive *jihád* is fully articulated in the later *Sháfi'í* legal compendium known as the *Al-Ḥáwí Al-Kabír* by Abú Al-Ḥasan Al-Máwardí (d. 450/1058). A very important question comes to the fore for

---

[11] Saḥnún, 1999, see *supra* note 9.

[12] Al-Sháfi'í, 2002, vol. 4, p. 247, see *supra* note 4.

[13] Al-Sháfi'í, 2005, p. 337–42, see *supra* note 2.

[14] Al-Sháfi'í, 2002, vol. 4, p. 248 and vol. 9, p. 490, see *supra* note 4.

[15] *Ibid.*, vol. 9, p. 491.

Al-Máwardí: does the *Qur'án* permit all-out fighting; that is, equally against those who initiate fighting and those who do not? Al-Máwardí documents the view of the early exegete and jurist 'Atá' Ibn Abí Rabáh (d. 115/733) who asserted that it was never permissible to fight those who do not fight. Al-Máwardí, however, takes exception to this view, because he maintains that the Qur'ánic articulation of the doctrine of combative *jihád* reaches its final form in the Qur'ánic text 2:193, 9:5, and 2:191, which, according to him, encode divine permission *to fight equally those who fight and those who desist from fighting.*[16]

There is disagreement among scholars, however, as to whether this obligation is individual or collective. It is not possible for us to reproduce in full Al-Máwardí's extensive and highly significant discussion here on account of length constraints. In summary, according to Al-Máwardí, the collective nature of *jihád* is established in the Qur'ánic text 9:41, which states: "Go forth [to battle], [armed] light and heavy!". The verse continues: "Struggle in God's way with your possessions and your selves". This may be understood, according to Al-Máwardí, as instructing the believer to supply himself or others, when unable to fight, with the provisions of war, such as a riding animal. The Qur'ánic text 9:122, which states: "It is not for the believers to go forth [to fight] totally", further establishes the collective obligation of *jihád.* The main purpose of the collective *jihád* is to protect Islamic realms from the incursions of the enemy and to thereby ensure the safety of the lives and property of Muslims. If the enemy were to encroach upon Muslim territory and threaten it, then the collective duty of *jihád* becomes an individual one for all those capable of engaging in combat.[17] To phrase it differently, before the onset of war, the combative *jihád* is a collective duty; after hostilities begin (literally, "when the two armies meet"), it becomes an individual obligation, says Al-Máwardí.[18]

Al-Máwardí's *Al-Ḥáwí Al-Kabír* is without doubt a highly important legal work, which shows the maturation and crystallisation of specific, legal rulings pertaining to conceptualisations of the military *jihád* and its conduct. Much of the earlier equivocation and debates regard-

---

[16] Abú Al-Ḥasan Al-Máwardí, *Al-Ḥáwí al-kabīr fi fiqh ma<u>dh</u>hab al-Imám a<u>sh</u>-<u>sh</u>afi'i raḍí alláhu 'anhu wa-huwa <u>sh</u>arḥ mu<u>kh</u>taṣar al-muzani*, Dár Al-Kutub Al-'Arabiyya, Beirut, 1994, vol. 14, p. 110.

[17] *Ibid.*, pp. 110–13, 142–51.

[18] *Ibid.*, p. 180.

ing the principle of non-aggression by his time appear to have been resolved. A general consensus on legal positions on these issues had clearly emerged by Al-Máwardí's time, which when compared to multiple, earlier views, can be fairly described as more aggressive and inflexible.

However, it is very important to note that a general immunity for non-combatants continued to be upheld by Al-Máwardí, as it was by later jurists, such as the *Ḥanafí* scholar Abú Bakr Al-Sarakhsí (d. 490/1096) from the fifth/eleventh century. In his influential *Kitáb Al-Mabsuṭ*, Al-Sarakhsí affirms this principle[19], as does the later *Ḥanbalí* jurist Ibn Qudáma (d. 620/1223) in his *Kitáb Al-Mughní*. Ibn Qudáma bases his position on the topic of granting immunity to non-combatants from attack on the well-known *ḥadíth* (recorded by Abú Dáwúd in his *Sunan*) in which the Prophet forbids the killing of frail (*fániyan*) elderly men, children, and women, while noting exceptions in the case of women and children being used as human shields, for example.[20]

4.3. Modern Scholars and Jurists

These legal developments during the classical period emphasising an overall belligerent perspective have been subjected to severe criticism by a number of modern and contemporary Muslim scholars, including jurists who have parted ways with many of their pre-modern counterparts. Such scholars and jurists include Muḥammad Abduh, Muḥammad 'Imára, Abú Zahra, and Al-Zuhaylí, among others. These scholars have emphasised that the *Qur'án* should be read holistically and that the critical verses which forbid the initiation of war by Muslims and which uphold the principle of non-coercion in religion categorically militate against the conception of an offensive *jihád* to be waged against non-Muslims *qua* non-Muslims.

This is a position forcefully articulated by the great modernist Egyptian scholar and reformer of the late nineteenth century, Muḥammad

---

[19] Muḥammad Al-Sarakhsí, *Kitáb Al-Mabsúṭ*, Dár Al-Kutub Al-'Ilmiyya, Beirut, vol. 10, pp. 3–4.

[20] Ibn Qudáma, *Kitáb Al-Mughní*, Hajar, Cairo, 1990, vol. 13, pp. 177–78. For a fuller discussion of some of these juridical positions, see Asma Afsaruddin, "The *Siyar* Laws of Aggression: Juridical Re-interpretations of Qur'ánic *Jihád* and Their Contemporary Implications for International Law", in Marie-Luisa Frick and Andreas T. Müller (eds.), *Islam and International Law: Engaging Self-Centrism from a Plurality of Perspectives*, Brill, Leiden, 2013, pp. 45–63.

'Abduh (d. 1323/1905). Appointed the Grand Mufti of Egypt in 1317/1899, a position he held until his death, he is counted as one of the greatest reformers of the modern Islamic world, whose thought is still considered highly influential in liberal, modernist circles.[21] Although 'Abduh did not write specifically on *jihád* itself, his views (as partially refracted through his disciple Rashíd Riḍá) may be reconstructed from his *Qur'án* commentary *Tafsír Al-manár*. 'Abduh's recorded commentary on the critical verses of the *Qur'án*, 2:190 and 9:5, allow us to gain a sufficiently comprehensive window into his perspectives on the purview of the combative *jihád*, as discussed below.

Like the early *Qur'án* exegetes discussed above, 'Abduh emphasises that the Qur'ánic text 2:190 allowed fighting as "defence in the path of God so as to allow unimpeded worship of Him in His house" and as a warning against those who break their oaths and seek to entice Muslims away from their faith. The Arabic command '*wa-lá ta'tadú*' ('do not commit aggression') is interpreted by him to contain both a proscription against initiation of hostilities by Muslims and attacking traditional non-combatants such as women, children, the elderly, the infirm, and "those who proffer you peace"; additionally, it prohibits causing destruction to crops and property.[22]

The next verse (that is, the Qur'ánic text 2:191) is understood to be a specific reference to the pagan Meccans who had driven the Prophet Muḥammad and his companions out of their homes in Mecca and prevented their subsequent attempt to peacefully perform the pilgrimage in the year of Al-Ḥudaybiyya. The right granted to Muslims to defend themselves in the face of Meccan hostility and faithlessness was therefore a divine act of mercy towards them in their hour of helplessness, comments 'Abduh. He says that the right to fight in self-defence, as is clearly the case here, undermines the assertions of those who maintain out of wilful ignorance that Islam was spread by the sword.[23] *Fitnah* in the Qur'ánic text 2:190 is specifically glossed as the torments visited upon the Muslims

[21] For a recent monograph-length study of 'Abduh's thought, see Mark Sedgwick, *Muhammad Abduh*, Oneworld Publications, Oxford, 2009.

[22] Muḥammad Rashíd Riḍá, *Tafsír al-Qur'án al-karím al-mashhúr bi-tafsír al-manár*, Dár Al-Kutub Al-'Ilmiyya, Beirut, 1999, vol. 2, pp. 169–70.

[23] This sharp rejoinder is clearly directed at a number of Orientalist scholars and Christian missionaries of his day who were prone to making such statements.

as a consequence of their beliefs – expulṣion from their homes and confiscation of their property, for example. 'Abduh cross-references here the Qur'ánic text 29:2[24] to underscore the meaning of *fitnah* as 'tribulations' and the Qur'ánic text 22:39[25] to establish the reasons (oppression, eviction from home, and so on) which render fighting in self-defence permissible.[26]

If the polytheist were to desist from fighting and violence, then hostility against him also ceases, because aggression against him is carried out only to make him renounce his violent, oppressive ways and for no other reason, he stresses.[27]

'Abduh rejects the interpretation that the so-called sword verse[28] had abrogated the more numerous verses in the *Qur'án* which call for forgiveness and peaceful relations with non-Muslims. 'Abduh argues that, in the specific historical situation with which the verse is concerned – with its internal reference to the passage of the four sacred months and to the pagan Meccans – other verses in the *Qur'án* advocating forgiveness and non-violence were not abrogated but rather in (temporary) abeyance or suspension (*laysa naskhan bal huwa min qism al-mansí*). *Naskh* implies the abrogation of a command, which is not the case here. Rather, the command contained in the Qur'ánic text 9:5 was in response to a specific situation at a specific time in order to achieve a specific objective and has no effect on the injunction contained in, for example, the Qur'ánic text 2:109, which states, "pardon and be forgiving, till God brings His command", which is in regard to a different set of circumstances and objec-

24 See the *Qur'án*, 29:2, *supra* note 3. It states: "Do the people reckon that they will be left to say 'We believe,' and will not be tried?".

25 See *ibid.*, 22:39–40. It states: "Leave is given to those who fight because they were wronged – surely God is able to help them – who were expelled from their habitations without right, except that they say 'Our Lord is God'".

26 Riḍá, 1999, vol. 2, pp. 170–71, see *supra* note 22.

27 *Ibid.*, pp. 171–72. Similar views are expressed by the Lebanese *Shí'í* scholar Muḥammad Ḥusayn Faḍl Alláh (d. 2010). With regard to *Qur'án* 2:193 in particular, he comments that the verse is not concerned with the cessation of unbelief, but with wrong-doing and hostility (*aẓ-ẓulm wa-'l-'udwán*), and pointedly adds that interpretation of Qur'ánic verses may generate meanings not previously mentioned by classical commentators, see Muḥammad Ḥusayn Faḍl Alláh, *Min waḥy al-Qur'án*, Dár Al-Malak, Beirut, 1998, vol. 4, pp. 74–83.

28 The *Qur'án*, 9:5; alternatively, 8:38. See *supra* note 3.

tives.[29] ‘Abduh therefore is appealing to the principle of *ta<u>kh</u>ṣíṣ* which restricts the applicability of certain Qur’ánic verses to the historical context of their revelation, with no general applicability beyond it.[30]

‘Abduh is critical of those who would see the injunction contained in the Qur’ánic text 9:5 with its clear reference to Arab polytheists applicable in any way to non-Arab polytheists or to the People of the Book. The latter are referred to very differently in the *Qur’án*, as in the Qur’ánic text 5:82,[31] and in *ḥadí<u>th</u>s*, such as the one which counsels leaving the Ethiopians (as well as Turks) alone as long as they leave the Muslims alone. He bemoans the fact that if jurists had not read these verses and *ḥadí<u>th</u>s* “from behind the veil of their juridical schools”, then they would not have so egregiously missed the fundamental point made throughout the *Qur’án* and in sound *ḥadí<u>th</u>s* that “the security to be obtained through fighting the Arab polytheists according to these verses is contingent upon their initiating attacks against Muslims and violating their treaties […]”.[32] ‘Abduh goes on to point out that the very next verse, the Qur’ánic text 9:6, offers protection and safe-conduct to those among the polytheists who wish to listen to the *Qur’án*.[33] The implication is clear – polytheists and non-Muslims in general who do not wish Muslims harm and display no aggression towards them are to be left alone and allowed to continue their ways of life.

These proof-texts (and others beside them) belie the arguments made by Orientalist scholars and those who follow them that *jihád* is reducible to fighting against non-Muslims in order to forcibly effect their conversion.[34] ‘Abduh points to the Qur’ánic text 2:256 (“No compulsion

---

29 Riḍá, 1999, vol. 10, pp. 161–62, see *supra* note 22.

30 For a helpful discussion of the concepts of *naṣṣ* and *ta<u>kh</u>ṣíṣ*, see Mohammad Hashim Kamali, *Principles of Islamic Jurisprudence*, Islamic Texts Society, Cambridge, 2005, pp. 149 ff.

31 This verse states: “[T]hou wilt surely find the nearest of them in love to the believers are those who say ‘We are Christians’”. See *supra* note 3.

32 Riḍá, 1999, vol. 10, pp. 162–63, see *supra* note 22.

33 *Ibid.*, vol. 10, pp. 171–75.

34 See, for example, Rudolph Peters, *Jihad in Classical and Modern Islam*, Markus Weiner, Princeton, 1996, p. 3: “[T]he ultimate aim [of the military jihad] is to bring the whole earth under the sway of Islam and to extirpate unbelief”. After September 11, 2011, some of these views have mutated into extremist statements of wholesale denunciation of Islam itself and its alleged exclusive penchant for violence; see, for example, Patrick Sookhdeo,

is there in religion") and other verses which allow fighting only against those who initiate fighting and which command Muslims to incline to peace when the adversary inclines to peace,[35] as proof-texts – all of them establish the falsity of imputing such a reductive meaning to *jihád*.[36]

The well-known Egyptian jurist and intellectual Muḥammad makes many similar points in his refutation of the militant screed titled *Al-Faríḍah Al-Ghá'ibah* ('The Lapsed or Neglected Duty') penned by the militant Abd Al-Salám Faraj, who murdered Egyptian president Anwar Sadat in 1981.[37] In this refutation, 'Imára takes strong exception to a number of positions adopted by Faraj and his cohort.

For example, 'Imára criticises Faraj and his supporters' invocation of the Qur'ánic text 9:5[38] as a verse that abrogates all other verses of 'forbearance' (*al-ṣabr*), 'forgiveness' (*al-'afu*), 'pardon' (*al-ṣafḥ*); and 'turning away' (*al-i'ráḍ*). They ignore the fact that the verse was revealed specifically concerning the polytheists (*al-mushrikún*) and that it has nothing to do with "those who believe in some [parts of] the Book and disbelieve in other [parts]", a description which may be understood to refer to the People of the Book. They also erroneously liken today's rulers to the *Khawárij* and those tribes who refused to pay *zakáh* to Abú Bakr in order to justify their militant campaign against governments in Muslim-majority societies. On all counts, they are guilty of deliberately distorting the meaning of the Qur'ánic text 9:5, which, 'Imára stresses once again, references only the polytheists and no other group. He points out that the well-known pre-modern scholar Al-Suyúṭí unambiguously stated that the

Understanding Islamic Terrorism: The Islamic Doctrine of War, Isaac Publishing, Pewsey, 2004; and a myriad of polemical essays found on the Internet in particular. For a critique and exposé of a number of these positions, see Afsaruddin, 2013, *supra* note 7.

35 The *Qur'án*, 8:61, see *supra* note 3.

36 Many of these points are also made strenuously by other modern Muslim scholars. See, for example, Muḥammad Abú Zahra, *Al-'Alaqat ad-dawliyya fí 'l-Islam*, Matba'at Al-Azhar, Cairo, 1964; Sobhi Mahmassani, "The Principles of International Law in the Light of Islamic Doctrine", in *Recueil des Cours*, 1966, vol. 117, pp. 249–79.

37 For a translation of Muḥammad Abd Al-Salám Faraj's text, *Al-Faríḍá Al-Ghá'iba*, see Johannes J.G. Jansen, *The Neglected Duty: The Creed of Sadat's Assassins and Islamic Resurgence in the Middle East*, Macmillan, New York, 1986.

38 This verse states: "Then, when the sacred months are drawn away, slay the idolators wherever you find them, and take them, and confine them, and lie in wait for them at every place of ambush. But if they repent, and perform the prayer, and pay the alms, then let them go their way, God is All-forgiving, All-compassionate". See *supra* note 3.

Qur'ánic text 9:5 did not abrogate, for example, the Qur'ánic text 2:109, which runs, "pardon and be forgiving, till God brings His command", a verse revealed in connection with the People of the Book as its Qur'ánic context clearly shows.[39]

To correct such fundamental misunderstandings of the purposes of *jihád*, 'Imára reviews the early historical circumstances which gradually allowed for the articulation of the combative *jihád* and its purview. In brief, he remarks that for thirteen years before the *Hijrah*, the Muslims in their weak state could not and did not fight; instead they were exhorted by the *Qur'án* to ward off evil with goodness[40] and other non-violent means of repelling aggression.[41] This state of affairs continued into the early Medinan period, even as Muslims became organised as a polity and finally achieved the freedom to practice and propagate Islam. Despite continuing persecution by the pagan Meccans and the growing treachery of certain Jewish tribes, the *Qur'án* still counselled showing forbearance with the former group[42] and forgiveness and pardon for the latter.[43] With the revelation of the Qur'ánic text 22:38–40, permission was finally granted to Muslims to fight back; these verses outlined the specific reasons (expulsion from their homes; defence of houses of worship) for the justification of physical retaliation. Exegetes commenting on these verses have pointed to the defensive nature of this combative phase of *jihád* permitted by God. The roughly twenty military encounters, which occurred in the seven years following the revelation of these verses, were all battles of self-defence intended to repel the wrong-doers who had expelled the Muslims from their homes.[44]

'Imára then deals with the cluster of verses in *Súrat Al-Baqara*[45] revealed after the signing of the Treaty of Al-Ḥudaybiyya. On the one hand, he comments, the directives in these verses were a response to the aggression of the polytheists and contain a reprimand for their violation of the

39 Muḥammad 'Imára, *Al-Faríḍá al-g͟há'iba: 'arḍ wa-ḥiwár wa-taqyím*, Dár Al-Wahda, Cairo, 1982, pp. 34–35.

40 The *Qur'án*, 23:96, see *supra* note 3.

41 For example, *ibid.*, 41:33–35; 88:21–22.

42 *Ibid.*, 73:10–11.

43 *Ibid.*, 5:13.

44 'Imára, 1982, pp. 35–37, see *supra* note 39.

45 *Ibid.*, 2:190–94.

terms of the Treaty and of the sanctity of the Sacred Mosque and its precincts. On the other hand, these verses offer assurance to the Muslims that they have the right to fight back under such circumstances while forbidding them from initiating aggression and from exceeding the original extent of harm done to them. Similar restrictions on the initiation of fighting and conduct during the waging of war are also clearly stipulated in regard to the Qur'ánic text 9:5, which is mistakenly understood by some to permit the propagation of Islam "by the sword". 'Imára stresses that the rest of the ninth chapter (*Al-Tawba*) unambiguously upholds these fundamental Qur'ánic principles:[46]

- Recourse to armed combat on the part of Muslims is contingent on prior aggression by the polytheists (and this is the only group referenced in this chapter); and
- It is a response to their hostile violation of their pacts with Muslims. Violence, our author affirms, cannot be justified otherwise; the propagation of religion is not a Qur'ánically-sanctioned reason for initiating hostilities.

He comments, "Islamic[ally sanctioned] fighting (*al-qitál al-islámí*) is not the objective of Islam nor of Muslims". It is rather the means to cripple the power of the oppressor against the weak, who suffer from the persecution of the polytheists". This is clearly stated in the Qur'ánic text 4:75–76:

> How is it with you, that you do not fight in the way of God, and for the the men, women, and children who, being abased, say, 'Our Lord, bring us forth from this city whose people are evildoers, and appoint to us a protector from Thee, and appoint to us from Thee a helper'? The believers fight in the way of God and the unbelievers fight in the idol's way [*al-ṭághút*]. Fight you therefore against the friends of Satan; surely the guile of Satan is ever feeble.

'Imára is anxious to drive this point home, and thus repeats for emphasis that this is the true purpose of "fighting in the path of God" – for the deliverance of the weak and to resist *al-ṭághút*, which refers to tyranny, aggression, arrogance, and extremism on the part of the polytheists. The Qur'ánic text 9:5 must be understood contextually as referring only to these polytheists specifically; to derive a broader and more general ap-

[46] 'Imára, 1982, pp. 30–40, see *supra* note 39.

plicability of this verse violates the rules of logic and proper understanding of the revelations of God.[47]

'Imára then turns his attention to explication of the term *jihád* and its multiple meanings, challenging those who would assert that it essentially means 'fighting' (*qitál*). He says that the term's basic meaning is the exertion of one's utmost ability and effort in order to defend oneself against enemies in the different spheres in which humans exert their ability and effort. It refers to various kinds of enemies, from thoughts to material acquisitiveness. It also refers to the different spheres of physical combat and its purview ranges from warding off external enemies to combating the lower self and attempting to conquer evil instincts. All of these are arenas for carrying out different kinds of *jihád*. In the revealed law, it possesses a general meaning, more general than war, fighting, and armed combat.[48]

In his influential work *A<u>th</u>ár Al-Ḥarb Fí Al-Fiqh Al-Islámí*, the well-known Syrian scholar of Islamic law and legal theory Al-Zuhaylí has similarly stated that all the Qur'ánic verses on fighting were revealed to allow Muslims to defend themselves against persecution and attack by their enemies.[49] As far as legitimate war is concerned in the Islamic context, Al-Zuhaylí identifies three specific types:

1. War against those who forcibly prevent the preaching of Islam and who foment internal disorder and strife;
2. War in defence of individuals and communities that are persecuted; and
3. War to repel a physical attack against oneself and one's country.[50]

Al-Zuhaylí points out that, types 2 and 3 are fully compatible with current principles of international law, which allow for self-defence against prior aggression and humanitarian intervention in conflict-ridden regions.[51]

47 *Ibid.*, pp. 40–41.

48 *Ibid.*, pp. 43–44.

49 Wahba Al-Zuhaylí, *A<u>th</u>ár Al-Ḥarb Fí Al-Fiqh Al-Islámí: Dirása Muqárana*, Dár Al-Fikr, Beirut, 1981, pp. 106–20.

50 *Ibid.*, pp. 93–94.

51 Compare with Article 51 and Chapter VII of the Charter of the United Nations, which refer to the principles of self-defence and humanitarian intervention, respectively; see Charter of

Type 1, however, has no clear parallel in international law since it is not confined to the boundaries of the modern nation-state; it is rather deployed as a moral instrument to ensure religious freedom and contain social instability in general. Such a justified war that may be waged on primarily moral grounds has its parallel in Christian notions of just war and is not based on positive international law.[52]

These three *casus belli* are widely accepted by modern Muslim jurists. The influential but controversial Egyptian-born scholar based in Qatar, Yúsuf Al-Qaraḍáwí, similarly states that "moderate" Muslims (*al-mu'tadilún*) are peaceful towards those who are peaceful towards them, and do not fight except those who fight them, prevent the peaceful propagation of the Islamic message, and persecute believers on account of their faith.[53] This position represents a significant departure from the classical juridical view that the Muslim ruler was obligated to carry out a military foray once a year as expansionist *jihád* in order to expand the territorial realms of Islam. Modern mainstream scholars largely reject this position as untenable because first, it violates the *Qur'án*'s prohibition against fighting except in self-defence, and, second, it reflects legal accommodation to a world predicated on *a priori* non-Muslim hostility to Muslims and in which war was the default situation between nations.

4.4. Conclusion

The discussion above makes it clear that, due to the concessions made by the classical Muslim jurists to *Realpolitik*, the *Qur'án*'s absolute prohibition on initiating military aggression was considerably watered down over time within the *siyar* literature. The gradual attenuation in later exegetical and legal literature of the categorical Qur'ánic prohibition against initiating aggression by Muslims is revelatory of the triumph of political realism over scriptural fidelity. Our survey reveals that early exegetes and jurists like 'Atá' Ibn Abí Rabáh, Mujáhid Ibn Jabr, and Muqátil Ibn Sulaymán and later scholars like Fakhr Al-Dín Al-Rází firmly maintained that the

the United Nations, 26 June 1945, in force 24 October 1945 (http://www.legal-tools.org/doc/6b3cd5/). There is also much debate on the 'responsibility to protect'.

52 See, for example, Neil Biggar, *In Defense of War*, Oxford University Press, Oxford, 2013, p. 310: "that military action can sometimes be morally justified in the absence of, and even in spite of, statutory or customary international law".

53 Yúsuf Al-Qaraḍáwí, *Fiqh Al-Jihád*, Maktabat Wahba, Cairo, 2009, vol. 1, p. 244.

Qur'ánic text 2:190 unambiguously forbade the initiation of military hostilities and that military activity could be launched only against actual, not potential, aggressors. Other scholars and jurists from the third/ninth century onwards like Al-Ṭabarí, Al-S͟háfi'í, Al-Máwardí and others who were close to the ruling elites served the cause of empire by articulating the principle of offensive *jihád.* By going back to our earliest sources and by undertaking a diachronic comparison of key exegetical and juridical works, it is possible to excavate an earlier and prominent layer of principled adherence to the Qur'ánic principle of non-aggression and trace its progressive transformation into primarily the legal principle of non-combatant immunity during the course of war, as we have shown.

Recuperation of this earlier strand of juridical thinking should goad contemporary Muslim jurists and scholars into re-examining the classical juridical views on the parameters of the combative *jihád* and laying bare their historically contingent nature. Modern Muslim jurists increasingly invoke the *Qur'án*'s pronouncements on military ethics to question some of the legal provisions that developed concerning warfare after the first century of Islam.

In doing so, a larger area of commonality with contemporary international law on the conduct of war becomes apparent.[54] On one significant point, however, we notice a strong continuity between classical and modern jurists – their insistence that civilian life and property be protected during warfare and that non-combatant immunity is a principle that may not be violated, except in severely circumscribed circumstances. This categorical proscription is meant to prevent the crime of mass killings and of genocide, commissions of which are declared to be beyond the moral limits of Islamic ethics and law. In a vastly altered world in which mutually binding international treaties exist positing peace rather than war as the default situation, the classical legal rules of war and peace both invite revisiting as well as endorsement of their key provisions that uphold the sanctity of human life and seek to protect defenceless civilians from senseless violence.

[54] Afsaruddin, 2013, pp. 71–75, see *supra* note 20.

5

Jus in Bello and General Principles Related to Warfare According to Islamic Law

Abdelrahman Afifi*

5.1. Introduction

In some parts of the Muslim world, the level of knowledge about Islam is basic. This makes such communities vulnerable to misleading teaching by religious and political leaders. Vulnerability in turn may lead to political extremism; and I would argue, despite what many in the West might say, the suffering that results from wrongful, violent practices and erroneous or misleading religious beliefs held by some Muslims is most severe among Muslims themselves.[1] The purpose of this chapter is, therefore, not primarily analytical. Rather, it seeks to empower those grappling to dispel those misconceptions in societies damaged by extremism by citing traditional Islamic texts and exploring their existing interpretations by legal scholars alert to the importance of spatial and temporal context, underlining the very real synergy between Islamic law and contemporary international criminal law.

The attitude that underlies extremism wilfully ignores an important point: Muslims cannot find every answer to every query directly in the *Qur'án* or the *Sunnah*, and that includes questions of law. Indeed, according to *fuqahah al-uṣúl* (the specialists in principles of Islamic jurisprudence) only 250 verses of the *Qur'án* from the total of 6,632 are related to legal questions. From these verses, however, the *fuqahah al-uṣúl* have extracted general rules and principles. From the second source, *Sunnah,*

---

* Dr. **Abdelrahman Afifi** has been working as an Investigator at the Office of the Prosecutor of the International Criminal Court since 2005. He has published many academic studies related to international law and international criminal law, including "On the Scope of Professional Secret and Confidentiality: The International Criminal Court Code of Professional Conduct for Counsel and the Lawyer's Dilemma", in *Leiden Journal of International Law*, 2007, vol. 20.

1 M. Cherif Bassouini, *The Sharí'ah and Islamic Criminal Justice in Time of War and Peace*, Cambridge University Press, Cambridge, 2013, p. 1.

the *fuqahah al-uṣúl* also extracted rules and principles from the authentic *ḥadí<u>th</u>*. These together establish the way revealed by God. But it is now the fundamental task of all scholars to work within these general rules to find solutions to particular legal problems, using all means possible. Rules are not created in a vacuum. They originate in a particular time and context and aim to regulate specific kinds of conduct. If a situation changes, rules need to change in such a way as to achieve the objective of regulating it; this idea is supported by the juristic principle that the ruling evolves with the effective cause.[2]

A legal framework to make this possible has existed within Islam since the tenth century, developed and enriched by the work of eminent scholars in the thirteenth and fourteenth centuries. It is a framework that allows Muslims to progress in their research and develop their skills in order to provide appropriate answers to the questions of their respective communities. It is grounded in the concept of *ijtihád*, a technical term of Islamic law that describes the process of making a legal decision by independent interpretation of the legal sources, the *Qur'án* and the *Sunnah*. The principal function of *ijtihád* is to maintain fidelity to the principles identified by the *fuqahah al-uṣúl* while formulating specific rules adapted to the historical and geographical context.

The opposite of *ijtihád* is *taqlíd,* the Arabic word for 'imitation'. For centuries, many dominant Muslim scholars have followed the path of blind *taqlíd* conformity. This has seriously disabled their capacity to rediscover the authentic and dynamic message contained in the *Qur'án* and *Sunnah.*[3] This failure to actively follow *ijtihád* has had the disturbing effect of moving people further away from the sources of *<u>Sh</u>arí'ah*. The tide of *taqlíd* has carried some so far as to say that there is no further need to interpret the *Qur'án* and *ḥadí<u>th</u>*, and that the door of *ijtihád* is now closed.[4] It is a disturbing prospect, as Muhammed Abú Zahrah notes:

[2] Mohammad Hashim Kamali, *Principles of Islamic Jurisprudence*, Pelanduk Publications, Selangor, 1989, p. 120.

[3] Tariq Ramadan, *Etre musulman Européen: Etude des sources islamiquesislamique à la lumière du contexte européen*, Tawihid, 1999, p. 82.

[4] Wael B. Hallaq, "Was the Gate of Ijtihad Closed?", in *International Journal of Middle East Studies*, 1984, vol. 16, pp. 3–4; Bernard G. Weiss, "Interpretation in Islamic Law: The Theory of Ijtihad", in *American Journal of Comparative Law*, 1978, vol. 26, pp. 199–212.

"Nothing is further from the truth – and we seek refuge in God from such excesses".[5]

This study is an attempt to clear some ground around a particular legal principle, that of *jus in bello,* the rules relating to the conduct of war. It asks: "What are the rules stipulated in the Islamic law in relation to the conduct of Muslims in war? How should Muslims behave? How can Muslims integrate the modern rules into Islamic law?". These questions seem to me to be paramount for two reasons. Firstly, as many scholars of Islamic law point out, classical Muslim jurists paid the greatest part of their attention to the Islamic *jus in bello* (rules regulating the conduct of war)[6] and far less to the Islamic *jus ad bellum* (justification for resorting to war).[7] Secondly, there is a particular problem in terms of Western understanding of the term *jihád.* This word literally means 'struggle or effort'. It can refer to internal psychological struggle or to the effort to build a just society, as well as armed struggle to protect Islam. Regrettably, *jihád* is often understood in Western literature as a holy war to convert non-Muslims by the sword or as a war to universalise the rule of Islam.[8] Even a brief glance at Muslim scholarship around *jus in bello* will indicate that the strict prohibition against targeting clergy on the one hand, and the protection granted to non-Muslim enemy combatants on the other hand, disprove any claim that *jihád* is a holy war to convert by force or to kill infidels.[9] However, more detail is necessary to dispel the deep roots of this misunderstanding.

In modern times, no one could dispute the fact that international humanitarian law, including the rules related to war, contains a level of

5 Muḥammad Abú Zahrah, *Úṣúl Al-Fiqh*, Dár Al-Fikr Al-'Arabi, Beirut. 2003, p. 318.

6 Rudolph Peters, *Jihad in Classical and Modern Islam: A Reader (Princeton Series on the Middle East)*, Markus Wiener Publishers, Princeton, 1996, p. 119.

7 See Sohail Hashmi, "Saving and Taking life in War", in Jonathan E. Brockopp (ed.), *Islamic Ethics of Life: Abortion, War and Euthanasia*, University of South Carolina Press, Columbia, 2003, p. 158; Elisabeth Kendall and Ewan Stein (eds.), *Twenty-first Century Jihad: Law, Society and Military Action*, I. B. Tauris, 2015; Asma Afsaruddin, *Striving in the Path of God: Jihád and Martyrdom in Islamic Thought*, Oxford University Press, Oxford, 2013.

8 Lester Sumrall, *Jihad: The Holy War, Timebomb in the Middle East*, Sumrall Publishing, 2002.

9 M. Cherif Bassiouni, "Evolving Approaches to Jihad: From Self-Defense to Revolutionary and Regime-Change Political Violence", in *Chicago Journal of International Law*, 2007, vol. 8, no. 1, pp. 119–46.

detail not found in the Islamic laws. This is because the means used in war in the past have completely changed, necessitating the creation of rules and principles to adapt to the new concepts of war. This study will demonstrate areas in historic Islamic law where there are considerable opportunities for adaptation, harmonisation, and the integration of international rules. It will go back to first principles, established at the time of the Prophet Muḥammad and his companions, and will also explore the principle of *jus in bello* from the perspective of *siyásah al-Sharí'ah* (*Sharí'ah*-oriented policy) and *maqaṣid al-Sharí'ah* (objectives of *Sharí'ah*).

It is here worth noting too that when it refers to *fuqahah al-uṣúl* (the specialists in principles of Islamic jurisprudence) it refers also to the sources of Islamic law highlighted in this study and in particular to the concept of *al-maṣlaḥah* (public good or public interest) in order to integrate the international rules related to warfare into the Islamic system.

Before debating *jus in bello*, it is important to provide a general idea about the meaning of *Sharí'ah,* Islamic jurisprudence *(fiqh) and* primary sources of Islamic law.

5.2. General Definitions

5.2.1. Meaning of *Sharí'ah*

Sharí'ah refers to that which God ordained in the *Qur'án* (and which is also reflected in the *Sunnah*); this includes, *inter alia*, general principles, guidance, prescriptions and proscriptions that define a Muslim and his or her relation with God, him- or herself, family, community, as well as the relation between the ruler and the people, and the nations in the international community.[10]

Islamic law refers to the legal discipline based on legislation, edicts of rules, *fiqh*, judicial interpretation, and valid *fatwás* (expert legal opinion). The issue to be explored here is the on-going struggle between progressive development and rigid adherence to *Sharí'ah* principles.

The 'Science of the Rules of *Fiqh*' means the accepted methodology of legal reasoning by means of which *fiqh* is developed.[11]

[10] Wael B. Hallaq, *An Introduction to Islamic Law*, Cambridge University Press, Cambridge, 2009, p. 14.

[11] Kamali, p. 572, see *supra* note 2.

5.2.2. Primary Sources of Islamic Law

5.2.2.1. The *Qur'án*

The *Qur'án* is the holy book of Islam, containing the revelations delivered to the Prophet Muḥammad by the angel Gabriel over a period of about twenty-three years. The *Qur'án* is, for Muslims, the word of God and comprises legislative proscriptions and rulings as well as spiritual guidance. It also constitutes the source of all law and legal obligation. The *Qur'án* consists of 114 chapters, which contain 6,236 verses.[12] It is the highest source of law, supreme over all other legal sources or evidence.

5.2.2.2. The *Sunnah*

The *Sunnah* refers to the deeds and practices of the Prophet. Many of the fundamental obligations of the *Qur'án*, such as the performing the prayer, paying *zakáh* (religious taxes), or performing the *ḥajj* (pilgrimage) could not possibly have been put into practice unless there were some practical demonstrations of how to do so. The obvious model was of course the Prophet. The *ḥadíth* comprises the narratives passed on from generation to generation about a particular occurrence. The *Sunnah,* the rule of law deduced from such *ḥadíth*, is the practice of the Prophet, his 'model behaviour'. In order to ensure a certain authenticity, each *ḥadíth* was traced through the chain of recognised narrators, back to the original tradition.[13] There are also subsidiary sources of Islamic law to which scholars might refer, such as *ijmá'* (consensus among Islamic scholars)[14] and *qiyás* (analogy).[15]

5.2.3. 'Legal Maxims' (*Al-Qawá'id Al-Fiqhíyyah*)

'Legal maxims' (*al-qawá'id al-fiqhíyyah)* is a term applied to a particular science in Islamic jurisprudence. Islamic legal maxims are theoretical abstractions, usually in the form of short epithetic statements expressive of the nature and sources of Islamic law. They encompass general rules in

---

12 Sheikh Wahbeh Al-Zuhili, *Úṣúl Al-Fiqh Al-Islamí*, Dár Al-Fikr, Beirut, 1986, p. 420.

13 Kamali, 2003, p. 48, see *supra* note 2.

14 Wael B. Hallaq, in "On the Authoritativeness of Sunni Consensus", in *International Journal of Middle East Studies*, 1986, vol. 18, pp. 427–54; Al-Zuhili, p. 481, see *supra* note 12.

15 Wael B. Hallaq, *A History of Islamic Legal Theories*, Cambridge University Press, Cambridge, 1997; Wael B. Hallaq, "Non-Analogical Arguments in Sunní Juridical Qiyas", in *Arabica*, 1989, vol. 36, no. 3, pp. 286–306; Al-Zuhili, 1986, p. 600, see *supra* note 12.

cases that fall under their subject. They are different from *úṣúl al-fiqh* (fundamental guiding principles of Islamic jurisprudence) in that they are based on the *fiqh* itself and represent rules and principles derived from the reading of the detailed rules of *fiqh* on various themes. One of the main functions of the Islamic legal maxims is to depict the general picture of goals and objectives of Islamic law (*maqáṣid al-Sharí'ah*).

The five generally agreed-upon maxims are as follows: (i) *al-umúr bi-maqáṣidhá*[16] ('acts are judged by their objectives and purposes'); (ii) *al-yaqín lá yazálu bi'l-shak* ('certainty is not overruled by doubt'); (iii) *al-mashaqqatu tajlib al-taysír* ('hardship begets ease'); (iv) *al-ḍararu yuzál* ('hardship must be removed'); (v) *al-'ádatu muḥakkamatun* ('custom overrides where there is no provision'); and (vi), *lá ḍarar wá-lá dirár* ('injury/harm shall not be inflicted or reciprocated').[17]

5.2.4. *Siyásah Al-Sharí'ah* and *Maqáṣid Al-Sharí'ah*

The objective of *siyásah al-Sharí'ah* might be included to carry out the *maqáṣid al-Sharí'ah*, the objectives of *Sharí'ah*, in protecting five human interests, namely freedom of faith, life, mind or reason, lineage and honour, and property. These five essential interests must be protected because their neglect will lead to disorder. Although the classical concept of *siyásah al-Sharí'ah* relates to the administration of the State, I would argue that this could be extended to describe an international humanitarian organisation that has an international legal personality. This extension is necessary because of the importance of protecting the five essential human interests.

5.2.5. *Asbáb Al-Nuzúl*

Finally, in order to understand the *Qur'án*, Muslims should have knowledge about several disciplines in order to be able to understand the

16 In *Sharí'ah*, one of the basic legal maxims agreed upon by Muslim scholars is *al-umúr bi-maqáṣidhá*, which implies that any action, whether physical or verbal, should be considered and judged according to the intention of the doer. The first element of the maxim, *umúr* (plural for *amr*), is literally translated as a matter, issue, act, physical or verbal. The second word is *al-maqáṣid* (plural of *maqaṣad*), which literally means willing, the determination to do something for a purpose. Thus, for an act to be punishable, the intention of the perpetrator has to be established.

17 Lukman Zakariyah, *Legal Maxims in Islamic Criminal Law: Theory and Applications*, Brill, Leiden, 2015, p. 235.

text itself. This would include *asbáb al-nuzúl* (causes of revelations) as many verses were revealed in response to particular incidents or questions directed to the Prophet. There should in principle be no conflict between the *Qur'án* and the authentic *Sunnah.* If, however, a conflict is seen to exist, they must be reconciled as far as possible and both should be retained. If this is not possible, the *Sunnah* in question is likely to be of doubtful authenticity and must therefore give way to the *Qur'án.*[18]

Understanding the *Qur'án, ḥadíth, al-qawá'id al-fiqhíyyah,* and *maqáṣid al-Sharí'ah,* will enable scholars to find new rules for emergent issues.

5.3. General Principles Governing Warfare under Islamic Law

There are many principles in Islamic law in relation to the conduct of Muslims in war. Four central principles can be highlighted: non-aggression, proportionality, justice, and amnesty. In the following, each principle will be addressed in turn.

5.3.1. Non-Aggression

Under Islamic rules, aggression against others, whether individual or collective, is strictly prohibited as a general principle. The Qur'ánic text at 2:190–191 generally discloses that there ought to be no transgression except against polytheists and the wrong doers. Numerous other verses underscore the *Qur'án*'s general attitude towards aggression and violence, including, "And if they incline to peace, do thou incline to it; and put thy trust in God; He is the All-hearing, the All-knowing".[19]

In a message to the leader of his armies, Sa'd Ibn Abí Waqas, Omar Ibn Al-Khaṭṭáb[20] said:[21]

> I order you and those accompanying you to be most careful about committing offences against your enemies, as the sins of the army are more fearful than their enemy. Muslims win because of their foe's disobedience to God; had it not been for this, we wouldn't have power over them, because their

18 Kamali, 2003, p. 61, see *supra* note 2.

19 *Ibid.*, 8:61.

20 Omar I, Second *Caliph* of Islam (634–644).

21 Jamal Ayyad, *Nuzum Al-Ḥarb Fí Al-Islamí* [Statutes of War in Islam], Maktabat Al-Khangi, Cairo, 1951, p. 43.

> numbers surpass ours, they are better equipped than we are. Hence, if we are equal in wrongdoing, they would be superior to us.

Jihád is lawful in Islam if necessary to suppress aggression. It was prescribed in the second year of the *Hijrah,*[22] after Muslims had borne for fourteen years the harm done to them by the pagans of Mecca: "Leave is given to those who fight because they were wronged – surely God is able to help them".[23] The prevalence of Islam as a religion was not the motive for warfare in *jihád,* nor was its purpose to subordinate others and compel them to convert to Islam. Islam was not spread by the sword. Compulsory conversion to Islam did not occur in the history of Islamic preaching, as underscored by God's words: "No compulsion is there in religion. Rectitude has become clear from error [...]".[24]

There are three kinds of circumstances that legitimise warfare in Islam, namely:

1. aggression against Muslims: God the Almighty says: "Leave is given to those who fight because they were wronged – surely God is able to help them [...]";[25]
2. assistance for the victims of injustice: God the Almighty says: "How is it with you, that you do not fight in the way of God, and for the men, women, and children who, being abased, say 'Our Lord, bring us forth from this city whose people are evildoers, and appoint to us a protector from Thee, and appoint to us from Thee a helper'?";[26]
3. self-defence: God the Almighty says: "And fight in the way of God with those who fight with you, but aggress not: God loves not the aggressors".[27]

---

[22] The *Hijrah* is the emigration of the Prophet from Mecca to Medina in AD 622 (that is, year 1 of the *Hijrah,* the first year of the Muslim Era).

[23] The *Qur'án,* 22:39–40, see *supra* note 19.

[24] *Ibid.*, 2:256.

[25] *Ibid.*, 22:39.

[26] *Ibid.*, 4:75.

[27] *Ibid.*, 2:190.

Islamic rules establish a strict balance between military necessity and respect for human life, in a manner that gives primacy to saving the lives of non-combatants.

5.3.2. Proportionality

The principle of proportionality is reflected in many of the verses of the Holy *Qur'án* previously cited, such as the following:

1. "And fight in the way of God with those who fight with you, but aggress not: God loves not the aggressors";[28]
2. "And if you chastise, chastise even as you have been chastised; and yet assuredly if you are patient, better it is for those patient";[29]
3. "[T]he recompense of evil is evil the like of it; but whoso pardons and puts things right, his wage falls upon God; surely He loves not the evildoers";[30] and
4. "O believers, prescribed for you is retaliation, touching the slain; freeman for freeman, slave for slave, female for female. But if aught is pardoned by his brother, let the pursuing be honourable, and let the payment be with kindliness. That is a lightening granted you by your Lord, and a mercy; and for those who commit aggression after that – for him there awaits a painful chastisement".[31]

5.3.3. Justice

Justice is one of the main essential principles. Almighty God says: "Surely God bids to justice and good-doing";[32] and also, "O believers, be you securers of justice, witnesses for God. Let not detestation for a people move you not to be equitable; be equitable – that is nearer to godfearing. And fear God; surely God is aware of the things you do".[33] The Divine

[28] *Ibid.*, 2:190.

[29] *Ibid.*, 16:126.

[30] *Ibid.*, 42:40.

[31] *Ibid.*, 2:178.

[32] *Ibid.*, 16:90.

[33] *Ibid.*, 5:8.

Saying related by the Prophet enjoins, "O My subjects! I forbade injustice to myself, and forbade it among you. Do not do others injustice".[34]

One of the rare examples of justice in dealing with other nations described in the *Qur'án* is the story of the Samarkand people. They had complained to the Omayyad *Caliph* Omar Ibn Abdul Azíz (717–720) about the Muslim commander Qutayba's injustice and discrimination when he conquered their country without any prior warning. Omar sent his judge to settle the matter. His decision was that Arabs had to withdraw from the conquered territory and to go back to their camps, unless a new conciliation pact was concluded or a conquest took place after due warning.[35]

5.3.4. Amnesty

Islam prescribes tolerance, mercy and the granting of amnesty when dealing with one's opponents and even enemies, in accordance with the nature of the Islamic Message described by Almighty God addressing the Prophet in these words: "We have not sent thee [Prophet Muḥammad], save as a mercy unto all beings".[36]

These principles should be the guidelines for analysing Islamic rules on how Muslim combatants should behave during war. Observation of these principles means an attitude of submission to Islam. Consequently, infringement of them corresponds to transgression against Islam.

5.4. *Jus in Bello* and Islamic Law

International humanitarian law is synonymous with *jus in bello*;[37] it seeks to minimise suffering in armed conflicts, notably by protecting and assisting all victims of armed conflict to the greatest extent possible.

There are some important rules in Islamic law related to *jus in bello*; they outline the manner in which Muslim combatants must conduct themselves during an armed conflict. Islamic rules as to the methods, means,

---

34 Related by Muslim Ibn Al-Hajjaj (according to Abú Dhar Al-Ghaffary), in his *Sahih* (The Genuine).

35 Sheikh Wahbeh Al-Zuhili, "Islam and International Law", in *International Review of the Red Cross*, 2005, vol. 87, p. 274.

36 The *Qur'án*, 21:107, see *supra* note 19.

37 See International Committee of the Red Cross ('ICRC'), "What are *jus ad bellum* and *jus in bello*?", 22 January 2015.

and permissible targets correspond to some degree to the *jus in bello* principles in that both are based on the pillars of proportionality and discrimination.[38] There are many other issues related to *jus in bello* in which it is important to understand some of the rules set by Islamic law. Understanding these issues is relevant when discussing contemporary issues, such as targeting non-combatants and killing civilians.

In formulating these rules, the jurists resorted first to the *Qur'án*, and second to the traditions of the Prophet and the practice of the Prophet's companions. They took into consideration two principles: on the one hand the sanctity of life, and on the other hand military necessity.

Because it is based on the *Qur'án*, Islamic law similarly embodies humanitarian principles applicable in warfare: the necessity to exercise patience,[39] restraint,[40] compassion,[41] and justice[42] towards fellow human beings, who are considered part of the same family, descended from a single person.[43]

5.4.1. Categories of Enemy Non-Combatant Not to be Targeted

Several *ḥadíth* of the Prophet prohibit targeting very specific categories of enemy non-combatants, namely women, children, the elderly, and the clergy. A non-combatant, who is not taking part in warfare, whether by action, opinion, planning or supplies, must not be attacked.[44]

---

38 Ahmed Zaki Yamani, "Humanitarian International Law in Islam: A General Outlook", in Hisham M. Ramadan (ed.), *Understanding Islamic Law: from Classical to Contemporary*, Altamira Press, Oxford, 2006, p. 65.

39 The *Qur'án*, 16:126–127, see *supra* note 19.

40 *Ibid.*, 16:128.

41 *Ibid.*, 5:32.

42 *Ibid.*, 16:90.

43 *Ibid.*, 4:1.

44 Ahmad Ibn Al-Husayn Ibn Ali Ibn Musa Al-Bayhaqi, *Sunan Al-Bayhaqi Al-Kubrá*, Turath for Solutions, 2013, *ḥadíths* 17932, 17933, 17934, 17935, 17936, 17937, 2613 and 2614; Sulaymán Ibn Al-Ash'ath Abú Dáwúd, *Sunan Abí Dáwúd*, Dar Us-Salám Publications, 2008, *ḥadíths* 2608 and 2663. See also Mohammad Abú Nimer, "A Framework for Nonviolence and Peace-building in Islam", in *Journal of Law and Religion*, 2000–2001, vol. 15, pp. 217–65; Ali Ahmad, "The Role of Islamic Law in the Contemporary World Order", in *Journal of Islamic Law and Culture*, 2001, vol. 6, pp. 157–72.

5.4.1.1. Women and Children

Muslim jurists unanimously agree that it is impermissible to target women and children in war.[45] They classify anyone who has not reached puberty or is under the age of fifteen as a child, and thus the beneficiary of non-combatant immunity.[46] Jurists deduce this age limit from *ḥadíth* that show that the Prophet refused to accept some Muslim male volunteers aged fourteen at the battles of Badr (March 624) and Uhud (March 625). He accepted them only when they reached the age of fifteen.[47]

The jurists justified not targeting women and children because women and children are not fit for fighting.[48] Some jurists further justified this prohibition by the principle of *al-maṣlaḥah* as women and children could be exchanged for Muslims prisoners or for ransom.[49] However, jurists deferred cases when women and children took part in hostilities. Some jurists advocate that if a woman attacks a man, it is permissible for him to kill her, although only in a situation of self-defence.[50] They deduce the wisdom of this prohibition from the incident when a woman was killed in the battle of Hunayn (630). When the Prophet found her killed in the battlefield, he stated that she was not the one who would initially have fought. When the

45 Muḥammad Ibn Idris Al-Shâfi'í, *Al-Qum*, vol. 4, Dár Al-Ma'rifa, Beirut, 1973, p. 240.

46 See Maryam Elahi, "The Rights of the Child under Islamic Law: Prohibition of the Child Soldier", in *Columbian Human Rights Law Review*, 1988, vol. 19, pp. 265–79.

47 Muhi Al-Dín Ibn Ashraf Al-Nawawi, *Al-Majmu: Sharh Al-Muhadhdhab*, Dár Al-Fikr, Beirut, 2000, vol. 21, p. 20.

48 Muḥammad Al-Ghazálí, *Al-Wasit Fí Al-Madhhab*, Dár Al-Salám, Cairo 1997, vol. 7, p. 19, cited in Ahmed Al-Dawoody, *The Islamic Law of War: Justifications and Regulations*, Palgrave Macmillan, Basingstoke, 2011; Ibn Qudáma, "Al-Mughní", in Sayed S. Haneef, *Homicide in Islam: Legal Structure and the Evidence Requirements*, A.S. Nordeen, Kuala Lumpur, 2000; Ahmad Z. Yamani, "Humanitarian International Law: A General Outlook", in *Michigan Yearbook of International Legal Studies*, 1985, vol. 7, pp. 189–215.

49 Muḥammad Al-Ghazálí, *Al-Wasit*, vol. 7, p. 19, cited in Al-Dawoody, 2011, see *supra* note 48.

50 Muhammed Ibn Al-Hassan Al-Shaybání, *As-Siyar Al-Kabír*, Matba'at Jami'at, Cairo, 1958, vol. 4, p. 1416; Mohamed A. Dayem and Fatima Ayub, "In The Path of Allah: Evolving Interpretations of Jihad and Its Challenges", in *UCLA Journal of Islamic & Near Eastern Law*, 2008, vol. 7, pp. 67–120; Ahmad Z. Yamani, "Humanitarian International Law: A General Outlook", in *Michigan Yearbook of International Legal Studies*, 1985, vol. 7, pp. 189–215; Sobhi Mahmassani, "The Principles of International Law in the Light of Islamic Doctrine", in *Recueil des Cours*, 1966, vol. 117, pp. 205–328.

Prophet questioned the man who killed her, the man replied that he had killed her because she tried to snatch his sword in order to kill him.[51]

5.4.1.2. The Elderly

Most jurists prohibit targeting the elderly. However, they agree that if the elderly support the enemy in planning war operations, they can be targeted during the war.[52] The jurists based this ruling on the incident of the killing of Durayd Ibn Al-Summah, who was brought to the battlefield to plan operations for the battle of Hunayn, even though he was over one hundred years of age.[53] Since the Prophet knew about the killing and did not condemn it, the jurist deduced that it was permissible to target the aged in such cases.[54]

5.4.1.3. The Blind, the Sick and the Incapacitated

The jurists are in agreement that it is impermissible for a Muslim army to target the blind, the sick, the incapacitated, and the insane, unless they are still physically able to fight or to support the enemy.[55] There is no Qur'ánic proscription or precedent set by the Prophet in this matter; it is therefore for the jurists to decide whether it is permissible to target specific individuals in this situation on the basis of the harm they can cause to a Muslim army.

5.4.1.4. The Clergy

The jurists unanimously grant non-combatant immunity to all hermits. This prohibition is based on the Prophet's commands and also on his ten commands to Yazid Ibn Sufyan, an army leader. Abú Bakr reiterated the

---

[51] Abdraziq Ibn Hammam Al-Sanani, *Al-Mousanaf*, vol. 5, Al-Maktab Al-Islamí, Beirut, 1982, *ḥadíth* 9383, p. 201.

[52] Ahmed Abou-El-Wafa, *Islam and The West: Coexistence or Clash?*, Dar An-Nahda, Cairo, 2006, pp. 263–78.

[53] Muḥammad Ibn Ali Muḥammad Al-Shawkani, *Nayl Al-Awtar*, Dár Al-Jalil, Beirut, 1973, vol. 8, p. 73.

[54] Muḥammad Ibn Ali Muḥammad Al-Shawkani, *As-Sayl Al-Jarrar Al-Mutadaffiq 'Ala Hadá'iq Al-Azhar*, Beirut, 1984, vol. 4, p. 533; Anke I. Bouzanita, "The *Siyar*: An Islamic Law of Nations", in *Asian Journal of Social Sciences*, 2007, vol. 35, pp. 17–46.

[55] Ala Al-Dín Al-Kasani, *Badá'i' al Ṣaná'i' fi Tartíb As-Sará'i'*, Dár Al-Kutub Al-Arabi, Beirut, 1982, vol. 7, p. 101. See also Dayem and Ayub, 2008, pp. 67–120, see *supra* note 50.

Prophet's prohibition against targeting hermits.[56] However, jurists agree that if hermits support the army of the enemy they can be fought.[57]

5.4.2. Further Prohibitions and Rules of Conduct in War

5.4.2.1. Mutilation

The Prophet would brief his soldiers on their responsibilities, instructing them thus: "Do not handcuff or tie up the prisoners. Do not mutilate. Do not kill the wounded. Do not pursue one retreating or one who throws down his weapon. Do not kill the old, the young or their women. Do not cut down trees, unless you are forced to do so. Do not deploy poison in lands. Do not cut off the water supply".[58] At the battle of Uhud, the bodies of many Muslims, including the Prophet's uncle, were horrifyingly mutilated; the Prophet and other Muslims vowed to mutilate the enemies' bodies if they had the chance. The Prophet exclaimed: "If God gives him power over Quraysh, he will mutilate thirty or seventy of their men in the next confrontation".[59] Yet soon afterwards, the Prophet received a revelation that indisputably prohibited disproportionate violence in the delivery of punishment and commended patience towards the enemy:[60] "And if you chastise, chastise even as you have been chastised; and yet assuredly if you are patient, better it is for those patient".[61] Following the Qur'ánic revelation,[62] as maintained by the majority of exegetes and jurists, the Prophet prohibited mutilation.[63]

Abú Bakr and Umar Ibn Al-Khaṭṭáb passed the instruction of the Prophet to their armies. Abú Bakr wrote to one of his governors in Hadramawt in Yemen: "Beware of mutilation, because it is a sin and disgusting act".

---

[56] Málik Ibn Anas, *Muwaṭṭá, ḥadíth* 965.

[57] Ahmed Ibn Taymiyyah, *Majmú' Fatáwa Shaykh Al-Islamí Ibn Taymiyya*, Cairo, vol. 28, p. 660.

[58] Majid Khadduri, *War and Peace in the Law of Islam*, Johns Hopkins Press, Baltimore, 1955, p. 106.

[59] Mahmoud Ayoub, *Quran and its Interpreter*, State University of New York Press, Albany, 1992, p. 369.

[60] Yadh Ben Achour. "Islam and International Humanitarian Law", in *International Review of the Red Cross*, 1980, vol. 20, pp. 64–65. See also, *ibid.*

[61] The *Qur'án*, 16:126, see *supra* note 19.

[62] *Ibid.*, 16:126; 16:128.

[63] Málik Ibn Anas, *Muwatta Al-Imám Málik*, Dár Al-Fikr, Beirut, vol. 2, p. 447, *ḥadíth* 966.

According to a *ḥadíth* reported by Abú Hurayrah, the Prophet instructed Muslims to avoid the enemy's face during the fighting.[64] In fact, the Prophet even prohibited the torture and mutilation of animals. According to *ḥadíth*, when the Prophet once passed a group of people shooting arrows at a sheep, he disliked their action and added to the text, "do not mutilate animals".[65]

At end of the fighting, the bodies of enemy fighters should be handed over to the enemy if they require it; otherwise, Muslims are to bury them. According to several reports, the Prophet always ensured the burial of the dead, irrespective of whether the bodies belonged to the Muslims or their enemy. It was obligatory for Muslims to bury enemy dead bodies.[66]

5.4.2.2. Property Destruction

The classical jurists debated the issue of destruction of the enemy property during the course of fighting. They based their discussion on two reports. The first of these was the Prophet's order for Muslims to cut down the palm trees of the tribe of Banu Al-Nadir in 625; according to the Qur'ánic reference to this incident,[67] the Prophet gave this order to force Al-Nadir to surrender during a bloodless siege. The second report is related to Abú Bakr's ten commands to his army commander, which included: do not destroy buildings, do not slaughter sheep or a camel except for food, do not burn or chop down palm trees.[68] The jurists tried to reconcile the two reports by saying that it is forbidden for the Muslim army to impose destruction on enemy property and that Abú Bakr gave these instructions based on his knowledge that the Prophet's order to cut down the palm tree was later abrogated.[69] Some jurists prefer to say that the Muslim army may impose damage on the lifeless property of the enemy only when the enemy is powerful.[70] The majority of the jurists agree that it is permitted to kill horses or other animals when the enemy are fighting while riding them,

64 Mahmassani, 1966, p. 303, see *supra* note 51.

65 Al-Dawoody, 2011, p. 120, see *supra* note 48.

66 Ali Ibn Ahmed Ibn Hazm, *Al-Mouhalla*, Dár Al-Afaq Al-Jadida, Beirut, vol. 5, p. 117.

67 The *Qur'án*, 59:5, see *supra* note 19.

68 Karima Bennoune, "*As-Salámu Alaykum?* Humanitarian Law in Islamic Jurisprudence", in *Michigan Journal of International Law*, 1994, vol. 15, p. 626.

69 Khadduri, 1955, p. 103, see *supra* note 59.

70 Mohamed Ibn Idris Al-Shâfi'í, *Al-Umm*, Dár Al-Ma'rifa, Beirut, vol. 4, p. 257.

because the horse was used as military equipment.[71] All religious sites are immune from attack.[72]

5.4.2.3. Prisoners of War

Qur'ánic revelation directly addresses the subject of prisoners of war and commands Muslims to "set them free, either by grace or ransom".[73] Muslims are obliged after the end of fighting to free their prisoners of war, either freely, or in exchange for Muslim prisoners of war or ransom.[74]

When the Prophet divided the prisoners of war taken at the battle of Badr to be housed with the Companions, he instructed them to "observe very good treatment towards prisoners". Some prisoners narrate the treatment they received during captivity: "[T]he Muslim captors ate their morning and evening meals; they gave me the bread and ate the dates themselves".[75] This humane treatment was described in the *Qur'án* as follows: "[T]hey give food, for the love of Him, to the needy, the orphan, the captive".[76]

Prisoners should be protected from the heat, cold, hunger, thirst and any kind of torture.[77] Muslim scholars agreed with regard to the illegality of inflicting degrading or inhumane treatment on enemy prisoners.[78] Under Islamic rules, prisoners should be granted humane treatment, which is "comparable to an act of charity".[79]

---

[71] *Ibid.*, p. 244.

[72] Bedjaoui Mohamed, "The Gulf War of 1980–1988 and the Islamic Conception of International Law", in Iger F. Dekker and Harry H.G. Post (eds.), *The Gulf War of 1980–1988: The Iran-Iraq War in International Legal Perspective*, Nederlands Instituut voor Sociaal en Economisch Recht, The Hague, 1992, p. 289.

[73] The *Qur'án*, 47:4, see *supra* note 19.

[74] Lena Salaymeh, "Early Islamic Legal Historical Precedents: Prisoners of War", in *Law and History Review*, 2008, vol. 26, pp. 521–44.

[75] Muḥammad Hamidullah, *Muslim Conduct of State*, 4th ed., Ashraf Press, Lahore, 1961, p. 214.

[76] The *Qur'án*, 76:8, see *supra* note 19; Saleem Marsoof, "Islam and International Humanitarian Law", in *Sri Lanka Journal of International Law*, 2003, vol .15, pp. 23–28.

[77] Hamidullah, 1961, p. 214, see *supra* note 75.

[78] Yadh Ben Ashoor, "Islam and International Humanitarian Law', in *International Review of the Red Cross*, 1980, vol. 20, p. 64.

[79] Said El-Dakkak, "International Humanitarian Law Between the Islamic Concept and Positive Interactional Law", in *International Review of the Red Cross*, 1990, vol. 275, p. 110.

At the battle of Badr, the Prophet Muḥammad is said to have recommended goodwill and fair treatment towards prisoners to his fellow fighters.[80] He ordered that prisoners of war who had been fighting under the heat of the sun be safeguarded from further suffering. They should not experience the heat of the day in addition to the heat of their weapons.[81] Jurists commonly agree that it is prohibited to execute enemy hostages. This prohibition is based on the Qur'ánic instruction: "No person earns any sin except against himself only, and no bearer of burdens shall bear the burden of another".[82] Jurists also agree that, in captivity, members of the same family should not be separated.[83]

5.4.3. 'I Give You Ten Rules': Specific Orders for Conduct in War

Muslims are obliged to abide unilaterally by these rules of warfare; irrespective of the enemy's conduct, the obligation is not owed to human beings but to God alone. Abú Bakr reiterated several commandments, inspired by Prophetic Guidance, to his commander Yazid Ibn Abí Sufyan:[84]

> Stop, O People, that I may give you ten rules for your guidance, in the battlefield. Do not commit treachery or deviate from the right path. You must not mutilate dead bodies. Neither kill a child, nor a woman, nor an aged man. Bring no harm to the trees, nor burn them with fire, especially those which are fruitful. Slay not any of the enemy's flock, save for your food. You are likely to pass by people′, who had devoted their lives to monastic services, leave them alone.

The practices of the orthodox *Caliphs* serve as a good example to demonstrate the observance of humanity. Al-Shaybání, an eminent scholar, reports in his *Siyar*[85] that *Caliph* Abú Bakr condemned the practices of

---

80 Yadh Ben Ashoor, 1980, see *supra* note 78.

81 *Ibid.*

82 The *Qur'án*, 6:164, see *supra* note 19.

83 Troy S. Thomas, "Prisoners of War in Islam: A Legal Inquiry", in *The Muslim World*, 1997, vol. 87, p. 50.

84 Muslim, *Sahih*, vol. 19, *ḥadíth* 4292.

85 *Siyar* is the plural form of the Arabic word *sirah*, which is in turn derived from the verb *sara-yasiru* (to move). *Sirah* is a technical term in the Islamic sciences meaning the biography of the Prophet. Mohammad T. Al Ghunaimi, *The Muslim Conception of International Law and the Western Approach*, Martinus Nijhoff Publishers, The Hague, 1968, pp. 34–35; Shaheen S. Ali, "Resurrecting *Siyar* through *Fatwás*?", in M. Cherif Bassiouni and Amna Guellali (eds.), *Jihad and its Challenges to International and Domestic Law*, The

mutilation, torture and drowning of combatants, whether in battle or as prisoners. Records indicate that he told the commander of his army:[86]

> You will find people who claim that they are safe because they stay inside the mosques. Let them be. [...] I give you ten orders: do not kill children, women or old people; [...] do not be tyrannical towards captives and do not put them in irons.

Ali, the fourth *Caliph* insisted that humanitarian principles be observed during his struggle against the Umayyad and at the battle of Siffin (657). During this first Muslim Civil War, Ali urged his soldiers to distinguish between enemy combatants and innocent civilians. In the battle of the Camel (656), Ali reportedly commanded his followers thus:[87]

> When you defeat them, do not kill their wounded, do not behead the prisoners, do not pursue those who return and retreat, do not enslave their women, do not mutilate their dead, do not uncover what is to remain covered, do not approach their property except what you find in their camp of weapons, beasts, male or female slaves: all the rest is to be inherited by their heirs according to the writ of God.

5.5. Conclusion

This chapter has not attempted to draw specific detailed analogies between individual Islamic rules of war and modern international humanitarian law. However, the Islamic principles outlined here are plainly not in contradiction with that law. Integrating the rules of international *jus in bello* into any Islamic system could be justified by the application of *siyásah al-Sharí'ah* and *maqáṣid al-Sharí'ah*;[88] it could equally be demonstrated that there is

Hague Academic Press, The Hague, 2010, p. 116; Bouzanita, 2007, p. 17–46, see *supra* note 54.

86 El-Dakkak, 1990, p. 10, see *supra* note 79.

87 Mohamed Hamidullah, *Muslim Conduct of State*, 5th ed., Ashraf Press, Lahore, 1968, p. 363; Hamid Sultan, "The Islamic Concept", in *International Dimensions of Humanitarian Law*, Pedone, UNESCO, Paris/Henry Dunant Institute, Geneva, 1986, pp. 47–60.

88 Mustafa Omar Mohammed and Omar Kachka, *Developing Al-Siyasah Al-Shariah Framework for Contemporary Public Policy Analysis*, Department of Economics & Center for Islamic Economics, Kulliyyah of Economics and Management Sciences, International Islamic University Malaysia, 2016; Abdul Wahhab Khallaf, *As-Siyasah Ash-Shar'iyyah, Muassasah ar-Risálah*, Beirut, 1984, vol. 2; Lukman Thaib, "Concept of Political Authority in the Islamic Political Thought", in *International Journal of Humanities and Social Science Invention*, 2012, vol. 1, no. 1, pp. 12–19; Al-Zuhili, 2005, p. 274, see *supra* note 35.

considerable basis for adaptation, harmonisation, and integration of contemporary international laws of conduct in wartime and historic Islamic law. However, to ignore the concept of *jus in bello* highlighted in this study, as some groups in the Muslim world have done, or to attribute to Islam acts of terrorism, or to justify violence as permissible in Islam, perverts the spirit and the letter of Islamic rules.

Adoption of international norms through the concept of *siyásah al-Sharí'ah* and *maqaṣid al-Sharí'ah* is completely compatible with Islam and poses no doctrinal or legal issues. Historically, there has always been an intellectual and legal framework in Islam that is adaptable. Reluctance to provide appropriate responses to international law is due to the negligence of some Muslims with excessive attachment to *taqlíd,* and has absolutely nothing to do with Islam, whose teachings constantly encourage legal research and adaptation to the geographic and temporal context.

To stem the tide of *taqlíd,* Muslims, jurists, *'ulama'* and religious leaders should be united their efforts to re-study the Muslim heritage and seek points of synergy between Islamic law and contemporary international law. Likewise, the West should seek to engage with dynamic Islamic legal scholastic traditions. There are many fields in which Islamic law can easily be read in harmony with national and international rules. David A. Schwartz has argued: "The *Sharí'ah* provides a genuine, workable framework for countering international terrorism [...] the *Sharí'ah* is a resource the West must no longer overlook".[89] Western academe should welcome interventions from Islamic legal scholars, which can enable intellectual engagement between modern international humanitarian law and international criminal law within the spirit of the Muslim religion and vice-versa. Creative understanding of Islamic law in the modern world is vital.

Rather than simply teaching matters which occurred centuries ago, Muslims need to engage in a combined intellectual effort to rebuild the way they think. How to move forward is a priority for Islam. There should be a clear vision of what is absolute and immutable and what, on the contrary, is subject to change and adaptation, drawing on the traditions that this chapter has presented.[90]

---

[89] David A. Schwartz, "International Terrorism and Islamic law", in *Columbia Journal of Transnational Law*, 1990, vol. 29, no. 3, p. 652.

[90] Tariq Ramadan, 1999, p. 177, see *supra* note 3.

6

Non-International Armed Conflicts under Islamic Law: The Case of ISIS

Ahmed Al-Dawoody*

6.1. Introduction

At the time of writing, 13 of the 16 United Nations ('UN') Peacekeeping Operations and two thirds of the International Committee of the Red Cross's operations take place in the Muslim world.[1] Most of the current conflicts taking place in the Muslim world are non-international armed conflicts, which are largely caused by the post-colonial state structure, dictatorship, and poor distribution of wealth and power. According to Common Article 3 of the Geneva Conventions of 1949 and Article 1 of Additional Protocol II,[2] a conflict is classified as a non-international armed conflict if it satisfies the following four requirements:

1. The conflict takes place "in the territory of one the High Contracting Parties";
2. The conflict is between the governmental armed forces and armed groups, or between non-governmental armed groups;
3. The conflict reaches a level of intensity such that military forces are used and not merely the police; and

* **Ahmed Al-Dawoody** is an Assistant Professor in Islamic studies and Islamic law at Al-Azhar University in Cairo, Egypt, and teaches at the Geneva Academy of International Humanitarian Law and Human Rights in Geneva, Switzerland. He was the Assistant Director of Graduate Studies for the Institute for Islamic World Studies and the co-ordinator of the M.A. programme in Contemporary Islamic Studies at Zayed University in Dubai, United Arab Emirates. He has published many articles, including several on the relationship between Islamic law and international humanitarian law, and is the author of the publication *The Islamic Law of War: Justifications and Regulations* (Palgrave Macmillan, 2011).

1 See United Nations Peacekeeping, "Peacekeeping Operations", available on the web site of the United Nations.

2 See, for example, Geneva Convention (I) for the Amelioration of the Condition of the Wounded and Sick in Armed Forces in the Field, 12 August 1949, in force 21 October 1950, Article 3 (http://www.legal-tools.org/doc/baf8e7/).

4. The armed groups possess organised force under a leader and exercise control over a certain territory.

Although classical Islamic law books did not use the categorisation international versus non-international armed conflicts, they treated their international armed conflicts under the chapters of *al-jihád* or *al-siyar* and, due mainly to certain historical precedents during the first four decades of the Islamic era, they treated four specific forms of non-international armed conflicts, namely: (1) fighting against *al-murtaddún* (apostates); (2) fighting against *al-bughāh* (armed rebels, separatists); (3) fighting against *al-Khawárij* (roughly, violent religious fanatics); and (4) fighting against *al-muḥáribún* (highway robbers, bandits, pirates, terrorists). The first three forms of conflicts fall under the definition of non-international armed conflicts under international humanitarian law, while the fourth could be also treated likewise if it includes the above requirements.

Fighting against *al-murtaddún* is used exclusively in Islamic law and history to refer to the incidents of groups apostatising from Islam or rejection of the payment of *zakáh* (poor due) by the tribes in Arabia following the death of Prophet Muḥammad in 632[3] and, therefore, Muslim scholars relate any form of organised use of force among Muslims to any of the remaining three forms of non-international armed conflicts. Therefore, this chapter studies briefly the characteristics or conditions of rules of engagement with, and the punishment if any for, those who take part in these remaining three forms of non-international armed conflicts in order to find out, first, if the case of the militants of the Islamic State of Iraq and Syria ('ISIS') can be categorised in any of these three forms of conflicts. Second, if the answer is positive, then will there be any grounds for prosecuting the ISIS militants in a fictitious *Sharí'ah* court that applies exclusively classical Islamic law and what would be the punishment, if any? The Islamic rules regulating these three forms of non-international armed conflicts will be studied here in order to find out, on the one hand, how far the conflicting Muslim parties abide by the Islamic restraints on the use of force and, on the other hand, how far these classical Islamic rules on the use of force correspond with the modern international humanitarian law. This chapter argues that the confusion between the laws of fighting

[3] See, for example, Michael Lecker, "Al-Ridda", in Peri Bearman *et al.* (eds.), *Encyclopaedia of Islam*, rev. ed., Brill, Leiden, 2004, vol. XII, pp. 692–94; Muḥammad Ibn Idrís Al-Sháfi'í, *Al-Umm*, 2nd ed., Dár Al-Ma'rifah, Beirut, 1973, vol. 4, p. 222.

against *al-bughāh* and *al-Khawārij* has been used and abused to criminalise opponents of the state.

6.2. Fighting Against *Al-Bughāh*

Examining the scriptural basis or historical background of the emergence and development of these four forms of non-international armed conflicts can largely help in avoiding the confusion and misuse of categorising any of these conflicts. Fortunately, the law of armed rebellion is based on the Qur'ánic text 49:9 and developed by the classical Muslim jurists following the precedents set by the Fourth *Caliph* 'Alí Ibn Abí Ṭálib in his treatment with those who rebelled against him in the battles of Al-Jamal (in 656) and Ṣiffín (in 657).[4] But the main reasons for confusing the law of fighting against *al-bugháh* with the law of fighting against *al-Khawárij* are that both cases of armed conflicts contain *khurúj* (using armed force) against the state authorities and the details regulating both cases emanated from the fighting that took place between the Fourth *Caliph* and those who took up arms against him. Moreover, the naming of this armed conflict as a war against *bugháh* (transgressors), which is usually inaccurately understood to refer to armed rebels/secessionists and not to state authorities, gives the wrong indication that armed rebellion is altogether prohibited in Islam. Although Ibn Taymiyyah, other *Ḥanbalí* jurists, and *Sháfi'í* jurists state that *baghí* (armed rebellion) is not a sin, strangely enough, the *Máliki* and *Ḥanbalí* schools of law mistakenly listed and treated armed rebellion among the *ḥudúd* crimes[5] (crimes for which punishments are prescribed in the *Qur'án* or *ḥadíth*), albeit that, because of the very nature

4 See Muḥyí Al-Dín Ibn Sharaf Al-Nawawí, *Al-Majmú': Sharḥ Al-Muhadhdhab*, Beirut, 2000, vol. 20, p. 337; 'Alí Ibn Muḥammad Ibn Ḥabíb Al-Máwardí, *Al-Ḥáwí Al-Kabír: Fí Fiqh Madhhab Al-Imám Ash-Sháfi'í Raḍí Allah 'anh wa huwa Sharḥ Mukhtaṣar Al-Muzní*, Dár Al-Kutub Al-'Ilmiyyah, Beirut, 1999, vol. 13, p. 104.

5 See, for example, from the *Máliki* school, Aḥmad Ibn Idrís Al-Qaráfí, *Adh-Dhakhírah*, Dár Al-Gharb Al-Islamí, Beirut, 1994, vol. 12, pp. 5–206; Muḥammad Ibn Yúsuf Ibn Abí Al-Qásim Al-'Abdarí, *At-Táj wa Al-Iklíl: Sharḥ Mukhtaṣar Khalíl*, 2nd ed., Dár Al-Fikr, Beirut, 1977, vol. 6, pp. 229–319; Muḥammad 'Arafah Al-Disúqí, *Ḥáshiyah ad-Disúqí 'alá Ash-Sharḥ al-Kabír*, Dár Al-Fikr, Beirut, 2013, vol. 4, pp. 237–358. See, for example, from the *Ḥanbalí* school, 'Alí Ibn Sulaymán Al-Mirdáwí, *Al-Inṣáf fí Ma'rifah ar-Rájiḥ min al-Khiláf 'alá Madhhab al-Imám Aḥmad Ibn Ḥanbal*, Dár Iḥyá' Al-Turáth Al-'Arabí, Beirut, 1986, vol. 10, pp. 150–353; Manṣúr Ibn Yúnus Ibn Idrís Al-Buhútí, *Ar-Rawḍ al-Murbi': Sharḥ Zád al-Mustaqni'*, Maktabah Al-Riyadh Al-Ḥadíthah, Riyadh, 1970, vol. 3, pp. 304–45; Al-Muṣṭafá Al-Suyúṭí Al-Raḥaybání, *Maṭálib Ulí an-Nuhá fí Sharḥ Gháyah al-Muntahá*, Al-Maktab Al-Islamí, Damascus, 1961, vol. 6, pp. 158–308.

of *ḥudúd* crimes, they did not and could not give a specific scriptural punishment for armed rebels since there is no such punishment prescribed in these two scriptural sources. This confusion is recurrent even more among many contemporary Muslim scholars, in particular the *Wahhábi* school, who prohibit not only armed rebellion, but also peaceful demonstrations and even criticism of the rulers arguing that this is a form of *khurúj* against the state authorities, although *khurúj* as used by classical Muslim jurists generally refers to actual use of armed force, as explained below.

The scriptural basis of regulating the law of fighting against *al-bugháh* refers generally to fighting between two Muslim groups and requests the rest of the Muslims to bring about reconciliation between the fighting groups and if one of these groups transgresses against the other, then Muslims are required to fight against the transgressor, but it does not mention any punishment for the transgressor. The Qur'ánic text 49:9 reads:[6]

> And if two parties of the believers fight each other, then bring reconciliation between them. And if one of them transgresses against the other, then fight against the one who transgresses until it returns to the ordinance of God. But if it returns, then bring reconciliation between them according to the dictates of justice and be fair. Indeed God loves those who are fair.

Although this text does not specify the nature of the conflict or the warring parties, classical Muslim jurists used it to regulate armed conflicts between rebels and secessionists and the state as can be deduced from their identification of the *bugháh* below. In their deliberations for the identifications of the *bugháh*, classical Muslim jurists of the four schools of Islamic law, stipulated three conditions for a group of Muslims to be treated as *bugháh*.

First, the armed group must possess military power and organisation, *shawkah, man'ah, fay'ah*. It is quite remarkable to find striking similarities between classical Islamic law and modern international humanitarian law in defining the limits of force that should be possessed or used for acts of hostility to be treated as respectively under the Islamic law of rebellion or as non-international armed conflict under international humani-

6 All translations of the Qur'ánic texts in this chapter are mine.

tarian law. While classical Muslim jurists used many parameters to measure the force of an armed group in deciding whether to treat them as rebels, such as different minimum numbers, or whether the armed rebels control a town or a stronghold, only some classical Muslim jurists stipulated that the armed group must have a leader. Even for those who do not refer to the existence of leadership, it is apparent in their writing that the use of force does not mean sporadic incidents by armed individuals but force by an armed group which constitutes an entity unified by a shared cause, as shown below. These parameters resemble the definition of non-international armed conflicts in Additional Protocol II, Article 1(1), describing as conflicts those conflicts, "which take place in the territory of a High Contracting Party between its armed forces and dissident armed forces or other organised armed groups which, under responsible command, exercise such control over a part of its territory as to enable them to carry out sustained and concerted military operations".[7] But the most practical determining factor according to both legal systems is that the government is obliged to call on the military forces against the armed groups and not the police forces only.[8] For modern international humanitarian law, these definitions aim at distinguishing non-international armed conflicts from less violent acts, such as riots or acts of banditry, while for classical Islamic law, these deliberations regarding the size or power of the armed group also distinguish between armed rebels and terrorists or other criminals on the one hand, and on the other indicate that the rebels may have a just cause because their power may be the result of popular support for their cause. Therefore, if an unidentified small number of armed individuals who have no popular support, and thus do not constitute a military challenge to the government, use force against state authorities, then they cannot enjoy the status of rebels and they will be punished under the Islamic law of *ḥirábah*, according to the *Ḥanafí* and *Ḥanbalí* schools,[9] or punished for the specific crimes they commit during the

[7] Protocol (II) Additional to the Geneva Conventions of 12 August 1949, and Relating to the Protection of Victims of Non-International Armed Conflicts ('Additional Protocol II'), 8 June 1977, in force 7 December 1978, Article 1(1) (http://www.legal-tools.org/doc/fd14c4/).

[8] See Al-Qaráfí, 1994, p. 6, see *supra* note 5; Al-Raḥaybání, 1964, p. 161, see *supra* note 5.

[9] 'Abd Allah Ibn Maḥmúd Ibn Mawdúd, *Al-Ikhtiyár li-Ta'líl al-Mukhtár*, Dár Al-Kutub Al-'Ilmiyyah, Beirut, 2005, vol. 4, p. 160; 'Abd Al-Qádir 'Awdah, *At-Tashrí' al-Jiná'í al-Islamí: Muqáraná bi-al-Qánún al-Waḍ'í*, Dár Al-Kitáb Al-'Arabí, Beirut, vol. 2, p. 681.

course of hostilities, according to Sháfi'í.[10] This distinction between rebels and armed criminals is of paramount importance, because both armed rebels and governmental armed forces are immune from punishment for acts of hostility, provided that both follow the Islamic restraints on the use of force stipulated for this specific form of armed conflict and the purposes of their use of force, as discussed below.

Second, the armed group must have a *ta'wíl*, a complaint about injustice inflicted upon them by the government, or a belief that the government violated the *Sharí'ah*, or a disagreement with the government policies. In a word, this condition resembles to a certain extent the just cause criterion in the Christian just war theory, although classical Muslim jurists were generous and neutral and did not stipulate that the armed group's cause should necessarily be justified or legitimate. Interestingly, for the classical Muslim jurists, it is sufficient that the armed group believe in the justness of their cause. Although classical Muslim jurists indicate that the armed groups may likely be unjustified in their use of force, if such a group manages to collect and organise such a sizable military power, then they deserve to be treated under the law of rebellion. These two conditions indicate that such armed groups are not bandits and potentially, though not necessarily, may have a just cause, and therefore the state must treat them under the specific regulations of the Islamic law of rebellion.[11]

Third, they must use armed force, *khurúj*. This means that in modern terms any peaceful opposition to the state authorities, such as peaceful demonstrations or sit-ins, do not fall under the law of rebellion and hence cannot be classified as conflicts. Moreover, if armed rebellion is not criminalised under Islamic law, provided the above conditions are fulfilled, then *a fortiori* such peaceful opposition to the state cannot be criminalised either.

If these three instructions and precedents set by the Fourth *Caliph* are met, a process of resolving such a potential armed conflict peacefully

---

10 Al-Sháfi'í, 1973, p. 218, see *supra* note 3; 'Awdah, p. 681, see *supra* note 9.

11 See, for example, Muḥammad Al-Khaṭíb Al-Shirbíní, *Al-Iqná' fí Ḥall al-Fáẓ Abí Shujá'*, Dár Al-Fikr, Beirut, 1994, vol. 2, p. 548; Khaled Abou El Fadl, *Rebellion and Violence in Islamic Law*, Cambridge University Press, Cambridge, 2006, p. 243; Ahmed Al-Dawoody, *The Islamic Law of War: Justifications and Regulations, Palgrave Series in Islamic Theology, Law, and History*, Palgrave Macmillan, New York, 2011, vol. 2, pp. 159 ff.

must be followed, and if the process fails, then the special regulations on the use of force in this form of armed conflict must be strictly followed by the conflicting parties. The jurists agree that the state must contact the armed rebels and engage in discussions and negotiations with them regarding their justifications for the use of force, and if it finds that they are indeed legitimate, then it has to make the necessary decisions to correct the wrong done by the state. If the state has done nothing wrong, it should clarify and explain its position to the rebels and correct any misunderstanding the rebels may have. This approach is stipulated in the Qur'ánic text 49:9 and was followed by the Fourth *Caliph* in the battles of Al-Jamal (in 656) and Ṣiffín (in 657).[12] Some classical Muslim jurists add that if the discussion and negotiations fail between the state and the rebels who remain persistent in their plans to use force, then they should be called for a public *munáẓarah* (debate) so that the public can judge on the justness of their cause.[13]

If this process of reconciliation and attempts to prevent the conflict all fail, then, according to the majority of Muslim jurists, governmental forces are not allowed to initiate acts of hostilities against the armed rebels; while according to Abú Ḥanífah, the governmental forces are allowed to start to use force only after the armed group assemble to use force, because if the governmental forces waited until the armed group had already used force against them, they might be unable to mount a defence.[14] If fighting becomes inevitable, then the objective of fighting on

---

12 See, for example, Muwaffaq Al-Dín 'Abd Allah Ibn Aḥmad Ibn Qudámah, *Al-Mughní: fí Fiqh al-Imám Aḥmad Ibn Ḥanbal ash-Shaybání*, Dár Al-Fikr, Beirut, 1984, vol. 9, p. 5; 'Awdah, p. 689, see *supra* note 9.

13 On this process of resolving the conflict peacefully, see, for example, 'Alá Al-Dín Al-Kásání, *Badá'i' al-Ṣaná'i' fí Tartíb ash-Shará'i'*, 2nd ed., Dár Al-Kitáb Al-'Arabí, Beirut, 1982, vol. 7, p. 140; Yúsuf Al-Qaraḍáwí, *Fiqh al-Jihád: Ḍirásah Muqáranah li-Aḥkámih wa Falsafatih fí Ḍaw' al-Qur'án wa as-Sunnah*, Maktabah Wahbah, Cairo, 2009, vol. 2, pp. 1002 ff.; 'Alí Ibn Muḥammad Ibn Ḥabíb Al-Máwardí, *Naṣíḥah al-Mulúk*, Maktabah Al-Faláḥ, Al-Safah, Kuwait, 1983, p. 255; Aḥmad Ibn 'Abd Al-Ḥalím Ibn Taymiyyah, *Al-Khiláfah wa al-Mulk, Min Rasá'il Shaykh al-Islam Ibn Taymiyyah*, 2nd ed., Maktabah Al-Manár, Az-Zarqá', Jordan, 1994, p. 65; Al-Sháfi'í, 1973, p. 218, see *supra* note 3; Al-Nawawí, 2000, p. 349, see *supra* note 4; Al-Qaráfí, 1994, p. 7, see *supra* note 5; Al-Mirdáwí, 1986, p. 312, see *supra* note 5; 'Awdah, p. 689, see *supra* note 9; Abou El Fadl, 2006, pp. 152–59, see *supra* note 11; Ibn Qudámah, 1984, p. 5, see *supra* note 12.

14 See Khaled Abou El Fadl, "Political Crime in Islamic Jurisprudence and Western Legal History", in *U.C. Davis Journal of International Law & Policy*, 1998, vol. 4, no. 1, p. 20.

the part of the governmental forces should be that of merely putting down the rebellion by bringing them under the obedience of the ruler, that is, not to terminate the rebels. On the part of the rebels, their fighting should be restricted to achieving its objectives. For these reasons, in addition to restrictions on the use of force in international armed conflicts, the classical Muslim jurists stipulated the following strict rules of engagement, which distinguish this specific form of non-international armed conflict from any other form of conflicts:[15]

1. The governmental forces cannot target the armed rebels to kill during the fighting. Put in modern terms, both parties should not aim to shoot at the head or chest, let alone use any weapons of mass destruction;
2. The rebels can be fought only while they are *muqbilún* (attackers), which means that the governmental force's use of force must be restricted to self-defence; and, therefore
3. *Lá yutba' mudbiruhum*, that is, the rebels cannot be followed if they are escaping the battlefield;
4. *Lá yujhaz 'alá jaríḥihum*, the injured rebels cannot be killed. Although all the jurists address the governmental forces here, the same rules should be followed by the rebels;
5. Rebels' women and children cannot be enslaved and their property cannot be taken as the spoils of war. Moreover, as an indication of the sanctity of the rebels' property, even weapons confiscated from the rebels during the combat cannot be used by the governmental forces except in case of military necessity and must be returned to the rebels after the cessation of violence;
6. The State cannot seek the military assistance of non-Muslim forces in fighting against the rebels; and
7. With the exception of Abú Ḥanífah, the jurists agree that captured armed rebels must be set free.

It is regrettable that when these humane rules of engagement with the armed rebels are compared with the brutal repression of the peaceful

[15] See, for example, Al-Sháfi'í, 1973, p. 218, see *supra* note 3; Al-Nawawí, 2000, pp. 250–52, see *supra* note 4; Muwaffaq Al-Dín 'Abd Allah Ibn Aḥmad Ibn Qudámah, *'Umdah al-Fiqh*, Maktabah Aṭ-Ṭarafayn, Taif, p. 149; Abou El Fadl, 2006, pp. 152–60, see *supra* note 11; Al-Dawoody, 2011, pp. 163–67, see *supra* note 11.

demonstrators during the Arab Spring revolutions of 2011, one reaches the conclusion that Islamic law here is either unheard of or is being deliberately ignored, not only by state authorities but even by Islamic scholars. It seems that even peaceful demonstrators and peaceful political opponents of the state cannot enjoy such privileged status in many Muslim countries at present. The Amnesty International fact-finding team in Egypt indicated that, on 4 April 2011, the number of those killed in the Egyptian 25 January 2011 revolution was estimated at 856 by the Egyptian Ministry of Health. It also "found extensive evidence of excessive use of force by security forces across the country, including lethal force against protestors and others posing no threat to their or others' lives".[16] Moreover, some of the peaceful protestors were shot dead in the head and chest by snipers who, according to Amnesty International, were part of the police force,[17] in flagrant violation of the rules above, which affirm that even armed rebels cannot be fought unless they are *muqbilún* (attackers) and even then they cannot be a target for killing – the purpose of using force against them should be to quell their violence.

Therefore, if both the governmental forces and the rebels abide by these strict regulations, none of them will be liable for punishment for any destruction caused to the lives and property during the course of hostilities[18]. It should be reaffirmed here that any use of force by either party – the rebels or state authorities – before or after the initiation of hostilities or even during the hostilities if not linked to the objectives indicated above, will be liable to punishment. However, classical Islamic jurists did not mention what punishment the rebels or state authorities should receive in this case.[19] No less important, the fact that the rebels must be set free, at

16 Amnesty International, "Egypt Rises: Killings, Detentions and Torture in the '25 January Revolution'", 19 May 2011 (http://www.legal-tools.org/doc/7edd2c/).

17 *Ibid.*, pp. 18, 33, 35.

18 Al-Kásání, 1982, p. 141, see *supra* note 13; Al-Qaráfí, 1994, p. 10, see *supra* note 5; Ibn Qudámah, 1984, pp. 8 ff., see *supra* note 12; Abou El Fadl, 2006, p. 238, see *supra* note 11; Al-Dawoody, 2011, pp. 166 ff., see *supra* note 11.

19 See, for example, Muḥammad Al-Khaṭíb Al-Shirbíní, *Mughní al-Muḥtáj ilá Ma'rifah Ma'ání Alfáẓ al-Minháj*, Dár Al-Fikr, Beirut, vol. 4, p. 125; Muḥammad Ibn Abí Al-'Abbás Aḥmad Ibn Ḥamzah Al-Ramlí, *Niháyah al-Muḥtáj ilá Sharḥ al-Minháj*, Dár Al-Fikr, Beirut, 1998, vol. 7, p. 405; Muḥammad Al-Ghazálí, *Al-Wajíz fí Fiqh al-Imám ash-Sháfi'í*, Dár Al-Arqam Ibn Abí Al-Arqam, Beirut, 1997, vol. 2, p. 164; Al-Shirbíní, 1994, p. 549, see *supra* note 11; Abou El Fadl, 1998, pp. 17 ff., see *supra* note 14; 'Abd Allah Al-Ba'lí,

least after the cessation of hostilities, and that they are not liable for punishment for any destruction caused to the lives and property, proves that armed rebellion is not criminalised under classical Islamic law, provided that the armed rebels meets the three conditions above, on the one hand, and abide by these strict regulations on the use of force, on the other.

Interestingly, these classical Islamic rules regulating the Islamic law of rebellion are in agreement with the modern definition of non-international armed conflicts under international humanitarian law. The concerns of humanising non-international armed conflicts are quite clear in both legal systems. For example, the Islamic law of armed rebellion and Common Article 3 of the Geneva Conventions of 1949 and Article 1 of Additional Protocol II ensure non-combatant immunity, humane treatment of captured adversaries, and prohibit torture and the taking of hostages. However, while captured rebels cannot be prosecuted for the mere fact of resorting to armed rebellion, as shown above, under international humanitarian law, adversaries captured in non-international armed conflicts do not enjoy the status of prisoners of war ('POWs') granted in international armed conflicts, and therefore can be prosecuted under national legislation for the mere fact of taking up arms. But, in an attempt to avoid the victimisation of the state's adversaries, Article 6(2) of Additional Protocol II stipulates that a fair trial is a must for the passing of sentences and execution of punishments.[20]

6.3. Fighting Against *Al-Khawárij*

The greatest challenge in examining the case of the *Khawárij* in the literature of the four *Sunní* schools of Islamic law is the lack of a systematic treatment that clearly sets the definition of the *Khawárij* and the conditions for identifying a group as such, as well as the punishment, if any, for such group. Unlike the cases of the other two forms of non-international armed conflicts studied here, the Islamic legal treatment of the *Khawárij* is not based on scriptural sources – the *Qur'án* and the *Sunnah* – since the *Khawárij* emerged after the death of the Prophet. Hence, the jurists refer to the *Khawárij* mainly during their discussion of the *bugháh* and, to a

Kashf al-Mukhaddarát wa ar-Riyáḍ al-Muzhirát li-Sharḥ Akhṣar al-Mukhtaṣarát, Dár Al-Bashá'ir Al-Islamiyyah, Beirut, 2002, vol. 2, p. 775.

20 Additional Protocol II, Article 6(2), see *supra* note 7 (http://www.legal-tools.org/doc/fd14c4/).

great extent, their treatment reflects a historical description rather than a legal one. In other words, the legal sources mainly relate the origin and characteristics of this group in the absence of elaborate rules that regulate how they should be treated under Islamic law. In fact, they even disagree over the origin of the emergence of the *Khawárij*: some relate the origin of their emergence to a situation in which a certain 'Abd Allah Ibn Dhí Al-Khuwaiṣirí Al-Tamímí objected against the Prophet's distribution of some property. Strangely enough, this is considered by some scholars as the first case of *khurúj* (literally: exit, going out), although this situation does not include any use of violence by this single individual. Others opine that their origin is with the groups who resorted to violence against the Third *Caliph* 'Uthmán Ibn 'Affán, while the majority of the jurists relate their origin to the group of the supporters of the Fourth *Caliph* who rejected his acceptance of the offer of resorting to arbitration in order to end the conflict suggested by Mu'áwiyah Ibn Abí Sufyán after the battle of Ṣiffín (in 657).[21]

The sources describe the *Khawárij* as pious and devout worshippers;[22] however, they had a very limited or narrow understanding, or were ignorant, of Islam and the *Qur'án*. Apart from the historical narration of the emergence of the *Khawárij* and for the purpose of this chapter, the main characteristics of the *Khawárij* which distinguish them from other groups are that, first, they target innocent civilian Muslims including women and children, while the *bugháh*'s use of force is directed at the state authorities and limited to achieving its objectives. Two, unlike the *bugháh* and similar to the *muḥáribún*, the *Khawárij* indiscriminately kill and commit terrorist acts against their Muslim victims. Third, they seize the property of their Muslim victims, which is also prohibited under the Islamic law of rebellion. Fourth, they believe that any Muslim who committed a major sin, including the Companions of the Prophet, is a *káfir* (unbeliever). Hence, *takfír* (excommunication) of Muslims who commit any sin has since then become one of their main characteristics and a rationale for dividing the Muslims into believers versus *kuffár*. In other

21 See Sulaymán Ibn Ṣáliḥ Ibn 'Abd Al-'Azíz Al-Ghuṣn, "Al-Khawárij: Nah'atuhum, Musammáhum, Al-Qábuhum, Firaquhum", in *Majallah Jámi'ah al-Imám*, 2010, vol. 48, pp. 85–145; Usama Sulaymán, "Al-Khawárij bayn Al-Máḍí wa Al-Ḥaḍir", in *At-Tawḥíd*, vol. 404, p. 57.

22 Al-Ghuṣn, 2010, pp. 94, 99–102, see *supra* note 20.

words, as pointed out by Ibn Taymiyyah, the *Khawárij* see themselves as representing the *dár al-Islam* while the rest of the Muslims represent the *dár al-ḥarb*. Their reading of the Qur'ánic text 64:2, "It is He Who created you, then some of you are unbelievers and some of you are believers", leads them mistakenly to this two-fold division, which results in excommunicating those who do not share their beliefs.[23]

If these four characteristics are met within a certain group, then what are the Islamic rules of engagement that must be followed in fighting against the *khawárij*? Classical Muslim jurists disagree on this question, giving three possible answers: the majority argue that they should be treated as rebels, while some jurists of the *Ḥanbalí* school argue that they are to be treated as apostates. Nonetheless, a group of jurists maintain that they are to be treated as *muḥáribún*.[24] These answers reflect the lack of developed rules regulating specifically the treatment of the *khawárij,* which again explains the confusion between them and other forms of non-international armed conflicts in early Islamic history. In fact, the majority opinion here is untenable, because giving the privileged status granted to rebels under Islamic law to the *khawárij*, who among their main characteristics include the indiscriminate slaughter of women and children and using "terror-oriented methods",[25] practically means, for example, that government forces are not allowed to initiate hostilities against them, aim to kill them during the combat, or follow them while they are escaping from the fighting. If this were the case, then governmental forces would not be allowed to stop the *khawárij*'s slaughter of

[23] On the *Khawárij* see, for example, Zayd Al-Dín Ibn Najím, *Al-Baḥr ar-Rá'iq Sharḥ Kanz ad-Daqá'iq*, 2nd ed., Dár Al-Ma'rifah, Beirut, 1983, vol. 5, p. 151; Ibn Qudámah, 1984, pp. 3 ff., see *supra* note 12; Muḥammad Amín Ibn 'Umar Ibn 'Ābidín, *Ḥáshiyah Radd al-Muḥtár 'alá ad-Durr al-Mukhtár: Sharḥ Tanwír al-Abṣár Fiqh Abú Ḥanífah*, Dár Al-Fikr, Beirut, 2000, vol. 4, p. 262.

[24] See Zakariyyá Ibn Muḥammad Ibn Aḥmad Ibn Zakariyyá Al-Anṣárí, *Manhaj al-Ṭulláb*, Dár Al-Kutub Al-'Ilmiyyah, Beirut, 1997, p. 123; Al-Mirdáwí, 1986, p. 310, see *supra* note 5; Ibn Qudámah, 1984, pp. 3 ff., see *supra* note 12; 'Alí Ibn Aḥmad Ibn Sa'íd Ibn Ḥazm, *Al-Muḥallá*, Dár Al-Āfáq Al-Jadídah, Beirut, 1964, vol. 11, p. 97; Tamara Sonn, "Irregular Warfare and Terrorism in Islam: Asking the Right Questions", in James Turner Johnson and John Kelsay (eds.), *Cross, Crescent, and Sword: The Justification and Limitation of War in Western and Islamic Tradition*, Greenwood, New York 1990, pp. 135 ff.; Abou El Fadl, 2006, p. 56, see *supra* note 11.

[25] Abou El Fadl, 2006, p. 56, see *supra* note 11.

innocent victims, a consequence the majority of the jurists certainly could not justify.

No less important, since the *Khawárij* were even, in the words of Abou El Fadl, "declared to be rebels, entitled to the treatment given to the *bugháh*, and not bandits",[26] does this also mean that the *Khawárij* are to be set free after the cessation of hostilities and thus receive no punishment just like the rebels? Again, certainly, if the answer is yes, then this is another untenable position from the classical Muslim jurists, because letting the *Khawárij* who perpetrate such terrorist acts and who are likened in some legal sources to the *muḥáribún* because both of them cause *fasád fí al-'arḍ* (corruption in the land) go unpunished is in stark violation of the Qur'ánic text 5:33–34, examined below. Although there is no specific *ḥadd* punishment prescribed for the *khawárij*, particularly if they are to be prosecuted according to a law of their own, simply because they emerged after the death of the Prophet, it is still unwarranted that, in the literature studied, classical Muslim jurists did not develop a set of punishments for the *khawárij*. Therefore, it is ironic that the *Máliki* and *Ḥanbalí* schools of law mistakenly listed and treated armed rebellion among the *ḥudúd* crimes, though they did not provide such a punishment, and they as well as the rest of the *Sunní* jurists fail to develop the punishment of the *khawárij*. That is because, as shown above, in light of the comparison between the *bugháh* and the *khawárij*, the former's use of force potentially has a just cause, unlike the latter's who even if they had a just cause, cannot go unpunished because of their indiscriminate killings and acts of terrorism.

6.4. Fighting Against *Al-Muḥáribún*

The law of fighting against the *al-muḥáribún*, known as the law of *ḥirábah* or *quṭṭá 'uṭ-ṭaríq* (highway robbery, brigandry, banditry), is the most developed and the least controversial among the four forms of the use of organised force treated under classical Islamic law, because of its basis in scripture, which includes specific punishments. Here, there is no disagreement among all Muslim jurists, classical and contemporary alike, that *ḥirábah* is a *ḥadd* crime. Although *ḥirábah* does not usually reach the level of an armed conflict in the modern sense of the word, classical Muslim jurists' discussions reflect a situation in which organised force is used

[26] *Ibid.*

and which endangers the security of society. The law of *ḥirábah* is based on the following Qur'ánic text:

> Indeed, the retribution for those who *yuḥáribún* [make war upon] God and His Messenger and strive to make *fasád* [corruption] in the land is that they be killed or gibbeted or have their hands and feet amputated from opposite sides or they be banished from the land; this is a degradation for them in this world and in the Hereafter they will receive a grave chastisement. Excluded [from this retribution] are those who repent before you capture them; and be sure that God is All-Forgiving All-Merciful.

At the outset, it has to be affirmed here that, unlike the *bugháh* and the *khawárij*, the *muḥáribún* have no *ta'wíl*, justification, for their use of force because, as described in the classical sources, they do not provide justifications: their motives are usually the taking of money by force or spreading terror and intimidation among their victims. As for the elements of this crime: first, the use or threat of use of force, since the culprits of *ḥirábah* are described as an armed group who possess *shawkah* and *man'ah* (force, might, strength, power) – the terms which describe the *bugháh* above – and this is used *mughálabah* (overtly, forcefully), that is, in a manner that shows a challenge to state authorities. Although force can be used by a small group or even an individual in the context of *ḥirábah*, usually the context involves an organised and overt use of force. Second, victims are innocent victims who do not expect an armed confrontation and thus are unable to defend themselves. In the words of the classical Muslim jurists, the victims *lá yalḥaquhum al-ghawth* (are helpless and cannot be rescued). Therefore, unlike the *bugháh* and similar to the *khawárij*, the *muḥáribún* use "terror-oriented methods" against their victims who are mainly innocent civilians.[27]

So the situation here describes an armed confrontation between the *muḥáribún* and governmental forces (the police or military, depending on

[27] On the definition, elements, and forms of the crime of *ḥirábah* see, for example, Al-Kásání, 1982, p. 90, see *supra* note 12; Al-Sháfi'í, 1973, vol. 6, p. 152, see *supra* note 3; Ibn Qudámah, p. 149, see *supra* note 15; Muḥammad Ibn Aḥmad Ibn Muḥammad Ibn Rushd, *Bidáyah al-Mujtahid wa Niháyah al-Muqtaṣid*, Dár Al-Fikr, Beirut, vol. 2, p. 340; Al-Qaráfí, 1994, p. 125, see *supra* note 5; Al-Dawoody, 2011, pp. 170–77, see *supra* note 11; Nik Rahim Nik Wajis, "The Crime of Ḥirába in Islamic Law", Ph.D. thesis, Glasgow Caledonian University, 1996.

the power of the former) and Islamic rules of engagement apply only to the governmental forces. In sharp contrast to the *bugháh*, the governmental forces can target to kill the *muḥáribún* during the fighting and if they escape the fighting, they are to be followed until they are captured or killed. If the *muḥáribún* collected taxes from a territory they controlled, these taxes have to be re-collected by the state, unlike the case of the *bugháh*. Furthermore, unlike the rules of engagement in international armed conflicts under Islamic law, the *muḥáribún* cannot be given *amán* (quarter).[28] Although this might appear in contradiction to the established framework of international law, since Article 8(2)(e)(x) of the Statute of the International Criminal Court includes among the list of war crimes "Declaring that no quarter will be given",[29] the meaning of *amán* (quarter) as regulated in classical Islamic law, would in the case of *muḥáribún* indicate amnesty. In the conduct of hostilities, *amán* is a sort of contract whereby an enemy is granted protection for his life and property until he returns to his territory. It describes a situation in which an enemy indicates, either by a gesture or verbally, that he will no longer continue the fighting.[30] This proves that these are the harshest rules of engagement in Islam.

Although the punishments for the culprits convicted of *ḥirábah* are prescribed in the above Qur'ánic text, jurists mainly disagree over the intended meaning of the Arabic proposition *aw* (or) separating each of the above punishments. In short, the majority of jurists maintain that this proposition indicates listing a specific order for each crime committed,[31]

[28] See, for example, 'Alí Ibn Muḥammad Ibn Ḥabíb Al-Máwardí, *Kitáb al-Aḥkám as-Sulṭániyyah wa al-Wiláyát ad-Díniyyah*, Maktabah Dár Ibn Qutaybah, Kuwait, 1989, p. 86.

[29] Statute of the International Criminal Court, 17 July 1998, in force 1 July 2001 ('ICC Statute'), Article 8(2)(e)(x) (http://www.legal-tools.org/doc/7b9af9/).

[30] For more information on the *amán* system see, Al-Dawoody, 2011, pp. 129–36, see *supra* note 11.

[31] See Muḥammad Ibn Aḥmad Ibn Abí Sahl Al-Sarakhsí, *Kitáb al-Mabṣúṭ*, Dár Al-Ma'rifah, Beirut, vol. 9, p. 195; Ibn Mawdúd, 2005, p. 121, see *supra* note 9; Ibn Najím, 1983, p. 73, see *supra* note 23; Al-Sháfi'í, 1973, vol. 6, p. 151, see *supra* note 3; Al-Ghazálí, 1997, p. 177, see *supra* note 19; Al-Shirbíní, pp. 181–83, see *supra* note 19; Ibn Qudámah, 1984, pp. 125, see *supra* note 12; Ibn Qudámah, p. 149, see *supra* note 15; Al-Mirdáwí, 1986, pp. 296–98, see *supra* note 5; Al-Buhútí, 1970, pp. 330 ff., see *supra* note 5; Al-Rahaybání, 1961, p. 254, see *supra* note 5; Ibn Rushd, p. 341, see *supra* note 27; Abou El Fadl, 2006, pp. 56 ff., see *supra* note 11; Frank E. Vogel, "The Trial of Terrorists under Classical Islamic Law", in *Harvard International Law Journal*, 2002, vol. 43, no. 1, pp. 58–61.

while *Máliki* jurists advocate that this proposition indicates that the judge has the freedom to choose the punishment commensurate with each convicted criminal.[32] But, in any case, there is no disagreement over the criminalisation of *ḥirábah* and the fact that its culprits receive the severest punishments prescribed in Islamic law.[33]

6.5. The Case of ISIS

The emergence of most terrorist and radical Muslim groups throughout Islamic history is mainly linked with armed conflicts (mostly among Muslims), dictatorships, or the decline of the Muslims' power in the twentieth century. The emergence of ISIS is a case in point. In fact, ISIS is the result of two armed conflicts in Iraq and Syria that were caused by two dictatorships: the Saddam regime in Iraq and the Assad regime in Syria. The US-led invasion of Iraq led to the formation of Al-Qaeda in Iraq in 2003 at the hands of the Jordanian Abú Muṣ'ab Al-Zarqáwí.[34] Some of the ISIS militants, particularly those from outside these two countries, joined this group in order to recover the glory and power of the Muslims by establishing the *Caliphate*. ISIS was formed by Abú Bakr Al-Baghdádí in April 2013 as a result of a merger between a number of militant forces in Iraq formed following the US-led invasion of Iraq with the militant groups in Syria following the outbreak of the civil war in Syria in 2011. The governmental armed forces of Iraq and Syria, in addition to the international community, had not yet managed to destroy ISIS at the time of writing, despite controlling most of the territories in both Iraq and Syria,[35] and

---

32 See Al-Qaráfí, 1994, p. 126, see *supra* note 5; Ibn Rushd, p. 341, see *supra* note 27; Muḥammad Ibn Muḥammad Ibn 'Abd Al-Raḥmán Al-Ḥaṭṭáb, *Mawáhib al-Jalíl li-Sharḥ Mukhtaṣar Khalíl*, 2nd ed., Dár Al-Fikr, Beirut, 1977, vol. 6, p. 315; Aḥmad Al-Dardír, *Ash-Sharḥ al-Kabír*, Dár Al-Fikr, Beirut, vol. 4, pp. 349 ff.; Al-Disúqí, 2013, pp. 349 ff., see *supra* note 5; Al-Máwardí, 1999, p. 353, see *supra* note 4; Al-Máwardí, 1989, p. 84, see *supra* note 28; 'Awdah, p. 647, see *supra* note 9; Sherman A. Jackson, "Domestic Terrorism in the Islamic Legal Tradition", in *The Muslim World*, September 2001, vol. 91, no. 3–4, p. 300; Vogel, 2002, p. 59, see *supra* note 31.

33 On the punishment of *ḥirábah* see also, Aḥmad Ibn 'Abd Al-Ḥalím Ibn Taymiyyah, *As-Siyásah ash-Shar'iyyah fí Iṣláḥ ar-Rá'í wa ar-Ra'iyyah*, Dár Al-'Āfáq Al-Jadídah, Beirut, 1983, pp. 68–74; Al-Dawoody, 2011, pp. 177–83, see *supra* note 11.

34 Ahmed Al-Dawoody, "ISIS and its Brutality Under Islamic Law", in *Kansai University Review of Law and Politics*, 2015, vol. 36, p. 102.

35 Dale Sprusansky, "Understanding ISIS: Frequently Asked Questions", in *The Washington Report on Middle East Affairs*, October 2014, pp. 19–20.

ISIS' claimed responsibility for terrorist attacks committed in the Muslim world and in Europe. Although ISIS proclaimed itself a state, according to former US President Barack Obama, in his speech of 11 September 2014 on combating ISIS and terrorism, it "is certainly not a state [...] It is recognized by no government, nor the people it subjugates. ISI[S] is a terrorist organization, pure and simple".[36]

However, in light of the above discussion of the three forms of non-international armed conflicts treated by classical Muslim jurists, I will attempt to classify the use of armed force by ISIS into one of these categories, and identify the rules of engagement in fighting against it, as well as the punishment if any for its captured militants.

	Military power and organisation	*Ta'wíl*	Use of force	Rules of engagement	*Takfír*
Bugh// áh	√	√	√	√	×
Khawárij	√	√	√	×	√
Muḥáribún	√	×	√	×	×
ISIS	√	√	√	×	√

ISIS undoubtedly possesses *shawkah*, *man'aḥ*, *fay'ah*, military power and organisation, which is a common condition set by the classical Muslim jurists for all the above three forms of conflict. According to the parameters set by classical Muslim jurists, they already constitute a large number,[37] they managed to control more than a city or a stronghold, and the armed forces of more than one country are called on to fight against it. Also, ISIS has a command and a structure that has already allowed it to conduct hostilities and run its ahistorical, barbaric version of a so-called state. Furthermore, under the command of its leader Abú Bakr Al-

36 *Ibid.*

37 See Al-Sháfi'í, 1973, p. 218, *supra* note 3; Al-Shirbíní, p. 123, *supra* note 19; Abou El Fadl, 2006, p. 151, *supra* note 11.

Baghdádí, ISIS has managed to receive allegiance from groups in Egypt, Libya, Yemen, Saudi Arabia, Nigeria,[38] Algeria, the Arabian Peninsula,[39] Afghanistan, Pakistan, Dagestan, and Chechnya,[40] in addition to the tribal leaders of the areas under control in Iraq and Syria.[41] Although recent reports indicate that ISIS's force is declining, in the face of international society's failure to destroy ISIS, it has gained recruits both from the Muslim world and the West, including born Muslims and converts, as announced in its magazine *Dabiq*, the mouthpiece of ISIS. According to some recent studies, the estimated number of foreign fighters who have joined ISIS is up to 15,000 from 80 countries; a maximum of 25 percent of these fighters have come from the West.[42]

ISIS also has a *ta'wíl*, which is a common characteristic of the *bug͟háh* and the *k͟hawárij*, but not of the *muḥáribún*. Its ultimate objective, or at least one of its justifications for the use of force, is the establishment of the Islamic *Caliphate*. Its leader, Al-Baghdádí, affirmed that the re-establishment of the *Caliphate* will put an end to the weakness and humiliation of the Muslims and bring about its lost glory. Therefore, in June 2014, he proclaimed himself as the *Caliph* of all the Muslims and asked them to give allegiance to him.[43] Hence, ISIS shares the above characteristics with the *bug͟háh* and the *k͟hawárij*.

Regarding Islamic rules of engagement, ISIS has violated them: it has committed horrible atrocities against its victims, including women; children; and religious, ethnic, or sectarian minorities. ISIS militants have committed war crimes. They committed ethnic cleansing against the "non-Arab and non-*Sunní* Muslim communities, killing or abducting hundreds, possibly thousands, and forcing more than 830,000 others to flee the areas

38 See Clarion Project, "Special Report on the Islamic State", 23 August 2016, p. 23.

39 The Islamic State, "Remaining and Expanding", in *Dabiq*, 2015, vol. 5, pp. 12, 22.

40 The Islamic State, "From Hypocracy to Apostasy", in *Dabiq*, 2015, vol. 7, pp. 34 ff.

41 The Islamic State, "The Return of Khilafa", in *Dabiq*, 2014, vol. 1, pp. 12–15.

42 See Daniel Byman and Jeremy Shapiro, "Be Afraid. Be A Little Afraid: The Threat of Terrorism from Western Foreign Fighters in Syria and Iraq", 2014, Foreign Policy at Brookings, Policy Paper No. 34, p. 9. See also International Centre for the Study of Radicalisation Insight, "Up to 11,000 foreign fighters in Syria; steep rise among Western Europeans", 17 December 2013.

43 See BBC News, "ISIS rebels declare 'Islamic State' in Iraq and Syria", 30 June 2014.

it […] captured since 10 June 2014".[44] In addition to the slaughter of innocent civilians, torture and mutilation of victims, they also committed massacres of hundreds of captured Iraqi soldiers and forced Yazidi and Christian persons into sexual slavery.[45]

Takfír has become a major justification for terrorist attacks and assassinations, particularly of government official or public figures, for the past half a century. But leaving aside *takfír*, because it will not have a legal effect in determining the rules of engagement and the punishment of ISIS captives, the fact that ISIS violates the rules of engagement and uses terrorist attacks against civilians among other crimes disqualifies its members from being treated under the privileged status of the *bugháh* and, as a consequence, they are to be treated either under the vague law of the *Khawárij* or the law of *ḥirábah,* which comprise the harshest rules of engagement and the severest punishments. Therefore, recalling that jurists disagreed over the treatment of the *Khawárij* as apostates, rebels, or *muḥáribún*, the more rational position here is that ISIS should be treated as *muḥáribún* as far as the rules of engagement and punishment are concerned, simply because the law of the *Khawárij* is not developed particularly regarding the punishment of war crimes and violations of the rules of engagement. In response to a question about the Islamic ruling regarding ISIS members, the Jordanian Dár Al-Iftá' (*Fatwá* Council) issued *fatwá* number 3065 on April 13, 2015, stating that ISIS is a terrorist organisation because of its shedding of blood, *takfír* of the Muslims, causing *fasád fí al-'arḍ*, and violating the Islamic rules of engagement.[46] The *fatwá* does not refer to ISIS as either *Khawárij* or *muḥáribún*, although it uses the terminology employed by the classical Muslim jurists in the description of both; and does not refer to the punishment for ISIS militants either.

Therefore, since the rules of fighting against the *muḥáribún* should apply against ISIS, governmental forces can target ISIS militants to kill during fighting, and they are to be captured or killed. Following the classical Muslim jurists' rulings, the taxes collected by ISIS from the territo-

44 Amnesty International, "Ethnic Cleansing on a Historic Scale: The Islamic State's Systematic Targeting of Minorities in Northern Iraq", MDE 14/011/2014, 2014, p. 4.

45 United Nations News, "'Barbaric' sexual violence perpetrated by Islamic State militants in Iraq – UN", 13 August 2014.

46 Jordanian Dár Al-Iftá' (*Fatwá Council*), "Fatwá number 3065" available on the web site of the Jordanian government.

ries under their control are to be re-collected by the Iraqi and Syrian governments after re-taking control of the territories controlled by ISIS. But this ruling of the classical Muslim jurists is unwarranted, because the same justifications for prohibiting re-collecting the taxes in the case of the *bugháh* exist here in the case of ISIS. This is because re-collecting taxes will result in undue financial hardships for the taxpayers, as the *Sháfi'í* jurists, Al-Shirbíní and Al-Ramlí argued;[47] but also, as the *Ḥanafí* jurist 'Alá Al-Dín Al-Kásání pointed out, because the government did not provide the protection in return for which it collects the taxes.[48]

Regarding the punishment for captured ISIS militants, bearing in mind that ISIS members are not entitled to combatant status because only the *bugháh* are entitled to combatant status according to the Islamic law of non-international armed conflicts, convicted ISIS militants will receive the prescribed *ḥirábah* punishment.[49] Therefore, whether in battlefield or non-battlefield crimes, ISIS members convicted of killing are to be sentenced to execution and gibbetting, although *Málikí* jurists maintain that gibbeting is optional to the judge.[50] It is worth adding here that in *ḥirábah* crimes, which do not include killing, the *Málikí* jurists give the judge the authority to choose any of the four prescribed punishments in the *Qur'án*, provided that it serves the interests of society. So, if ISIS members are prosecuted and convicted for only terrorising and intimidating their victims without being convicted of killing or causing bodily injury or any other crimes, they are to be exiled or imprisoned.[51] Rape, torture, mutilation, forced expulsion, and other crimes committed in the context of the crime of *ḥirábah* receive the same punishment, even though not listed by name in classical Islamic criminal law books, because they fall within the

47 Al-Shirbíní, pp. 125, see *supra* note 19; Al-Ramlí, 1998, p. 405, see *supra* note 19.

48 Al-Kásání, 1982, p. 142, see *supra* note 13.

49 See, for example, Al-Dawoody, 2011, pp. 170–93, see *supra* note 9; Ahmed Al-Dawoody, "International Terrorism and the Jurisdiction of Islamic Law", in *International Criminal Law Review*, 2015, vol. 15, no. 3, pp. 565–86.

50 See Al-Qaráfí, 1994, p. 126, see *supra* note 27; Ibn Rushd, p. 341, see *supra* note 27; Al-Ḥaṭṭáb, 1977, p. 315, see *supra* note 32; Al-Dardír, pp. 349 ff., see *supra* note 32; Al-Disúqí, pp. 349 ff., see *supra* note 5; Al-Máwardí, 1999, p. 353, see *supra* note 4; Al-Máwardí, 1989, p. 84, see *supra* note 4; 'Awdah, p. 647, see *supra* note 9; Jackson, 2001, p. 300, see *supra* note 32; Vogel, 2002, p. 59, see *supra* note 31.

51 See Al-Sarakhsí, p. 195, see *supra* note 31; Al-Sháfi'í, 1973, vol. 6, pp. 151 ff., see *supra* note 3; Ibn Qudámah, 1984, p. 125, see *supra* note 12.

description of committing *fasád* in the land. Bearing in mind that *Máliki* jurists give the judge the authority to choose any of the four punishments prescribed in the *ḥirábah* Qur'ánic text, the judge can sentence ISIS members to execution if they have the intellectual ability to plan the attacks, while if they have only the physical ability to carry out the attacks, then the judge can sentence them to amputation of the right hand and left foot. But if ISIS members lack both intellectual and physical abilities, the judge can give them a discretionary punishment or send them to exile.[52]

As for accomplices, while the majority of jurists maintain that they should receive the same punishment as the actual perpetrators, Al-Sháfi'í argues that they should only receive a discretionary punishment left to the authority of the judge and imprisonment.[53] It should be pointed out here that it is only in the case of *ḥirábah* crimes that accomplices receive the same punishment as the actual perpetrators, because these crimes are considered as an aggression against the whole of society and not against the victims and their families only. For this reason, it is also only in *ḥirábah* crimes that the families of the murdered victims have no right to pardon the killers and waive their executions. But it should be added here that, concerning the question of the jurisdiction of Islamic courts, if such terrorist crimes are committed by ISIS members outside the Muslim world, then only a judge in an Islamic court that applies the *Ḥanafí* school of law will refuse to adjudicate such cases because, according to the *Ḥanafí* school of law, Islamic courts have no jurisdiction over crimes committed outside the Islamic world.[54]

6.6. Conclusion

The above discussion shows that the classical Muslim jurists developed detailed rules regulating the use of force in the cases of both armed rebellion and terrorism. Within the context of their primitive conflict situations, the classical Muslim jurists succeeded in terms of defining these two forms of conflict, setting the rules of engagement, and tackling the question of punishment. However, they failed to address the question of pun-

[52] See Al-Qaráfí, 1994, p. 126, see *supra* note 5; Ibn Rushd, p. 341, see *supra* note 27; 'Awdah, p. 647, see *supra* note 9.

[53] Al-Sarakhsí, p. 198, see *supra* note 31; Al-Sháfi'í, 1973, vol. 2, pp. 641 ff., 666–68, see *supra* note 3.

[54] See Al-Dawoody, 2015, pp. 565–86, see *supra* note 47.

ishments for the violations of the rules of engagement and developing punishments for the *khawárij*. Hence, the main challenge here for a classical Muslim judge who would attempt to enforce the Islamic rules in this area is the contradictory rulings developed by jurists of different, and even the same, schools of law. Additionally, the confusion between the laws of fighting against *al-bugháh* and *al-Khawárij* in Islamic legal and non-legal literature has led the *Máliki* and *Ḥanbalí* schools to mistakenly list armed rebellion among the *ḥudúd* crimes and, disappointingly, in the present time, this confusion and the fact that the *Khawárij* used acts of terrorism in early Islamic history have been capitalised on by many contemporary scholars who generally denounce and criminalise opposition to the state, whether in the form of expression of opinion or peaceful demonstrations, let alone armed rebellion.

It goes without saying that the forms and nature of conflict do change and hence modern forms of non-international armed conflict cannot be identical to the four forms regulated by the classical Muslim jurists. The case of ISIS shows some similarities with the forms of conflict discussed above, but its violation of the rules of engagement and use of acts of terrorism subject its members to the Islamic law of terrorism, particularly in light of the undeveloped law of the *khawárij*. Without a doubt, ISIS has committed numerous war crimes and human rights abuses including ethnic cleansing, massive murder, torture, forced marriages, sexual abuses and sexual slavery, use of child soldiers, and executions without due process. Although all these crimes are outrageous violations of Islamic law, ISIS still finds its way to the classical texts and claims that its acts represent true interpretations of Islamic sources. Less than a decade ago, I called for a codification by Muslim scholars and jurists of an Islamic law of war that is applicable in our present warfare contexts, in order to curb such violations "when the warriors or perpetrators of acts of warfare or terrorism are not in regular state armies".[55] This is intended to be no more than an authentic scholarly representation of the Islamic rules on the use of force in modern warfare situations, which can counteract the misunderstanding and misrepresentation of classical Islamic sources.

In fact, both classical Muslim jurists and modern international humanitarian law share the same concerns of humanising armed conflicts,

[55] Al-Dawoody, 2011, p. 105, see *supra* note 11.

with striking similarities; yet the classical sources can be misused on the one hand by radical groups and terrorists to justify indiscriminate use of force and terrorist attacks, and on the other hand, the confusion between the laws of fighting against *al-bughâh* and *al-Khawârij* has been used and abused by state authorities to criminalise opponents of the state and even sentence them to death. The current situation of lip-service adherence to Islamic law by some countries and of its being considered merely archaic and too scholarly by some, as well as the literalist interpretations and applications of it by radical groups, leads to the conclusion that the renewal and codification of Islamic law in its surrounding contexts is a must. Otherwise, since it seems that many Muslim societies will continue to struggle between the Islamisation versus the de-Islamisation of their societies, at least for the foreseeable future, the Muslim world and the West will continue to bear the consequences.

7

Arab and Islamic States' Practice: The *Sharí'ah* Clause and its Effects on the Implementation of the Rome Statute of the International Criminal Court

Siraj Khan*

7.1. Introduction

International law has changed drastically over the last century. Islamic law, in contrast, is at times conceived of as a monolithic bloc of laws derived from pre-modern revelations, with little or no relevance to modern societies, poorly suited, as it were, to the modern international legal framework.[1] This dichotomy begs a simple question: can a state whose legal system requires adherence to and compliance with Islamic laws adequately discharge its obligations under international law, particularly international criminal law? This chapter looks at the ways in which Islamic law complicates the adaptation of international law, specifically international criminal law, and adherence to it and to the International Criminal Court ('ICC').

7.2. The Convergence of the Islamic Legal Horizon with International Law

In the second part of the twentieth century, international law has emerged as a substantial force that demands the compliance of national laws. The

---

* **Siraj Khan** is an expert on the laws and legal traditions of various states in the Middle East and North Africa, focusing particularly on comparative constitutional law. He has extensive experience working on constitutional processes, the rule of law and judicial development in Yemen, Sudan, Libya and Jordan. He holds degrees in Law, International Law and Islamic & Middle Eastern Studies, and is reading for his Ph.D. focusing on the convergence of international law, constitutional law and Islámic Law. He was called to the Bar of England & Wales in 2010 (Lincoln's Inn) and received training in classical Islámic law and legal methodology (*úṣúl al-fiqh*) with scholars in Egypt and Jordan.

1 Meghan E. Tepas, "A Look at Traditional Islam's General Discord with a Permanent System of Global Cooperation", in *Indiana Journal of Global Legal Studies*, 2009, vol. 16, no. 2, p. 695.

question of international law's compatibility with national laws, which, for the purposes of this contribution focuses exclusively on national laws derived from the *Sharī'ah*, relies on three independent tiers. The dilemma itself is not limited to international law and the *Sharī'ah* in particular,[2] but rather, this balancing act between state sovereignty on the one hand, and international law's dominance over domestic law on the other, is perhaps one of the consequences of the accelerated globalisation of constitutional law in the twentieth century.

The first tier requires an assessment as to whether a general international legal obligation exists for states. This obligation could take the form of a unilateral, bilateral or multilateral treaty; or be derived from other sources of international law, such as customary law.[3] In order to understand the dynamic between Islamic law and the international obligations of a state, one needs to first determine what obligations exist for the state. If there is no international legal obligation then the question of its compatibility with Islamic law remains a merely theoretical question. In this case, the issue is whether Islamic law provides principles and norms for the protection of human rights at the domestic level alternative to those provided by international law.

The second tier requires an assessment of whether Islamic/Muslim-majority states have accepted these obligations. This can happen through constitutionally recognising the validity and superiority of international law over domestic laws. It can also occur by enacting secondary implementing legislation, thereby incorporating the international legal rules into national legal systems. If the latter option is chosen, the constitution or relevant domestic laws must be amended and brought into conformity with the relevant international laws, ideally prior to ratification. The state can enter reservations or declarations to limit the application of its international legal obligations, but the validity of these limitations will be determined by the extent of the derogation. A number of international legal obligations, particularly those concerning the protection of fundamental rights and freedoms, have now been regarded – in scholarly opinion as

---

2 For instance, see Helen Duffy, "National Constitutional Compatibility and the International Criminal Court", in *Duke Journal of Comparative & International Law*, 2011, vol. 11, pp. 5–38.

3 Statute of the International Court of Justice, 26 June 1945 (http://www.legal-tools.org/doc/fdd2d2/), Article 38(1).

well as in the jurisprudence of many national supreme and constitutional courts – as non-derogable. Limitation of and derogation from these can be considered to inherently obfuscate the purpose and intention of the ratification of the treaty and would, thereby, constitute invalid derogations and limitations.

The third tier assesses the level of congruity between international legal obligations and the *Sharīʿah*. This third step may also incorporate part of the second step, for instance, in states whose national legal systems require international laws and treaties to be approved by parliament. This ratification usually takes place through the enactment of a law giving legal effect to the international treaty obligations at the domestic level. This is particularly relevant in states that are 'dualist' as regards the process of ratifying international treaties.

States that require no further enactment by parliament for the enforcement and applicability of treaty obligations, so-called 'monists', have found alternative ways of accommodating international law. Some have installed bureaus for 'legislative opinion/interpretation'. These bureaus check the legitimacy and constitutionality of laws and provide interpretative guidance, usually while the law is still in draft or bill stage. In the absence of a supreme or constitutional court, the bureau can also review the legitimacy and constitutionality of laws post-enactment. In most states, the only way to assess the compatibility of international law with Islamic law – where both international and Islamic law are legally or constitutionally mandated – would be to challenge the law for unconstitutionality. At this third step, courts will likely be involved in checking the compatibility of the legal obligations under international law with the Constitution, national laws and Islamic law, particularly where national laws give effect to, or are derived directly from, Islamic legal principles and provisions.

In relation to both international law and Islamic law, particularly in the context of Muslim-majority states and those that apply Islamic law to some extent, one may ask which international law and which Islamic law is being referred to? The first question can be answered using the jurisprudence of domestic supreme courts, especially their decisions related to the status and interpretation of international law. These decisions often refer to the jurisprudence of international and regional courts (such as the European Court of Human Rights, the African Court of Human and Peoples' Rights and the Inter-American Court of Human Rights) or the jurisprudence of the International Court of Justice. The second question as to which Islamic law is more complex because Islamic law and jurisprudence are not wholly, nor uniformly, codified into domestic laws and codes in all states.[4] Indeed, the jurisprudence in a specific state as to what constitutes Islamic law may be inconsistent.

Building upon other scholarly contributions,[5] it is my contention here that a more measured and methodological approach to Islamic law and its application would be beneficial and would have the potential to indigenise international law to the Islamic legal context. Such culturally-sensitive approaches have the potential to achieve greater buy-in from Muslim-majority states in which the *Sharí'ah* features strongly in the legal system.

International law and the *Sharí'ah* may not be reconcilable with a purely textual and black-letter law approach, or at all in some limited cases. Such incongruence may occur purely as a result of a difference in conceptions of the origins of law from an Islamic worldview as compared with the origins of law elsewhere. This does not necessitate re-visiting anachronistic readings of the 'abode of war' and 'abode of peace' paradigms as dictated in classical Islamic literature, but we must understand that Islamic law accentuates an inherent consideration of normative values, which are derived from religious beliefs and sacred scriptures, around which the legal system functions. These normative values are inseparable from the law, particularlyparticularly in the Islamic legal tradition, whereas in non-Islamic and Western legal traditions, it is no longer the case that the normative value of a law should derive from scriptural or religious values. They may be derived merely from current social norms and political theologies without a normative moral value rooted in a religious, moral or ethical tradition.

---

[4] For example, one of the few instances where Islamic Law has been systematically introduced into codified law is the codification of Islamic family law in the 1958 'Code of Personal Status' (the 'Mudawwanat Al-Aḥwál Al-Shakhṣiyyah') in Morocco. See Léon Buskens, "Shariah and National Law in Morocco", Jan Michiel Otto (ed.), *Shariah Incorporated*, Leiden University Press, Leiden, 2010, p. 100.

[5] Ahmad E. Nassar, "The International Criminal Court and the Applicability of International Jurisdiction under Islamic Law", in *Chicago Journal of International Law*, 2003, vol. 4, no. 2, pp. 591–92.

The normative values in Islamic legal traditions are derived from religious beliefs and sacred scriptures and structure the legal system. At times, Islamic legal traditions are inseparable from the law. In non-Islamic and Western legal traditions, at least with the rise of liberal legal orders beginning from the nineteenth century, the law no longer looks to religion as a source for its legitimacy. Laws are believed to be outcomes of current social norms and political theologies without deep roots to a religious tradition. Hence, certain scriptural proscriptions in the *Sharíʿah* on various issues – some of which are subject to change, while others remain strict outliers to amendment – may not meet modern sensibilities amongst secular, liberal audiences, but nevertheless will be dominant in dictating what the law will be on a particular issue.

The Islamic legal tradition is hospitable to accommodating international law and allows for interpreting the *Sharíʿah* through a qualitative and objective-driven interpretative licence, as in the *maqáṣid* approach. This is one of the many approaches that can be used to encourage harmonisation, as well as to justify an informed and valid incongruence stemming from substantive reasoning for derogating from international law. So far, most international treaties and conventions that are drafted do not take adequate cognisance of Islamic legal proscriptions. A rare exception to this is the United Nations ('UN') Convention on the Rights of the Child. In Article 20 of the Convention we find references to Islamic law in the context of adoption. In doing so, the Convention specifies the varieties and equivalents of *kafálah* – akin to foster-care – as valid forms of adoption.[6] Even with this pluralistic accommodation, some Muslim-majority member-states still entered reservations to the provision, whereas others removed their reservations overnight without any substantive changes to

---

[6] Convention on the Rights of the Child, 2 September 1990, Article 20 (http://www.legal-tools.org/doc/f48f9e/), reads:

1. A child temporarily or permanently deprived of his or her family environment, or in whose own best interests cannot be allowed to remain in that environment, shall be entitled to special protection and assistance provided by the State.
2. States Parties shall in accordance with their national laws ensure alternative care for such a child.
3. Such care could include, *inter alia*, foster placement, *kafálah* of Islamic law, adoption or if necessary placement in suitable institutions for the care of children. When considering solutions, due regard shall be paid to the desirability of continuity in a child's upbringing and to the child's ethnic, religious, cultural and linguistic background.

their domestic laws or highlighting any revolutionary development in their understanding of Islamic law. This example illustrates well that in fact there was nothing in the provision that was contrary to the *Sharīʿah* after all.[7]

In the background of analysing the effect of the *Sharīʿah* on the applicability of the Statute of the ICC ('Rome Statute') in Muslim-majority states where the *Sharīʿah* is applied, attention must also be directed to the intention of some states in becoming signatories to the Rome Statute, especially where states have not fully ratified and likely will not in the near future. To understand why such states may have signed the Rome Statute but not applied or effected its principles at the domestic level towards full ratification, we have to re-assess the timing of the signatures. According to the rules of the ICC, only signatory states can have a say in the development process of the ICC. At the time of its establishment, out of a total twelve Muslim-majority states that eventually signed the Rome Statute, five signed ten days before the deadline. It is therefore a simple assumption that many of the states that signed at a late stage did so to be able to influence the final text of the Statute.[8] Somalia, Mauritania, Pakistan, Iraq,

---

[7] Egypt had entered reservations against the provisions related to adoption in the Convention on the Rights of the Child 1989. The reservation read as follows: "Since The Islamic Shariah is one of the fundamental sources of legislation in Egyptian positive law and because the Shariah, in enjoining the provision of every means of protection and care for children by numerous ways and means, does not include among those ways and means the system of adoption existing in certain other bodies of positive law, The Government of the Arab Republic of Egypt expresses its reservation with respect to all the clauses and provisions relating to adoption in the said Convention, and in particular with respect to the provisions governing adoption in articles 20 and 21 of the Convention". On 31 July 2003, the Government of Egypt informed the Secretary-General that it had decided to withdraw its reservation made upon signature and confirmed upon ratification in respect of articles 20 and 21 of the Convention. See the United Nations Treaty Collection, available on the UN website.

[8] Algeria signed the Rome Statute on 28 December 2000; Bahrain signed on 11 December 2000; Egypt signed on 26 December 2000; Iran signed on 31 December 2000; Jordan signed on 7 October 1998 and ratified/acceded on 11 April 2002 (Jordan was a founding member and therefore preceded other Muslim-majority states); Nigeria signed on 1 June 2000 and acceded on 27 September 2001; Oman signed on 20 December 2000; the Philippines signed on 28 December 2000 and acceded on 30 August 2011; Sudan signed on 8 September 2000; Syria signed on 29 November 2000; the United Arab Emirates signed on 27 November 2000; the Kingdom of Morocco signed on 8 September 2000; Yemen signed on 28 December 2000; and Kuwait signed on 8 September 2000. Tunisia was the latest State to sign and ratify the Statute on 24 June 2011, but notably does not specify the *Sha-*

Libya, Lebanon, Qatar, and Saudi Arabia have not signed the Rome Statute.

At a very conceptual level, it is understood that the development of international criminal law stems from the laws of armed conflict, once referred to as the laws of war. This specific need for regulation of war and armed conflicts emerged rapidly following the world wars in the twentieth century, when the initial development of international criminal law occurred, pushed mainly by Western powers that had participated in the two world wars.[9] The initial development of the League of Nations occurred after the First World War and the ratification of numerous treaties regulating armed conflict and the unlawful use of force thereafter. Between the First and Second World Wars, the laws relating to protection of humans and non-combatants from unlawful and illegal use of force were developed to provide substantive protection to states and their citizens against the unlawful use of force.[10] They also criminalised certain acts, recognising them as international crimes, or crimes with an international character when perpetrated by the authorities of one state against another. Along with criminalising certain acts, the laws also provided guidance on when the use of force would be legitimate and exceptions to this effect. It is not surprising, therefore, that the crimes recognised by international criminal law during its early development until the present age have been distinctly defined in the context of the types of crimes committed in the two world wars, and therefore cover a very specific experience of the use of force.

An oft-cited concern of some Muslim-majority states regarding joining the ICC has been that to do so would usurp the *Sharī'ah*'s exclusive jurisdiction in those states, effectively deferring this area of law to the Rome Statute, thereby substituting the law of God for the law of man. Though it is accepted that joining the ICC would involve a degree of jurisdictional deference in favour of the ICC, it need not necessarily involve an absolute abdication of the power to prosecute criminals domestically.

rī'ah as a source of law in its Constitution. See Coalition for the International Criminal Court, "Status of Ratification of the Rome Statute", 10 November 2011 (http://www.legal-tools.org/doc/21cfec/); Nassar, 2003, p. 593–94, see *supra* note 5.

9 Farhad Malekian, *International Criminal Responsibility of States: A Study on the Evolution of State Responsibility with Particular Emphasis on the Concept of Crime and Criminal Responsibility*, University of Stockholm, Stockholm, 1985, pp. 55–67.

10 *Ibid.*, pp. 103–13.

Once notified of an impending prosecution, a state can, in good faith, itself prosecute the accused domestically. This ensures that countries fearful of incompatibility between the *Sharīʿah* and international criminal law have the possibility of avoiding ICC jurisdiction by domestically prosecuting those cases. This principle of 'complementarity', established under Article 17(1) of the Rome Statute,[11] provides that the ICC will only investigate and prosecute cases in which national courts are unwilling or genuinely unable to investigate or prosecute. This inadvertently limits the invocation of the ICC's jurisdiction and allows the state to apply the relevant domestic laws. However, this system has been criticised since the complementarity regime envisaged by the ICC was conceived from a Western conception of justice, not taking into account Islamic criminal law and its rules of evidence, procedure and the system of retribution and punishments. This means that states imposing a system of criminal evidence and procedure based on the *Sharīʿah*, or those with relatively less 'developed' systems of criminal justice, would almost always fall foul of the requisite standards of criminal justice as applied in Western legal jurisdictions, and of the principles that establish whether a state is or is not able to investigate and prosecute cases as required by the ICC. Such states would therefore be unable to find protection by the complementarity regime under the Rome Statute.[12]

Article 21(1)(c) of the Rome Statute expressly allows for the application of "general principles of law derived by the Court from national laws of legal systems of the world including, as appropriate, the national laws of States that would normally exercise jurisdiction over the crime" at such trials. Therefore, though the Rome Statute allows for trials to apply Islamic criminal laws and principles, it would only do so provided that "those principles are not inconsistent with this Statute and with international law and internationally recognized norms and standards". However, since most Islamic criminal laws and principles would likely be judged as falling below the necessary norms and standards referred to in Article 21(1)(c) above, and the qualifications stated in Article 21(3) to "be con-

11 Statute of the International Criminal Court ('Rome Statute'), 17 July 1998, in force 1 July 2001, Article 17(1) (http://www.legal-tools.org/doc/7b9af9/).

12 Adel Maged, "Arab and Islamic Shariah Perspectives on the Current System of International Criminal Justice", in *International Criminal Law Review*, 2008, vol. 8, no. 3, pp. 485–86, fn. 37, and corresponding text.

sistent with internationally recognized human rights", these provisions are unlikely to provide any rapid confluence between the legal traditions to allow for trials based on Islamic criminal laws and principles.

The triggering mechanisms for the ICC to invoke its jurisdiction are quite clear, but the application of these mechanisms has not occurred without concern. The three triggering mechanisms are:[13]

1. The State complaint, where every State Party can refer a situation to the prosecutor;[14]
2. The Prosecutor's *proprio motu* power to initiate an investigation on the basis of information received[15] and then a referral to the pre-trial chamber to request authorisation to proceed to full prosecution; and
3. The referral of a situation to the ICC by the UN Security Council by a resolution under Chapter VII of the UN Charter.[16]

This third option is known to have its flaws; particularly, awarding a political body the right to initiate criminal justice proceedings at the international level is susceptible to abuse through politicised prosecutions. Article 16 of the Rome Statute also gives the Security Council the power to halt investigations and prosecutions for a period of twelve months, in cases where the Council deems that in complex situations, an investigation or prosecution may hinder international peace and security whilst pursuing international criminal justice. This power was particularly criticised when the Security Council, at the behest of the United States of America (which famously has not ratified the Rome Statute), invoked Article 16 in two Resolutions which exempted UN peace-keepers who were not nationals of a State Party to the Rome Statute from the jurisdiction of the ICC for two consecutive periods of twelve months each.[17] This was seen by many States Parties to be inconsistent with the letter and spirit of the Rome Statute, particularly when, on the expiry of the second twelve-month peri-

---

13 Hans-Peter Kaul, "International Criminal Court (ICC)", in *Max Planck Encyclopedia of Public International Law*, Oxford University Press, December 2010.

14 See Rome Statute, Article 13(a) (http://www.legal-tools.org/doc/7b9af9/), *supra* note 11.

15 See Rome Statute, Articles 13(c) and 15 (http://www.legal-tools.org/doc/7b9af9/), *ibid.*

16 See Rome Statute, Article 13(b) (http://www.legal-tools.org/doc/7b9af9/), *ibid.*

17 United Nations Security Council Resolution 1422 (2002), UN Doc. S/RES/1422(2002), 12 July 2002 (http://www.legal-tools.org/doc/1701d5/); United Nations Security Council Resolution 1487 (2003), UN Doc. S/RES/1487(2003), 12 June 2002 (http://www.legal-tools.org/doc/20e269/).

od, efforts were made once again to extend it further – though these efforts ultimately failed due to lack of support from Security Council members.

Mention must also be made of the difference in theoretical conceptions and definitions of crimes in the Rome Statute and in Islamic criminal law. These have been covered in detail by others and would in any case be too extensive to detail here. It should suffice to say that under both international criminal law and the Islamic criminal legal system, various crimes of an international character are understood and regulated somewhat differently. The regulation of these crimes is largely dictated by the circumstances through which such crimes develop. The history of policing such crimes involves the attempt of state authorities to regulate and criminalise those offences against the specific backdrop of the regional political and historical environments from which they emerged.[18]

7.3. The *Sharīʿah* Law Clause

Many Muslim-majority states recognise the validity of both the *Sharīʿah* and Islamic law. This finds mention to varying degrees: in the Constitution's preamble, the provision on determination of a state religion, the principle of conformity of legislation to the principles and rulings of the religion, and the conditions to be satisfied by the Head of State. Most pertinent to this chapter is the conformity of legislation to the principles and rulings of the religion, which often finds expression in what is termed the 'source of law clause' or the '*Sharīʿah* law clause' in the Constitution. The 'source of law clause' refers to the normative legal value for the *Sharīʿah* or for the principles and rules that are derived from it.[19] It establishes the

[18] For a substantive treatment of the various crimes under both international criminal law and Islamic criminal law (including those recognised by one system and not the other under shared conceptual frameworks), see Farhad Malekian, *Principles of Islamic International Criminal Law: A Comparative Search*, Brill, Leiden, 2011, pp. 171–91 (aggression), 193–207 (war crimes), 210–12 (unlawful use of weapons), 213–23 (crimes against humanity), 225–36 (slavery), 237–41 (genocide), 243–50 (apartheid), 251–63 (torture), 265–70 (crimes against internationally protected persons), 271–74 (taking of hostages), 275–80 (drug offences), 280–88 (trafficking in persons and pornography), 295–97 (criminalisation of alcohol consumption), 299–302 (piracy), 331–37 (humanitarian protection of prisoners of war).

[19] Clark B. Lombardi, "Designing Islamic Constitutions: Past Trends and Options for a Democratic Future", in *International Journal of Constitutional Law*, 2013, vol. 11, no. 3, pp. 615–45; Dawood I. Ahmed and Moamen Gouda, "Measuring Constitutional Islamization:

principles and sources by which laws are drafted and written, and eventually applied by the executive and administrative authorities in the state as well as, importantly, by the judicial authorities.

The term 'Islamic law' is no longer adequate to designate both the religiously-inspired laws of a Muslim-majority country and 'the continuity of legal doctrine' (*fiqh*) as it once used to. In modern legislative and governance practice, 'Islamic law' has been downgraded to refer merely to laws enacted by parliaments composed of non-specialists in the *Sharí'ah* who make up the legislative organs. They are advised by boards of scholars as to which laws do or do not comply with the *Sharí'ah*. The lack of proper juristic method and consideration of juristic opinions (*fiqh*) in modern legislative processes is detrimental to the purpose and methodologies of deriving sound Islamic legal opinions on legislative and other matters. This dilution of Islamic law to a black-letter, overly textual and literal derivation of rulings from one main source (scripture) at the expense of a holistic methodology, has resulted in obscurantist formulations of Islamic legislation in the nation-state. The mere fact that the Constitution of the state has a *Sharí'ah*-law clause and a board of Islamic scholars advising Parliament, is considered sufficient by many to conclude that laws are therefore compliant with the *Sharí'ah*.[20]

Muslim-majority countries that have enacted criminal laws on the basis of the *Sharí'ah* law clause within their respective constitutions and have subsequently codified them within their domestic legal systems are fairly numerous: Libya first enacted Islamic criminal laws in 1972, the United Arab Emirates in 1978, Iran in 1982, Sudan in 1983 and the northern states of Nigeria in 2000–2002. In Somalia also, the rise of local Islamic courts, originally through the Islamic Courts Union, has resulted in the *de facto* imposition of Islamic criminal law, now largely controlled by non-state actors such as Al-Shabáb.[21] Islamic criminal laws have been

The Islamic Constitutions Index", in *Hastings International and Comparative Law Review*, 2015, vol. 38, pp. 1–74.

20 Baudouin Dupret, "The Relationship between Constitutions, Politics, and Islam: A Comparative Analysis of the North African Countries", in Rainer Grote and Tilmann Röder (eds.), *Constitutionalism, Human Rights, and Islam after the Arab Spring*, Oxford University Press, Oxford, 2016, pp. 234, 238.

21 Cedric Barnes and Harun Hassan, "The Rise and Fall of Mogadishu's Islamic Courts", in *Journal of Eastern African Studies*, 2007, vol. 1, no. 2, pp. 151–60; Global Security, "The

enacted in Saudi Arabia, Qatar and Yemen for much of their recent history, proceeding from the adoption and seemingly uninterrupted assimilation of tribal customs into a modern monarchic nation-state framework (with the exception of Yemen, which is still based on an intricate and large-scale system of tribal alliances). Another model exists in Afghanistan where the punishment for apostasy, though not specified as a *ḥadd* offence in the *Qur'án*, and therefore not listed in the penal code, can be applied by virtue of a constitutional provision, which permits courts to directly apply Islamic legal punishments as derived from the *Ḥanafī* school of jurisprudence in matters that are not specified by the constitution or other laws.[22] But there are aberrations and inconsistencies in the manner of application of Islamic criminal laws, from selective and arbitrary, religiously- or politically-motivated convictions, to criminalising actions that support ideological movements and trends. In Sudan, some positive trends have been witnessed over the past decade, which evidence 'undeclared moratoriums' through creative application of procedural rules on some *ḥudúd* punishments, largely through judicial activism.[23]

Islamic criminal laws have also been enacted through negative 'repugnancy clauses', such as in Article 227(1) of the Constitution of Pakistan 1973 (amended 2015) which requires that:[24]

> [a]ll existing laws shall be brought in conformity with the Injunctions of Islam as laid down in the Holy *Qur'án* and *Sunnah*, in this part referred to as the Injunctions of Islam, and

Supreme Islamic Courts Union (ICU)", 10 May 2013; Stanford University, Mapping Militant Organizations Project, "Islamic Courts Union", 30 March 2016.

22 Said Mahmoudi, "The Sharî'a in the New Afghan Constitution: Contradiction or Compliment?", in ZaöRV, Max Planck Insistut Für Auslandisches Öffentliches Recht Und Völkerrecht, 2004, vol. 64, pp. 871–72; Constitution of the Islamic Republic of Afghanistan, 3 January 2004, Article 130 (http://www.legal-tools.org/doc/9aa221/): "In cases under consideration, the courts shall apply provisions of this Constitution as well as other laws. If there is no provision in the Constitution or other laws about a case, the courts shall, in pursuance of *Ḥanafī* jurisprudence, and, within the limits set by this Constitution, rule in a way that attains justice in the best manner." See Adeel Hussain, "Afghanistan's Constitution between Shariah Law and International Human Rights", in *Verfassungsblog*, 22 May 2017.

23 Redress, "The Constitutional Protection of Human Rights in Sudan: Challenges and Future Perspectives", January 2014 (http://www.legal-tools.org/doc/4430b8/).

24 Constitution of the Islamic Republic of Pakistan, 12 April 1973 (as amended 7 January 2015), Article 227(1) (http://www.legal-tools.org/doc/dc9f9d/).

> no law shall be enacted which is repugnant to such Injunctions.

This model requires *ex-post-facto* determinations of whether actions done in compliance with existing laws go against Islamic legal principles and rulings and whether, therefore, the laws themselves contravene the *Sharīʿah*, in which case they are duly repealed. In Pakistan such determinations are delivered by the Federal *Sharīʿat* Court bench at the Supreme Court.

The '*Sharīʿah* law clauses' in most constitutions are vaguely formulated and offer little in the way of guidance to legislative bodies regarding the sources and principles of the *Sharīʿah*. After enactment of the legislation, the task of ensuring that laws comply with the Constitution and its provisions – such as with international law where this is obliged by the constitution – rests with the Constitutional Court or other apex court.

The following section provides a short excursus on the status of the *Sharīʿah* in the constitutions of some Muslim-majority states. This includes: (1) states that have not ratified the Rome Statute, but whose constitutional and legislative frameworks have been altered recently; (2) states that have recently entered into communications with the ICC regarding the status of their membership to the Rome Statute; and (3) states that have, by virtue of an application to the ICC, invited the ICC to exercise its jurisdiction to investigate acts committed on their territory. The case studies presented in this chapter suggest that the existence of the *Sharīʿah* clause does not substantively affect the decision of states on whether to ratify the Rome Statute, or the international legal obligations of states that have already ratified the Rome Statute. On this basis alone, it would suggest that there is no inherent incompatibility between the *Sharīʿah* and the Rome Statute when it comes to the fundamental principles of the *Sharīʿah*.

7.4. Case Studies and Recent Developments

The case studies below provide an overview of selected states whose constitutional and domestic legislative framework has expressly recognised the normative and legislative value of the *Sharīʿah*. It further elaborates on the potential of this recognition to allow for accession to, and full compliance with, the Rome Statute.[25] I have chosen to include only those states whose legislative and constitutional frameworks have undergone substantial changes, or have received little scholarly attention in this context.

7.4.1. Egypt

Egypt first introduced the *Sharí'ah* into the Constitution as a normative device for the institutional, governance and legislative framework in 1971, by enshrining in Article 2 of the Constitution that "the principles of the Islamic *Sharí'ah* are a main source of legislation". In 1980, Article 2 was amended to include the definite article, to read: "the principles of the Islamic *Sharí'ah* are *the* main source of legislation". Following the protests and turbulences that overthrew Mubarak in 2011, a new Constitution was passed, which adopted Article 2, but added a new Article 219, which added that "the principles of the Islamic *Sharí'ah* include its general evidence and its fundamental and doctrinal rules, as well as its sources considered by schools of the People of tradition and consensus (*ahl al-Sunnah wa'l-jamá'ah*)". This insertion serves two purposes. Firstly, it limits the role of the Constitutional Court in extrapolating the principles of the Islamic *Sharí'ah* to that accepted by the four *Sunní* schools of jurisprudence, by virtue of the sentence "considered by schools of the People of tradition and consensus". Secondly, it adds that the principles of the Islamic *Sharí'ah* include evidence, and fundamental and doctrinal rules. This clause implies a link to the comprehensive and explicit evidence in the revealed text (*al-adillah al-kulliyah*), fundamental rules in terms of legal methodology (*al-qawá'id al-uṣúlíyyah*), fundamental doctrines of law and rules of jurisprudence (*úṣúl al-fiqh* and *al-qawá'id al-fiqhíyyah*), as well as a subtle reference to juristic orthodoxy in relation to the "sources considered by schools of the People of tradition and consensus", which usually refers only to the *Sunní* schools of jurisprudence. Though this was a novel approach, it was not implemented, since the 2012 Constitution was suspended in July 2013 through a military coup, and the new Constitution approved by referendum in January 2014 repealed Article 219 and re-

[25] This could be on the basis of the State's constitutional recognition of Islam as either the official religion of the State or its people, or by virtue of expressly recognising the legislative value of the *Sharí'ah* as an official source of law in the State in its Constitution or domestic laws.

instated Article 2, as amended in 1980. The source of law clause (Article 2) now reads: "Islam is the religion of the state and Arabic is its official language. The principles of Islamic *Sharí'ah* are the principal source of legislation". Article 219 went some way in intimating what the phrase "the principles of Islámic *Sharí'ah*" could include. Its repeal takes us back to a vague formulation, which allows for the inclusion of an unlimited number of sources with which legislation could be justified as being compliant to the *Sharí'ah*.

The ICC does not have jurisdiction over Egypt, since it has only signed and not yet ratified the Rome Statute.[26] Egypt has been a longstanding proponent of the idea of a permanent international criminal court and occupied an influential role in the drafting of the Rome Statute, which established the ICC.[27] Despite this, and despite being a signatory, it has still not ratified the Statute, thereby ensuring that the Rome Statute cannot be enforced in Egypt's domestic legal framework. Many states claim that Egypt's failure to ratify the Statute in their domestic legal systems stems from a fear of politically-motivated prosecutions, particularly in countries that have a heightened level of civil unrest. Since the date of its signature in 2000, there was no official relationship or communication between Egypt and the ICC, until recently when, in 2013, an attempt was made at invoking the jurisdiction of the ICC in Egypt.

In December 2013, things took an interesting turn in Egypt. The Freedom and Justice Party ('FJP') – effectively the political wing of the Muslim Brotherhood in Egypt – petitioned the ICC to investigate alleged crimes against humanity in Egypt, based on the number of supporters of one-time President Mohammed Morsi, who were allegedly killed after the ousting of Morsi. Lawyers on behalf of the FJP called on the ICC to accept jurisdiction since Morsi, according to them, was still the legitimate President of the Republic of Egypt; hence they should accept jurisdiction under Article 12(3) of the Rome Statute with respect to alleged crimes committed since 1 June 2013, with allegations of murder, unlawful imprisonment, torture, persecution against an identifiable group and the enforced disappearance of persons. It is important to note that Article 12 of

26 Coalition for the International Criminal Court, 2011, see *supra* note 8 (http://www.legal-tools.org/doc/21cfec/).

27 Roy S.K. Lee, *The International Criminal Court: The Making of the Rome Statute – Issues, Negotiations, Results*, Kluwer Law International, The Hague, 1999, pp. 591–92.

the Rome Statute is also known as "[p]erhaps the most difficult compromise in the entire negotiations" for the Rome Statute.[28] This is due to the fact that subsections 2 and 3 of Article 12 allow states that are non-parties to the Statute to accept the exercise of jurisdiction by the Court, for instance if crimes are committed on the territory of, or by nationals of, a State Party.[29]

The FJP's application was dismissed as not having been submitted on behalf of the state concerned, based, *inter alia*, on the lack of 'effective control' exercised by the Morsi government. The ICC Prosecutor's Office ('OTP') refused to accept the request to investigate, stating that it had not been submitted by the ruling government.[30] This was the case even though, as argued by the lawyers appointed by the FJP, the African Union had decided to suspend Egypt from participating in its activities during that period and collectively refused to recognise the military government that took control on 3 July 2013. The OTP refused to accept that the African Union's suspension of Egypt amounted to effective recognition of the continuation and validity of Morsi's government at the time of the application. On 18 September 2014, lawyers on behalf of the FJP filed an application to request the Pre-Trial Chamber to review both the decision of the Prosecutor and of the Registrar not to open an investigation into the crimes alleged in Egypt. This was, perhaps, the first application of this type to ask for the appointment of a Chamber to review the decision of the Prosecutor not to conduct a preliminary examination. The Pre-Trial Chamber refused both arguments to review the original decision and to give leave to appeal the original decision on the grounds that the "Pre-Trial Chambers have constantly denied subsequent requests for reconsideration as having no statutory support".[31] They reasoned that the right to

---

28 Philippe Kirsch QC and Darryl Robinson, "Reaching Agreement at the Rome Conference", in Antonio Cassese, Paola Gaeta, and John R.W.D. Jones (eds.), *The Rome Statute of the International Criminal Court: A Commentary*, Oxford University Press, Oxford, 2002, p. 83.

29 William A. Schabas, *The International Criminal Court: A Commentary on the Rome Statute, Commentaries on International Law*, Oxford University Press, Oxford, 2010, pp. 277–91.

30 ICC, Office of the Prosecutor, Press Release, "The Determination of the Office of the Prosecutor on the Communication Received in Relation to Egypt", 8 May 2014.

31 ICC, Situation in the Democratic Republic of the Congo, *Prosecutor v. Thomas Lubanga Dyilo*, Pre-Trial Chamber I, Decision on the Prosecution Motion for Reconsideration, ICC-01/04-01/06-123, 23 May 2006, p. 3 (http://www.legal-tools.org/doc/365c0b/); ICC, Situa-

lodge an interlocutory appeal is only given to parties to the relevant proceedings, and since in the previous decision the Applicant lacked *locus standi,* the Applicant could not be considered to be a party to the present proceedings within the meaning of Article 82(1)(d) of the Rome Statute.[32] Not only was the refusal of the application by the OTP controversial in raising serious questions about the relationship between Egypt and the Court, it shows that the ICC has been hesitant in getting involved in politically-sensitive cases.[33] It also raises serious questions about the scope of applicability of Article 12(3) of the Rome Statute.

Since the Arab Spring and Egyptian revolution of 2011 that led to the fall of President Mubarak's regime, there have been multiple calls for Egypt to join the ICC as a full member, and, indeed, it has been announced that Egypt will take the necessary steps to join and ratify "all

tion in the Democratic Republic of the Congo, *Prosecutor v. Thomas Lubanga Dyilo*, Pre-Trial Chamber I, Decision on the Prosecution Motion for Reconsideration And, in the Alternative. Leave to Appeal, ICC-01/04-01/06-166, 23 June 2006, paras. 10–12 (http://www.legal-tools.org/doc/a2d89a/); ICC, Situation in the Republic of Kenya, *Prosecutor v. William Samoei Ruto and Joseph Arap Sang*, Pre-Trial Chamber II, Decision on the "Defense Request for Leave to Appeal the Urgent Decision on the 'Urgent Defense Application for Postponement of the Confirmation Hearing and Extension of Time to Disclose and List Evidence' (ICC-01/09-01/Ll-260)", ICC-01/09-01/11-301, 29 August 2011, para. 18 (http://www.legal-tools.org/doc/84374a/); ICC, Situation in the Republic of Kenya, *Prosecutor v. William Samoei Ruto and Joseph Arap Sang*, Pre-Trial Chamber II, Decision on the Application by the Government of Kenya Challenging the Admissibility of the Case Pursuant to Article 19(2)(b) of the Statute, ICC-01/09-01/11-101, 30 May 2011, para. 42 (http://www.legal-tools.org/doc/dbb0ed/); ICC, Situation in the Republic of Kenya, *Prosecutor v. William Samoei Ruto and Joseph Arap Sang*, Pre-Trial Chamber II, Decision on the "Prosecution's Application for Extension of Time Limit for Disclosure", ICC-01/09-01/11-82, 10 May 2011, para. 11 (http://www.legal-tools.org/doc/098503/); ICC, Situation in the Democratic Republic of Congo, *Prosecutor v. Bosco Ntaganda*, Pre-Trial Chamber II, Decision on the Defense Request for Leave to Appeal, ICC-01/04-02/06-207, 13 January 2014, para. 39 (http://www.legal-tools.org/doc/fbb86a/).

32 ICC, Regulation 46(3) of the Regulations of the Court, Pre-Trial Chamber II, Decision on a Request for Reconsideration or Leave to Appeal the "Decision on the 'Request for Review of the Prosecutor's Decision of 23 April 2014 Not to Open a Preliminary Examination Concerning Alleged Crimes Committed in the Arab Republic of Egypt, and the Registrar's Decision of 25 April 2014'", ICC-RoC46(3)-01/14, 22 September 2014, paras. 5-8 (http://www.legal-tools.org/doc/7ced5a/).

33 Mark Kersten, "ICC Says No to Opening Investigation in Egypt", in *Justice in Conflict*, 1 May 2014.

United Nations agreements on human rights".[34] Egypt has since made similar commitments, each time stipulating exclusions to its full ratification of the ICC, such as ratifying whilst guaranteeing immunity for President Bashir by way of establishing a Bilateral Immunity Agreement between Egypt and Sudan. Such a process would be pursuant to Articles 27 and 98 of the Rome Statute, which recognise that immunities may exist on the basis of a state's other obligations under international law (such as a bilateral treaty agreement), which would provide the state with the option of a waiver of immunity and would require consent to surrender, and that this would exist alongside the state's ratification of the Rome Statute.[35]

Egypt has not ratified the Rome Statute, but it has taken significant steps to ratify most international treaties that regulate crimes, and has criminalised many offences even though they are not defined as international crimes in international criminal law, and all of this despite its constitutional commitments to retain the *Sharīʿah* as a source of law.[36]

7.4.2. Palestine

The most recent signatory to the Rome Statue from the Middle East and North Africa region was the State of Palestine, which accepted ICC jurisdiction in June 2014 and formally acceded to the Rome Statute on 2 January 2015, entering into force on 1 April 2015. The extent to which the State of Palestine will engage with the ICC is yet to be seen. Palestine's Basic Law of 2003 (equivalent to the Constitution) was passed by the Palestinian Legislative Council in 1997, and ratified by President Yasser Arafat in 2002. It has subsequently been amended twice: in 2003, the political system was changed to include a Prime Minister, and in 2005 major changes were made to the system of elections.

---

[34] Foreign Minister of Egypt, Al-Araby Nabil, quoted in *Al-Rakoba.net Newspaper*, "Egyptian Foreign Minister Announces the Start of the Procedures for His Country's Accession to the ICC", 20 April 2011; Human Rights Watch, "Egypt: Important Commitment to Ratify Rome Statute", 29 April 2011.

[35] Mark Kersten, "Egypt to Join the ICC but Also Guarantee Bashir Immunity", in *Justice in Conflict*, 20 February 2011; Schabas, 2010, pp. 1037–45, see *supra* note 29.

[36] Egypt ratified the 1949 Geneva Conventions on 10 November 1952, and the two Additional Protocols on 9 October 1992. It also ratified the 1948 Convention on the Prevention and Punishment of the Crime of Genocide on 8 February 1952 and acceded to the UN Convention against Torture and Other Cruel, Inhuman or Degrading Treatment or Punishment on 26 June 1987. Egypt further acceded to the International Convention on the Suppression and Punishment of the Crime of Apartheid on 13 June 1977.

Article 7 of the Basic Law stipulates that "the principles of the Islamic *Sharí'ah* are a main source for legislation" and, therefore, the criminal laws for Muslims are also to be legislated in accordance with Islamic criminal laws.[37] The Basic Law, like all other constitutions, which include comparable source of law clauses, leaves it vague as to what the principles of the Islamic *Sharí'ah* are, though the clause is widely understood by scholars to refer to both the sources of Islamic law as well as widely-accepted principles applied by Muslim jurists. Article 18 of the Basic Law indicates Palestine's adherence to the Universal Declaration of Human Rights ('UDHR'), as well as a specific intent to "seek to join other international covenants and charters that safeguard human rights". Notwithstanding the above, the *Sharí'ah* law clause and Article 18 of the Basic Law would not preclude or prevent full ratification and implementation of the Rome Statute in Palestine. However, other recent developments may have implications for Palestine's full compliance with the Rome Statute.

On 22 January 2009, under Article 12(3) of the Rome Statute, Ali Khashan, Minister of Justice of the Government of Palestine, applied to the OTP to investigate "acts committed on the territory of Palestine since 1 July 2002" by Israel related to the on-going conflict between the two states.[38] The then-Prosecutor, Luis Moreno-Ocampo, was wary of the fact that an admission of the complaint to full investigation would have been tantamount to the recognition of Palestine as a state. As a result, the OTP refused to admit the application to investigate any alleged crimes until such time as the question of the statehood of Palestine was resolved – an issue that took more than three years to resolve at the ICC.[39] This is no longer an issue, with Palestine's accession to the Rome Statute on 2 January 2015 rendering it a State Party.

7.4.3. Tunisia

Tunisia was only the fourth member of the Arab League (out of a total of 22 Member States), and the 116th state overall to join the Rome Statute. In

---

[37] The Palestinian Basic Law, "2003 Permanent Constitution Draft", 17 February 2008, available on the web site of the Palestinian Basic Law.

[38] Palestinian Ministry of Justice, Office of the Minister Ali Khashan, "Declaration Recognising the Jurisdiction of the International Criminal Court", 21 January 2009 (http://www.legal-tools.org/doc/d9b1c6/).

[39] ICC, Office of the Prosecutor, "Situation in Palestine", 3 April 2012 (http://www.legal-tools.org/doc/f5d6d7/).

addition, it has the distinction of being the first North African state to accede to the Rome Statute, on 24 June 2011.

Tunisia is only the second most-recent country in the Middle East and North Africa to accede to the Rome Statute. While the congratulatory messages that were sent by the High Representative of the European Union to the world regarding Tunisia's accession made reference to the Arab Spring, it made no reference to Islamic law or the *Sharíʿah,* and for very good reason. After the revolution in Tunisia, the newly-written Constitution that was adopted makes reference in Article 1 to the fact that the religion of the State of Tunisia is Islam, but there is no 'source of law', '*Sharíʿah* law', or repugnancy clause, as found in the constitutions of other states that apply Islamic law. Furthermore, there is no mention whatsoever of Islamic law being a source of legislation. This would presume that Tunisia's criminal and other laws would quite easily be compliant with the Rome Statute and would not face the problems of other states that have acceded. But the clear reference in the Constitution establishing the religion of the State of Tunisia as Islam qualifies it for inclusion in our comparative analysis. Though the clause itself does not obligate consideration of the *Sharíʿah* for the purposes of enacting new legislation, it may serve as a legitimate reference point for existing indigenous and long-standing Islamic customs and traditions derived from the *Sharíʿah*. These traditions may not have been codified but could be afforded legislative protection under Article 1. The effect of Article 1 on enacting domestic legislation and ratifying international treaties is yet to be fully tested.

7.4.4. The Maldives

The Maldives is well-known for its beautiful natural landscapes and sweeping shorelines, but less so for the fact that the *Sharíʿah* is one of the sources of its laws. Article 10(a) of its Constitution states:[40]

> The religion of the State of the Maldives is Islam. Islam shall be one of the basis [*sic*] of all the laws of the Maldives.

Article 10(b) compounds this with a repugnancy clause:[41]

---

[40] Constitution of the Republic of Maldives, 7 August 2008, Article 10(a) (http://www.legal-tools.org/doc/93aff7/).

[41] *Ibid.*, Article 10(b).

No law contrary to any tenets of Islam shall be enacted in the Maldives.

Not only does the Constitution explicitly provide for laws based on the *Sharīʿah,* the Penal Code of the Maldives came into effect on 16 July 2015, repealing the law of 1968. The new Penal Code was initially drafted through a commissioned project by the UN Development Programme, under the supervision of Professor Paul Robinson and a team of researchers at the University of Pennsylvania in 2006.[42] The draft legislation was not passed in the 16th *Majlis* (Parliament) in 2008, but was re-submitted to Parliament in late 2009 in the 17th Majlis. It remained with the *Majlis* until December 2013, was rejected in the first vote and then finally passed in April 2014. Its enforcement was delayed until April 2015 to allow institutions to amend their regulations and by-laws to ensure they were in compliance with the new Penal Code.[43]

The Code is particularly unique since it was specifically drafted to take consideration of the *Sharīʿah* and common law principles in criminal law, by experts from both the Islamic and common law legal traditions. It is perhaps not a mere coincidence that the Maldives acceded to the Rome Statute on 21 September 2011, in the run-up to the criminal law reforms, which culminated in the new Penal Code in April 2014. The Maldives does not have a history of civil war or violent conflict so it is not surprising for it to have escaped scholarly attention, particularly for the purposes of international criminal law.

The Islamic criminal system of the Maldives serves as an example of a successful effort between Islamic law specialists and those with Western legal backgrounds. They created a penal code that takes elements of both legal jurisdictions whilst remaining cognisant of modern conceptions of fairness, justice, fair trial principles and a combination of the law of evidence in criminal procedure in both Islamic law and the common law system.[44] The extent to which the domestic Islamic criminal legal

---

42 Paul H. Robinson *et al.*, "Codifying Shariah: International Norms, Legality and the Freedom to Invent New Forms", in *Journal of Comparative Law*, 2007, vol. 2, no. 1, pp. 1–53.

43 Hassan Mohamed, "Maldives Celebrates Historic Penal Code", in *Maldives Independent*, 16 July 2015; *Penn Law News*, "Penal Code Drafted by Prof. Paul Robinson and Students Is Enacted in the Maldives", 8 May 2014.

44 For a comparable exercise in enabling a dialogue between the two legal systems as far as the modern application of Islamic criminal law is concerned, see Sadiq Reza, "Due Process

provisions in the new Penal Code and the domestic criminal law courts' architecture are coherent, comprehensive and able to prosecute crimes of an international character is yet to be assessed.

7.4.5. Sudan

On 8 September 2000, Sudan signed the Rome Statute, but roughly eight years later, Sudan's government submitted to the Secretary-General of the United Nations that, "Sudan does not intend to become a party to the Rome Statute. Accordingly, Sudan has no legal obligation arising from its signature".

Sudan's body of criminal laws has long been noted to suffer from a substantial lack of reference to international crimes and has gained in prominence since the conflict in Darfur, in which many crimes stipulated in the Rome Statute were said to have been committed. It was subsequently alleged that the criminal justice system in Sudan was incapable, from a purely technical and capacity standpoint, to hold suspects accountable for such crimes, even if there was political will to support such prosecutions. Some of the accused for whom warrants were issued voluntarily presented themselves to the ICC's Pre-Trial Chambers.[45]

Prior to the Darfur conflict, it is noteworthy that many of the changes in the criminal laws in Sudan were ushered in by a military, and not a civilian government. Between November 1983 and June 1999, the Nimeiri Military Regime (1969–1985) repealed the Armed Forces Act of 1957 and introduced the People's Armed Forces Act of 1983. The new Act dealt with the repression of many war-related crimes and included them in a section of the Act on crimes and punishments (Section 10). Some of the crimes that were made punishable included looting, pillaging, and inhumane treatment of prisoners of war and the wounded. The Armed Forces Act of 1983 represented a measure of progress but was soon revoked by the civilian government that took power after the collapse of the Nimeiri regime, and was then replaced by the People's Armed Forces Act of 1986. During the short period of civilian rule in Sudan (1986–1989), the latter

in Islamic Criminal Law", in *George Washington International Law Review*, 2013, vol. 46, no. 1, pp. 1–27.

45 See the case of Bahar Idriss Abú Garda, who voluntarily appeared at the pre-trial chambers in response to the warrant against him, and who was acquitted for insufficiency of evidence. Details of the case are available on the ICC web site.

Act has been widely regarded as one of the worst legislative acts that regulated the conduct of the armed forces in Sudan. It is clear that the purpose of this was to provide immunity to armed forces personnel from prosecution under national laws.

National courts were *de facto* precluded from prosecuting international crimes, which resulted in a serious gap in repressing the crimes of genocide and other war crimes. The ICC's investigation in respect of the Situation in Darfur, pursuant to a Security Council referral – since Sudan signed the Rome Statute but is not a State Party – originated because Sudanese laws were not deemed to adequately regulate the prosecution of international crimes. They also lacked adequate legal procedures to hold those accused of such crimes accountable. Undoubtedly, this has affected the ICC's approach with regard to the complementarity regime with Sudan and the Court's determination of whether it has jurisdiction over the international crimes allegedly committed in Darfur.

On 29 June 2005, pursuant to Security Council Resolution 1593 of 2005, information was sought from Sudanese institutions on any proceedings that had taken place in relation to the alleged crimes in Darfur. Some of the institutions approached included the Committees against Rape, the Special Courts, the Specialised Courts that replaced them, the National Commission of Inquiry, and other *ad hoc* judicial committees and non-judicial mechanisms. On the basis of this information, the then-Prosecutor of the ICC outlined in his statement to the Security Council that there were cases that would be admissible in relation to the Darfur situation.[46] Notwithstanding the inability of the criminal laws to deal with this issue, after the Security Council referred the Darfur situation to the ICC, Sudan did make changes by enacting the Armed Forces Act in 2007 and the Criminal Act in 1991 (as amended in 2009). These amendments were designed, it is claimed, to ensure that the armed forces acted within the recognised boundaries of the use of force. The amendments also incorporated crimes against humanity, genocide and war crimes.[47] The Armed Forces Act of 2007 contains provisions on these crimes within a whole

---

[46] ICC, Office of the Prosecutor, "Statement to the United Nations Security Council on the Situation in Darfur, the Sudan, pursuant to UNSCR 1593 (2005)", 8 June 2011 (http://www.legal-tools.org/doc/f2676c/).

[47] See further Lutz Oette, *Criminal Law Reform and Transitional Justice Human Rights Perspectives for Sudan*, Ashgate, Burlington, 2011, pp. 163–72.

chapter on international humanitarian law. The Criminal Law amendments of 2009 added an entire chapter (Chapter 18) incorporating a total of seven articles which were drafted by a special committee formed in the Ministry of Justice following the ICC intervention in the Darfur situation.[48]

These are perhaps the latest in a series of amendments to the situation in Sudan that allow for the incorporation and recognition of international crimes in Sudan, and therefore, from the perspective of the state, obviate the need to ratify the Rome Statute. Though designed to end impunity for such crimes, mere incorporation is insufficient and there are serious challenges related to the level of implementation of these provisions by the Judiciary and ordinary courts in Sudan.

To summarise, notwithstanding the differences between Islamic law and international criminal law, states such as Sudan that have references to Islamic law in their domestic legislation are able to pass amendments to laws that can provide for the prosecution of such crimes. Therefore, the focus in such states should move away from the issue of compatibility of the various provisions in the codified Islamic laws and the Rome Statute. Instead, they should focus on providing for domestic laws, mechanisms for prosecution, evidential procedures and evidentiary rules that are coherent and substantial. This would allow for legitimate and fair trials for prosecuting such crimes without reference to the ICC, particularly where there are political and other strong objections to the ICC in certain countries due to the particular legal or political system that is in operation.

7.5. Conclusion

Article 18 of the Vienna Convention on the Law of Treaties 1969 requires a "state that has signed but not ratified a treaty to refrain from acts that would defeat its object and purpose".[49] This means that, irrespective of the fact that a state has not fully ratified the Rome Statute, if it is a signatory it must, at the very least, not act contrary to its provisions, even if it cannot act in total conformity with it. In any case, it must not act in contravention to the extent that it would frustrate the purpose and intent of the Statute. This is implied by the act of signature. Even if there is no interna-

48 *Ibid.*, for greater detail.

49 Vienna Convention on the Law of Treaties, 23 May 1969, in force 27 January 1980, Article 18 (http://www.legal-tools.org/doc/6bfcd4/).

tional legal obligation, which can be cited in case of breach, the signatory state must show elementary signs of compliance, even if only through ensuring that its actions do not breach any of the provisions of the Statute. Similarly, due to non-ratification, the ICC cannot exercise its jurisdiction over breaches of the Statute in the state. There are, however, other ways of invoking jurisdiction where, for example, the perpetrator of an act considered unlawful under the Rome Statute is a national of a State Party and is alleged to have carried out the unlawful act on the territory of another state, whether the latter is a State Party or not.

The procedures by which investigations and prosecutions are initiated at the ICC are also subject to some scrutiny by Arab states, and are perceived to counter the principles of the *Sharí'ah* related to accountability and trial of perpetrators of international crimes. The recent history of many Arab and Islamic nations that have achieved independence from foreign occupation has led to the making of a distinction by many states in the Middle East and North Africa region between the act of terrorism and the struggle for self-determination and independence.[50] Notably, on 1 July 1999, the Organisation of the Islamic Conference convened to conclude the Convention on Combating International Terrorism and specified in Article 2(a) that:

> Peoples' struggle including armed struggle against foreign occupation, aggression, colonialism, and hegemony, aimed at liberation and self-determination in accordance with the principles of international law shall not be considered a terrorist crime.[51]

Some states still consider that struggles of nations for independence and sovereignty are legitimate and fully compliant with international law. In doing so, they support the recognition of, and differentiation between, terrorism and the right to self-determination against foreign occupation in international conventions. This distinction has been incorporated in at

---

[50] See Organisation of the Islamic Conference, Resolution No. 58/26-P, on the convention of an international conference under the auspices of the UN to define terrorism and distinguish it from the peoples struggle for national liberation, adopted by the Twenty-Sixth Session of the Islamic Conference of the Foreign Ministers, Session of the Peace and Partnership for Development, 28 June to July 1999, para. 6 of the Preamble, available on the web site of the Organisation of the Islamic Conference.

[51] Convention of the Organisation of the Islamic Conference on Combating International Terrorism, 1 July 1999 (http://www.legal-tools.org/doc/e8a798/).

least three regional conventions whose membership includes states that apply the *Sharīʿah.* Distinctly relevant to this is the international law norm of '*uti possidetis*' governing territorial delimitations, the modern and evolved concept of which prevents newly-independent states from altering their physical borders to pre-colonial borders.[52] The application of this norm, whose meaning and application has evolved according to time and geographical application,[53] has exacerbated widespread conflict among states throughout the Middle East and particularly in North Africa.

It is unfortunate that there is a discernable pattern of exclusionary behaviour that seeks to disqualify consideration of non-Western legal traditions in the debates and drafting of international conventions and treaties. A prime example of the effect of excluding perspectives from Muslim and Arab states, and especially Islamic legal perspectives, can be gleaned from the work papers of the drafting of the UDHR, whose records are meticulously preserved. Though almost all Muslim and Arab states have now adopted the UDHR, the implementation of its provisions in most states is severely lacking, and there are clear reasons why this may be the case. The general sessions of the drafting of the UDHR were attended, among others, by representatives of Arab states from Lebanon and Saudi Arabia, both of whom were Arab Christians. Their religious persuasion is not a substantive problem in its essence, and there is nothing objectionable to non-Muslims advising on such issues. In this case, however, what is relevant is that these non-Muslim delegates were not experts in Islamic law and, therefore, the treaty deliberations failed to highlight pertinent issues, which would be objectionable from an Islamic legal perspective. This hits directly at the issue of compatibility of the *Sharīʿah* with international law.

This is also clear from the objections of many Muslim states' representatives on the clauses related to the freedom to change one's religion, and was indicative of a wider reticence, to put it mildly, to accept views or contributions from religious perspectives and legal traditions that were

52 Giuseppe Nesi, "Uti Possidetis Doctrine", in *Max Planck Encyclopedia of Public International Law*, Oxford University Press, 2011.

53 *Ibid.*

inherently tied to a religious ethical foundation.[54] For instance, a cursory analysis of the *travaux préparatoires* of the UDHR informs us that the first session of the Commission on Human Rights was composed of eighteen members, included Dr. Charles Ḥabíb Malik of Lebanon as a representative of Arab states, notably not a specialist on Islamic law; Mr. Osman Ebeid from Egypt; and Dr. Ghassame Ghani from Iran, who attended many of the initial sessions.[55] The only constant representative that remained was Dr. Charles Malik. What is extremely revealing of the attitude of the committee against including the perspective of peoples or states that applied Islamic law, or any ideas inspired from religious principles and law, can be ascertained by perusing the narratives of the choice of candidate sent by Britain. They sent Charles Dukes, described as "a retired trade unionist whose mind was unencumbered by the least knowledge of international law […] [a] gifted amateur".[56] Charles Dukes was chosen over Professor Hersch Lauterpacht on the recommendation of the Legal Adviser of the British Foreign Office who said that Professor Lauterpacht would be a "very bad candidate […] Professor Lauterpacht, though a distinguished and industrious international lawyer is, when all is said and done, a Jew recently come from Vienna. I think the representative of HMG on human rights must be a very English Englishman".[57]

On a more substantive level, during the discussions and the working groups, around 18 European constitutions were considered, 18 from Latin America, 5 Middle Eastern Constitutions (Iran, Iraq, Lebanon, Saudi Arabia, and Syria) and 4 African Constitutions (Egypt, Ethiopia, Liberia, and South Africa).[58] Though Saudi Arabia abstained in voting for the adoption of the UDHR (along with Belorussian SSR, Czechoslovakia, Poland, Ukrainian SSR, Union of South Africa, USSR, and Yugoslavia), they gave no reason for abstention, leading to assumptions that it was due to Article 18, which recognised the right to change one's religion. What is further

---

54 William A. Schabas, *The Universal Declaration of Human Rights: The Travaux Préparatoires: October 1946 to November 1947*, vol. 1, Cambridge University Press, Cambridge, 2013, p. lxxxiii.

55 *Ibid.*, pp. 155–56.

56 A.W. Brian Simpson, *Human Rights and the End of Empire: Britain and the Genesis of the European Convention*, Oxford University Press, Oxford, 2001, pp. 350–52.

57 *Ibid.*

58 Schabas, 2013, p. lxxxix, see *supra* note 54.

surprising is that Saudi Arabia chose to be represented by Jamil Baroody, a Lebanese Christian, who represented the state's opposition to both Article 16 (related to family and marriage rights) and Article 18, stating that domestic laws should govern these matters, and suggested (for Article 16) replacing "equal rights" with "full rights as defined in the marriage laws of their country".[59] He also criticised the draft for having "for the most part, taken into consideration only the standards recognized by western civilization and had ignored those of more ancient civilizations which were past the experimental stage, and the institutions of which, for example marriage, had proved their wisdom through the centuries [...] It was not for the Committee to proclaim the superiority of one civilization over all others or to establish uniform standards for all the countries of the world".[60]

One possible solution to this issue could be to quite simply include representatives of Muslim states, and specifically independent experts of Islamic law and accomplished Muslim jurists, to partake in the discussion on the drafting of treaties and international legal documents to ensure that Islamic legal viewpoints are properly advocated and considered prior to finalising the draft covenant, declaration or treaty, and opening them for adoption.

There are other reasons that also explain and add to the level of animosity of Arab and Islamic states (as well as those in Africa) towards the ICC and its regime, notwithstanding the fact that the ICC may be a necessity where domestic legal systems are especially *unable* or *unwilling* to prosecute international crimes. This points us towards an argument made by many African states that can explain the attitude of some African states towards the ICC. The argument claims that African states, "unlike their powerful European and North American counterparts, are not allowed to uphold their primacy of jurisdiction". This provides the OTP with a convenient reason to reject a claim based on the principle of complementarity on the ground that the criminal courts of the relevant territorial state are unable or unwilling to prosecute. This is sometimes the case even where states have incorporated international crimes into domestic legislation,

59 United Nations General Assembly, Official Records of the Third Session of the General Assembly, Part I, Third Committee. Summary Records of Meetings, 21 December 1948, pp. 890–92.

60 *Ibid.*, p. 370.

showing the state's intent to prosecute such crimes.[61] This reductivist attitude towards African and non-Western legal traditions has understandably been received with contempt. This is somewhat balanced by the precedents of the ICC in justifying their intervention in cases of 'genuine' inability to prosecute (Rwanda), and unwillingness (Libya, in respect of the Lockerbie bombers).

Related to this discussion is the difference between the conceptions of retributive justice and restorative justice in both Islamic criminal law and in Western legal systems (and in the ICC). Both the Islamic criminal legal system and the mechanisms of the ICC contain elements of retributive and restorative justice. The Rome Statute also envisages procedures for societies and victims that are largely restorative in their approach by including victims within aspects of the trial process. The level of restorative justice at the ICC could be further enhanced by recognising and offering methods that may seem trivial and inadequate to some, but for traditional societies – not only traditional Muslim societies – are a very important factor in the healing and transitional justice process.

61 For the example of Sudan, see also Luke Moffett, *Justice for Victims before the International Criminal Court*, Routledge, 2014, pp. 251–53; Sarah M.H. Nouwen, *Complementarity in the Line of Fire: The Catalysing Effect of the International Criminal Court in Uganda and Sudan*, Cambridge University Press, Cambridge, 2014, pp. 284–91.

8

What is the Measure of 'Universality'? Critical Reflections on 'Islamic' Criminal Law and Muslim State Practice *vis-à-vis* the Rome Statute and the International Criminal Court

Shaheen Sardar Ali and Satwant Kaur Heer*

8.1. Introduction

Contributions in this edited collection have explored a range of substantive and procedural aspects of international and Islamic criminal law regimes and the extent to which these resonate with the Rome Statute establishing the International Criminal Court ('ICC'). The present chapter digresses from this line of enquiry to focus on *actual Muslim state*[1] *practice* in relation to the Rome Statute and the ICC. In doing so, we hope to deepen our understanding of the multiple factors informing positions adopted by states in multilateral treaty negotiations. Drawing upon primary source materials in the form of official records of deliberations at the United Nations ('UN') Diplomatic Conference of Plenipotentiaries on the Establishment of an International Criminal Court, Rome 15 June – 17 July 1998 (the 'Rome Conference') in drafting the Rome Statute, this chapter challenges the viewpoint that relatively few ratifications by Muslim states is the direct result of incompatibility of Islamic law and *S̲harīʿah* with 'international' and 'universal' conceptions of criminal justice. Noting from

---

* **Shaheen Sardar Ali** is a Professor of Law at the University of Warwick, United Kingdom. Professor Ali has received a number of national and international awards. In 2012, she was named one of the 100 most influential women of Pakistan. Professor Ali has published extensively in a number of areas including human rights, women's rights, children's rights, Islamic law and jurisprudence, international law, and gender studies. Her latest monograph is *Modern Challenges to Islamic Law* (Cambridge University Press, 2016). **Satwant Kaur Heer** is a Ph.D. candidate at the University of Warwick. Her research focuses on the effectiveness of the Office of the Prosecutor at the International Criminal Court. She has previously obtained an LL.M. in International Development Law and Human Rights from the University of Warwick, and an M.Sc. and LL.B. from the University of Leicester.

1 When referring to Muslim states, we refer to all states that are members of the Organisation of Islamic Cooperation.

records[2] that not once were the words 'Islam', 'Islamic criminal law' or *Sharí'ah* uttered by any delegate from Muslim states, the present chapter poses the following three questions: Is there a basis for suggesting a definitive link between Islamic criminal law and a small number of Rome Statute ratifications by Muslim states? In the absence of a homogenous regime of 'Islamic' criminal/penal laws in most Muslim states, and in view of the inherent plurality of the Islamic legal traditions, which version of 'Islamic criminal law' is being referred to when it is argued that Islamic criminal law and its international counterpart are incompatible, and why? Finally, well aware that declarations of the supremacy of Islamic law and *Sharí'ah*[3] in national constitutions in most Muslim states is by and large rhetorical and window dressing, is this perspective itself indicative of hegemonic international politics?

This chapter advances the argument that in seeking to understand why so few Muslim states have ratified the Rome Statute, it is more useful to place state practice in international law at the centre of the debate rather than Islam and Islamic criminal justice. Using formal acceptance of the Rome Statute as the only indicator would imply that all common and civil law jurisdictions that failed to ratify the Statute have done so due to their incompatibility with 'international' and 'universal' criminal law principles – a position few would hold to be tenable. 'Muslim' states do not always vote as a bloc despite the Organisation of Islamic Cooperation's attempts to present a unanimous approach to issues; neither do Arab States. Preconceived factors are therefore being attributed to why particular states or groups of states fail to ratify international treaties in the areas of human rights and humanitarian law broadly defined. For instance, when the United States of America does not ratify international treaties, it is said to be due to their 'intransigence' or 'internal politics' and not due to incompatibility with her national laws. Contrast this with the position taken when a state with a majority Muslim population does the same; it is somehow

2 See United Nations Diplomatic Conference of Plenipotentiaries on the Establishment of an International Criminal Court Rome, 15 June – 17 July 1998 ('Rome Conference'), Official Records, UN Docs. A/CONF.183/13 (Vol. I) (http://www.legal-tools.org/doc/ee97ab/), A/CONF.183/13 (Vol. II) (http://www.legal-tools.org/doc/253396/), A/CONF.183/13 (Vol. III) (http://www.legal-tools.org/doc/656f32/).

3 *Sharí'ah* is the overarching umbrella of rules, regulations, values and normative frameworks, covering all aspects and spheres of life for Muslims. Islamic law is only one aspect of *Sharí'ah*; hence the use of both *Sharí'ah* and Islamic law.

directly or indirectly attributed to Islam, Islamic law and *Sharīʿah* – as in the case of the Rome Statute.

This chapter comprises three main parts. The first part presents a brief contextual and historical overview of the Islamic criminal law regime, why it is relevant to distinguish between doctrinal and theoretical conceptions of Islamic criminal law, its historical ebb and flow, and partial revival in a few Muslim states today (Section 8.2.). The second part introduces the discussion on Muslim state practice in international law through the lens of interventions made by delegates from Muslim states during the drafting process of international treaties, focusing on the Rome Statute. The third part presents some analytical observations based on the drafting process of the Rome Statute and Muslim states' interventions. As the concluding section, it proposes ways of claiming universality of norms and principles by adopting an inclusive approach towards all legal systems in honest and serious dialogue across regional, political, religious and cultural divides. Lastly, it suggests acknowledgement that religious, legal and cultural traditions are dynamic and evolving, and that the way forward is to focus on actual state practice rather than narrowing it to religious precepts alone.

8.2. Islamic Criminal Law: A Brief Contextual Journey

This section presents a brief contextual journey of the Islamic criminal law regime and why a simple comparison with 'universal' or international principles of criminal law is futile in understanding why Muslim states have not ratified the Rome Statute in large numbers. It also attempts to displace some deeply-entrenched notions in academic writings on Muslim States and the ICC by conflating classical principles of Islamic criminal law with penal codes in a handful of Muslims states. Others are unable to differentiate between 'Arab' and 'Muslim', employing these terms interchangeably. But what appears to be universally accepted among critics of Muslim states' engagement with international law in general is the assumption that there exists general and unanimous consensus among Muslim communities regarding what constitutes Islamic criminal law and that all Muslims subscribe to an identical, uncontested and homogenous legal system.

In seeking to articulate the plurality and dynamism of the Islamic legal traditions and *Sharīʿah*, and to adopt a different line of enquiry, we are guided by Rudolph Peters's approach to the study of Islamic criminal law in his excellent work, *Crime and Punishment in Islamic Law: Theory and Practice from the Sixteenth to the Twenty-first Century.* His remarks are particularly apt in the present enquiry:[4]

> I do not compare Islamic criminal laws with modern criminal laws [...] A completely comparative approach is in my opinion, not meaningful and not feasible. It is not meaningful because it is not clear with what system of criminal law it must be compared. With a modern European or American system? Or, with a pre-modern European system? Neither comparison will be very helpful in understanding the Islamic doctrine whose early origins date back to the seventh century. Moreover we are dealing with a fluid and often contradictory body of opinions and not with a uniform unequivocal doctrine of criminal law. This makes comparison even more complicated.

The criminal laws of societies, communities and states offer insights into what core values a society cherishes[5] and what interests they seek to protect.[6] Just as societies evolve, so do their values and laws. Islamic law is no exception in this regard. We use this term with some caution and by default, as Islamic law is not a uniform body of laws akin to common and civil law systems but more in the form of a scholarly discourse with varying, equally legitimate principles, viewpoints and opinions on the basis of which legally-enforceable laws may be formulated.[7]

---

4 Rudolph Peters, *Crime and Punishment in Islamic Criminal Law: Theory and Practice from the Sixteenth to the Twenty-first Century*, Cambridge University Press, Cambridge, 2005, p. 2. Despite the pitfalls identified by Peters, a growing body of literature has emerged in the area of comparative criminal law (between theoretical and doctrinal conceptions of Islamic criminal law and its 'universal' or 'international' counterpart), the purpose of which is mainly to highlight commonalities and differences between the two traditions. That is not to say that this research is not useful or that it ought not to be undertaken. Comparative research is important and valuable but has its challenges in fluid and dynamic areas such as the Islamic legal traditions.

5 *Ibid.*

6 M. Cherif Bassiouni, *The Shari'a and Islamic Criminal Justice in Times of War and Peace*, Cambridge University Press, Cambridge, 2014, p. 118.

7 See Mohammad Hashim Kamali, "Legal Maxims and Other Genres of Literature in Islamic Jurisprudence", in *Arab Law Quarterly*, 2006, vol. 20, p. 77; Gamal Moursi Badr, "Islamic Law: Its Relationship to Other Legal Systems", in *American Journal of Comparative Law*, 1978, vol. 26, p. 187; Bassiouni, 2014, see *supra* note 6; Mohammad Hashim Kamali, *Sharí'ah Law: An Introduction*, Oneworld Publications, Oxford, 2008; Wael B. Hallaq, *The Origins and Evolution of Islamic Law*, Cambridge University Press, Cambridge, 2005.

Based on the primary sources of Islamic law – the *Qur'án* and *Sunnah* and supplemented by secondary sources and juristic techniques, that is, *ijmá'*, *qiyás* and *ijtihád*, provisions of Islamic criminal law are plural. This plurality emerges from the fact that Islamic law developed through juristic schools of thought headed by scholars who commanded a wide following and, over time, only drew upon the approaches and interpretations of these 'Masters'.[8] Thus, despite common sources, the Islamic legal traditions convey differing legal formulations depending upon the school of thought (*madhhab*) to which the scholar belongs.[9] Even within the *madháhib* (plural of *madhhab*), there exist variations; hence the difficulty of describing a coherent body of 'Islamic criminal law'.

Lying at the intersection of religion, culture, tradition, and politics, Islamic criminal law is thus informed by centuries of history and civilisational baggage, including the description 'Islamic criminal law'. Within the Islamic legal traditions as mandated by the Qur'ánic text, *'adl* (justice) is the driving force behind dispute resolution. Seen as the opposite of *ẓulm* (injustice), Islamic criminal regimes strive to do justice and legal rules are tools for achieving *'adl*. This in turn implies that Islamic criminal law is malleable and contextual, not immutable and fixed. For instance, suspension of the death penalty and amputation of limbs in times of famine amount to modification of Islamic criminal or penal laws because implementing it during famine would not be *'adl* but tantamount to *ẓulm*. The moratorium on *ḥudúd* laws for theft during the reign of *Caliph* Omar Ibn al Khittab due to famine in the Arabian Peninsula is an example. In contemporary times, Tariq Ramadan, a Muslim scholar, has called for a moratorium of the death penalty, arguing from within the Islamic legal tradition that so long as all the pre-requisites for a just, equitable and well-governed Muslim society are not fulfilled, implementing *ḥudúd* punishments would not amount to *'adl* but *ẓulm*.[10]

---

8 We refer here to the founders of schools of juristic thought in Islam including more prominently, Imám Abú Ḥanífa, Imám Málik, Imám Sháfi'í, Imám Ḥanbal and Imám Jafar.

9 Muslims are broadly divided into *Sunní* and *Shí'ah*. *Sunnís* subscribe to the *Ḥanafí*, *Málikí*, *Sháfi'í* or *Ḥanbalí* school of juristic thought. *Shí'ah* follow the *Al-Ithná'ashariyyah*, *Zaydí* and *Ismá'ílí* schools of thought.

10 Tariq Ramadan, "An International call for Moratorium on corporal punishment, stoning and the death penalty in the Islamic World", 5 April 2005, available on his web site.

Islamic criminal law is composed of three categories of crimes – *ḥudúd*, *qiṣáṣ*, and *ta'zír*. These categories cover substantive, procedural, evidentiary matters. *Ḥudúd* (singular *ḥadd*) means limit(s) drawn in the religious text of Islam where penal action and penalty are mandatory as these offences are deemed extremely serious. *Ḥadd* offences include *ḥirábah* (highway robbery or banditry); *ziná'* (sexual relations outside marriage); *sariqah* (theft); *sharb al-khamr* (drinking alcohol). Two other *ḥadd* offences are contested and there is no consensus as to their *ḥadd* nature including *baghí* (rebellion against a legitimate ruler) and *riddah* (renunciation of one's belief in Islam). Due to the serious penalties involved (death, amputation of limbs for instance), stringent evidentiary requirements and safeguards are in place for all *ḥadd* offences.[11]

The second category – *qiṣáṣ* – literally means 'equivalence' and refers to offences against individual life or physical integrity. The penalty is based on the principle of 'eye for eye', meaning that if a person has been killed their heirs may take the life of the killer. But this category is fluid due to the fact that compensation in lieu of life may also be permissible, such as *diyát* (blood money) or forgiveness. The third category, *ta'zír*, implies those offences for which there are no *ḥadd* (mandatory) punishments and discretion of the judge is permitted. Often, offences where evidentiary requirements are not fulfilled drop into the *ta'zír* category and hence lesser penalties.[12] Historically, as a predominantly jurists' law, it is important to understand that procedurally, the Islamic legal traditions were inquisitorial; hence vast discretion was afforded to judges (*quḍáh*).

From the nineteenth century onwards, in Muslim-majority jurisdictions – particularly those colonised by European powers – Islamic criminal law was slowly replaced by European penal codes, 'eclipsed' as Peters terms it, and remaining suspended from statute in many Muslim states to this day. So what is being debated, discussed and studied in most scholarly offerings today in relation to its (in)compatibility with international norms and principles is the combination of doctrinal Islamic criminal law

---

[11] For an excellent collection of essays on the subject see, M. Cherif Bassiouni (ed.), *The Islamic Criminal Justice System*, Oceana Publications, New York, 1983; Muḥammad Abdel Haleem, Adel Omar Sherif and Kate Daniels (eds.), *Criminal Justice in Islam: Judicial Procedure in the Shariah*, I. B. Tauris, London, 2003; Bassiouni, 2014, see *supra* note 7.

[12] *Ibid.* Islamic criminal law is a complex subject and due to word limitations, we present the rules at their simplest.

and actual criminal law of some Muslim states. Islamist parties and groups, when coming into power, consider it their priority, as it contains instruments of power and hegemony in the form of corporal punishments of extreme harshness and cruelty. This is evident in the so-called 'Islamisation' process in Pakistan, Sudan, Northern Nigeria, and Malaysia. Saudi Arabia is the sole Muslim country where Islamic criminal regime has applied uninterrupted.

The 'Islamisation' drive in some Muslim states has resulted in the enacting of penal codes supposedly based on the *Qur'án* and *Sunnah* reviving the classical doctrine of criminal laws of the pre-modern era. It is without doubt that provisions of these laws are in conflict with international human rights conventions in several areas. But what is not being highlighted as explicitly and robustly is that these so-called 'Islamic criminal laws' are contested within Muslim states and communities themselves, due to plurality of interpretations and lack of essential pre-requisites for these offences and punishments. These laws are also in conflict with the constitutions and other national laws of these states. Pakistan is a case in point. Peters is of the view that: "When Islamic criminal law was reintroduced in the various countries, it did not meet with much opposition. In most countries it was supported by large groups in Muslim society. This is due to the powerful ideological discourse surrounding it, which holds promises for the 'ordinary people'".[13] Whilst this may be an accurate inference, the constituency of those who actually happily subscribe to it is minimal, mostly political and ideological elites. It is those very 'ordinary people' who are at the receiving end of the so-called Islamic criminal law regimes in Muslim countries where it has been re-introduced. The *ḥadd* offences and punishments for sexual relations outside of marriage (*ziná'*) were massively abused to the point that, following large scale public debates, the law was 'disabled' by the enacting of the Women Protection Act 2006 in Pakistan. Further, whilst many Muslims welcome Islamisation of state and society, their understanding of what this means is neither monolithic nor homogenous, as most Muslims when questioned seek both Islam and democracy, equality, freedom of religion and freedom from corrup-

[13] Peters, 2005, see *supra* note 5, p. 14.

tion (see, for example, the slogans from the Muslim street during the Arab Spring).[14]

Re-introduction of aspects of Islamic criminal law in these jurisdictions is not motivated by an honest religious spirit or desire to live by the Qur'ánic text and *Sunnah*. As more than one writer on the subject has shown, this move was and remains guided by political and cultural motivations and to gain legitimacy and authority in the public domain. In Pakistan, General Zia-ul-haq introduced his agenda of Islamisation and Islamic criminal laws to appease his right-wing Islamist supporters and gain a political foothold to counter his seizure of power in a military coup. In Iran, Áyátulláh Khomeini had a similarly political motive, as did Nimeiri in the Sudan.

Arguments made by some that Islam and *Sharí'ah* are inherently incompatible with international conceptions of rights including criminal law are factually incorrect. Islamic legal traditions are plural, evolving and dynamic and open to development, just as international norms are changing, and changes to the *ḥudúd* laws in Pakistan are an example of this fluidity. How long ago was it that armed invasion of land belonging to others was a legitimate way of acquiring territory? When did international law prohibit slavery? Does international law allow colonialism, torture, inhuman and degrading punishment today when not more than a century ago these were countenanced?

The fact that common principles of law and justice can be and are evolving is demonstrated by the number of states of various persuasions who engage with international treaties. What makes these convergences challenging is the views of both Muslim apologists as well as some Western scholars who argue that human rights regimes reflect Western ideals and are not universal norms; hence the wariness of Muslim states towards treaties reflecting these norms. A reality check is in order here too: if only a literal interpretation and application of the *Qur'án* and *Sunnah* were applied and could not be changed, why have all Muslim states prohibited

[14] There are several Pew Foundation surveys that support our position where Muslims have expressed huge support for democratic regimes as well as Islamic law. Also see the study by Amaney Jamal and Mark Tessler, "The Democracy Barometers: Attitudes in the Arab World", in *The Journal of Democracy*, 2008, vol. 19, pp. 97–110; Mark Tessler, Amaney Jamal and Michael Robbins, "New Findings on Arabs and Democracy", in *Journal of Democracy*, 2012, vol. 23, no. 4, 2012, pp. 89–103.

slavery – an institution present in the *Qur'án* but with explicit guidance for its gradual waning away? Similarly, in the sphere of family law, Qur'ánic verses relating to laws of inheritance have been modified in keeping with societal and contextual demands of Muslim communities. Why can a similar approach not be adopted for other aspects of Islamic law, including criminal law?

In terms of criminal law, there are areas where international norms on criminal justice and those within classical Islamic criminal law doctrine clash. But that clash is not a 'Muslim' attribute alone. For instance, the death penalty is applied in the United States of America as well as most Muslim states. Prohibition of abortion and, until recently, of contraception is not confined to Muslim traditions but prevalent in a number of European and Latin American states. Corporal punishment too is an area where serious debate is required. Most importantly, it is the legal and judicial systems of many Muslim states that require attention. Access to legal aid, prompt, fair and impartial judicial proceedings and due process need strengthening and these are not being kept away from the population by Islam. Indeed, were Islamic principles to be strictly adhered to, equality of arms, and prompt, effective and speedy justice would be the priority of any Muslim government.

8.3. Muslim State Practice in National, International Law and Treaty Formation: Connecting the Dots

This section engages with the argument presented by scholars such as Ahmad Nassar,[15] Steven Roach and others,[16] that focus on the position of Islamic and *Sharíʿah* being the supreme laws of Muslim states and that hence Muslim state practice in the national and international arenas will always be informed by these sources even in situations where the states themselves ratify or agree during deliberations to international norms.

[15] Ahmad Nassar argues many Muslim countries shun the ICC. A "common concern with joining the ICC has been that it would usurp Islamic law's exclusive jurisdiction, and substitute the law of man for the law of God", see Ahmad E. Nassar, "The International Criminal Court and the Applicability of International Jurisdiction under Islamic Law", in *Chicago Journal of International Law*, 2003, vol. 4, no. 2, pp. 587–96.

[16] Steven Roach, "Arab States and the Role of Islam in the International Criminal Court", in *Political Studies*, 2005, vol. 53, pp. 143–61; Mohamed Elewa Badar, "Islamic Law (Shariah) and the Jurisdiction of the International Criminal Court", in *Leiden Journal of International Law*, 2011, vol. 24, pp. 411–33.

This approach yet again mixes doctrinal plural Islamic legal norms with actual application on the ground and assumes that Islamic law is a fixed, homogenous category fossilised in time.

An oft-repeated statement regarding Muslim state practice *vis-à-vis* international treaty drafting and deliberations is that few Muslim states are active participants and shun the process and ratification processes.[17] The inference is that, since Muslim states adhere strictly to Islamic law and *Sharī'ah*, which runs counter to 'universal' norms, Muslim states are therefore reluctant to engage in these processes. However, an examination of the participants at the Rome Conference dispels the notion that Muslim states shunned the process. The table below (Table 1) identifies the number of Muslim state representatives present at the negotiations in Rome and demonstrates that Muslim states, by sending delegations ranging from one (Uzbekistan) to fifteen (Iran and Egypt) members, wanted to be involved in the negotiations.

Number	**Name of Muslim State**	**Number of representatives at the Rome Conference**
1.	Afghanistan	4
2.	Azerbaijan	6
3.	Bahrain	10
4.	Bangladesh	5
5.	Brunei	6
6.	Egypt	15
7.	Iran	15
8.	Iraq	6
9.	Indonesia	14
10.	Lebanon	3

[17] See discussion in Shaheen Sardar Ali, *Modern Challenges to Islamic Law*, Cambridge University Press, Cambridge, 2016, pp. 146–83.

11.	Libya	5
12.	Jordan	6
13.	Kazakhstan	7
14.	Kyrgyzstan	3
15.	Malaysia	3
16.	Kuwait	10
17.	Morocco	12
18.	Niger	4
19.	Oman	9
20.	Pakistan	5
21.	Qatar	6
22.	Saudi Arabia	11
23.	Syria	5
24.	Tajikistan	2
25.	Turkey	7
26.	Tunisia	6
27.	United Arab Emirates	11
28.	Uzbekistan	1
29.	Yemen	7

Table 1: Number of Muslim States and their Representatives at the Rome Conference.[18]

While numbers in and of themselves may not always translate into meaningful and effective participation, they cannot be easily dismissed either. International diplomacy has factors and indicators of the serious-

[18] Rome Conference, Official Records Volume II, Summary Records of the Plenary Meetings, p. 92, paras. 23–27, see *supra* note 2 (http://www.legal-tools.org/doc/253396/).

ness with which events are gauged; of these, making one's presence felt through strong delegations (in numbers as well as participation) is one. Therefore, irrespective of whether this active presence translated into ratifications or not, it is indicative of the intention to engage with the processes leading to the adoption of the Rome Statute and the ICC. A number of prominent Muslim scholars and diplomats were also deeply involved in the negotiations, including Professor M. Cherif Bassiouni as Chair of the Drafting Committee and Prince Zeid Ra'ad Zeid Al Hussein of Jordan, later the UN High Commissioner for Human Rights. Finally, it is relevant to make the point that, of the Muslim states present, at least three represented countries with the largest Muslim populations – Indonesia, Pakistan and Bangladesh. These non-Arab states did not always follow the line of Arab-Muslim states; neither were they in the elite club of 'Arab group of states'.

Table 2 below shows the number of Muslim states that have signed and ratified the Rome Statute; currently this stands at twenty-four states, out of a total of 123 State parties. These states are a mixture of those who were present and participated in the negotiations and many who signed and ratified the treaty subsequently.

Number	**Name of State**	**Date of Signature/Ratification**
1.	Afghanistan	10 February 2003
2.	Albania	18 July 1998/ 31 January 2003
3.	Bangladesh	16 September 1999/ 22 January 2002
4.	Benin	24 September 1999/ 22 January 2002
5.	Burkina-Faso	30 November 1998/ 16 April 2004
6.	Comoros	18 August 2006 (into force: 1 November 2006)
7.	Cote D'Ivoire	30 November 1998/ 15 February 2013
8.	Djibouti	7 October 1998/

		5 November 2002
9.	Gabon	22 December 1998/ 20 September 2000
10.	Gambia	7 December 1998/ 28 June 2002
11.	Guinea	8 September 2000/ 14 July 2003
12.	Guyana	28 December 2000/ 24 September 2004
13.	Jordan	7 October 1998/ 11 April 2002
14.	Maldives	21 September 2011
15.	Mali	17 July 1998/ 16 August 2000
16.	Niger	17 July 1998/ 11 April 2002
17.	Nigeria	1 June 2000/ 27 September 2001
18.	Palestine	2 January 2015 (into force: 1 April 2015)
19.	Senegal	18 July 1998/ 2 February 1999
20.	Sierra Leone	17 October 1998/ 15 September 2000
21.	Surinam	15 July 2008
22.	Tajikistan	30 November 1998/ 5 May 2000
23.	Tunisia	24 June 2011
24.	Uganda	17 March 1999/ 14 June 2002

Table 2: Signatures/ratifications of the ICC Statute by Muslim states.[19]

[19] See ICC, "The States Parties to the Rome Statute", available on the web site of the ICC.

Having looked at the statistical evidence of Muslim states' presence during the drafting stages and the eventual ratification of the Rome Statute, we now investigate their levels of participation and the content of their interventions. Here too, official records of their deliberations offer credible primary evidence upon which to draw inferences regarding Muslim states' perceptions and approaches to the Rome Statute and the ICC. This section offers examples of interventions by Muslim state delegations, supporting the argument advanced in this chapter that Islamic law is not the focus of interventions of Muslim states in these treaty deliberations. On the contrary, it is guarding national jurisdiction, the principle of complementarity, restricting (or extending) the scope of the ICC to internal or external conflicts and so on.

The drafting process of the Rome Statute is not an isolated case of these complexities. During the course of her research on the drafting processes of the UN Convention on the Elimination of All Forms of Discrimination Against Women ('CEDAW'), and the UN Convention on the Rights of the Child ('CRC'), Shaheen Ali discovered the complexity and multi-layered discourse of balancing national laws, culture, custom, tradition and religion with competing international human rights norms. In studying the CEDAW drafting process, she observed elsewhere:[20]

> Socio-economic, religious, political, and ideological posturing at the global level evidently contribute to a treaty during its drafting as well as after its adoption, and in the context of the present inquiry this was manifested through the wider capitalist–socialist polarity, since CEDAW was drafted at the height of the Cold War. Divisions were also visible in those developed and developing countries' concerns and priorities under the umbrella of the burgeoning 'non-aligned' movement, as well as in the positions adopted by Muslim states.

Similar disparate approaches to the CRC through voting patterns at the drafting process as well as subsequent ratification and reservations are evident from official records and academic writings on the subject.[21] It

[20] Ali, 2016, p. 156, see *supra* note 17.

[21] The CRC became unique in that it is the first international human rights treaty to make specific mention to Islamic law and *Sharīʿah*. For a detailed analysis of Muslim state practice regarding the CRC, see Shaheen Sardar Ali and Sajila Sohail Khan, "Evolving Conceptions of Children's Rights: Some Reflections on Muslim States' Engagement with the United Nations Convention on Rights of the Child", in Nadjma Yassari, Lena-Maria Möl-

must be acknowledged that positions adopted by Muslim majority states regarding CEDAW and the CRC were at times informed by Islamic law and *Sharíʿah* whilst no similar mention is made during deliberations of the Rome Statute.

Reading through official records of the drafting process of the Rome Statute, a few facts emerge that reinforce the main argument of this chapter – that Muslim states are not necessarily driven towards a particular position on a treaty by virtue of their affiliation to Islamic law and *Sharíʿah.* They engage with the process as any other state would – defending their territory, sovereignty and political alignments at national, regional and international levels. This is evident in the discussion below, as an 'Arab Group', an 'African Group' and a 'Like-minded Group' of states developed during the deliberations and negotiations. In a lively and informative account of the negotiations, the late Professor M. Cherif Bassiouni, Chair of the Drafting Committee and himself an eminent Muslim scholar, brings to the fore the complex alignments, groupings, quality of delegates as well as levels of expertise at the negotiating table and in respective capitals. He observes:[22]

> The Arab States formed one of the most active informal groups; they met frequently and adopted common positions that were not necessarily supportive of the ICC, although some states (such as Egypt and Jordan) were part of the 'like-minded states'. The 'like-minded states' met most frequently and were the driving force for completing the Draft Statute and for establishing the ICC.

Not a single word about Islamic law and *Sharíʿah*, although he points to the different levels of skills and authority in delegates from what he calls the 'developed' and 'developing' worlds. He also makes comparisons between their levels of preparedness, clarity of instructions as well as authority to conduct negotiations.[23]

Furthermore, in some earlier treaty drafting processes, Muslim states have not hesitated in adopting positions informed by the Islamic

ler, Imen Gallala-Arndt (eds.), *Parental Care and Best Interest of the Child in Muslim Countries*, T.M.C. Asser Press, The Hague, 2017, pp. 285–324.

22 M. Cherif Bassiouni, "Negotiating the Treaty of Rome on the Establishment of the International Criminal Court", in *Cornell International Law Journal*, 1999, vol. 32, p. 443, fn. 25.

23 *Ibid.*, p. 456.

legal traditions and expressly making claims for modification or removal of certain formulations, stating that these are unacceptable on the basis of conflict with their religious and cultural traditions. By not invoking Islamic law and *Sharīʿah* at all during the deliberations for the Rome Statute, did Muslim states indicate acceptance of international criminal law provisions on the basis that these were in conformity with the Islamic legal traditions? If the Islamic criminal law regime was so central to the policy of Muslim States parties, then why was there no flagging up of contradictions between the draft Statute and domestic criminal regimes – at least by some Muslim states? Alternatively, is this a tacit acknowledgement by Muslim states of the fluidity and evolving nature of the Islamic legal traditions and the variation with which it is applied in their countries and movement towards a responsive and contextual understanding of Islamic law and *Sharīʿah*?

Bearing in mind these questions, we now turn our attention to what Muslim states did say during the deliberations and ways in which these interventions may be interpreted.

8.4. Statements of Support from Muslim States for the Draft Rome Statute: Token 'Universality' or Shared Criminal Law Principles?

None of the Muslim states spoke against the setting up of the ICC, although delegates varied in the warmth with which they greeted and supported the initiative. More importantly, no one raised any issues of conflict between substantive provisions of criminal law and Islamic criminal law principles, despite divergence in some areas.

Examples of statements made by Muslim states include the following: Mr. Zarif (Islamic Republic of Iran) stated that "the establishment of an international criminal court, independent, universal, effective and impartial, would be a milestone towards achieving peace with justice".[24] The Bangladeshi delegates were one of the most enthusiastic and supportive, observing that: "the Conference offered a rare opportunity for the international community to put in place a system of justice to redress unspeakable crimes".[25] The Afghan delegate too made known the strong support of

---

[24] Rome Conference, p. 92, paras. 23–27, see *supra* note 18 (http://www.legal-tools.org/doc/253396/).),

[25] *Ibid.*, p. 107, para. 25.

their government by reaffirming his delegation's "support for the establishment of an international criminal court".[26]

A reading of interventions from delegates other than Muslim states supports the view that there was universal support for the establishment of the ICC – albeit with provisos, reservations and trepidation. There is no single instance of Muslim states arguing against the ICC. Consensus-building to ensure universality of principles as well as unanimous support to strengthen the ICC was also visible in these interventions, not least from Muslim states, although this general support did not translate into unanimity when it came to signatures and ratifications.

8.5. Protecting National Interests through Principles of Complementarity: A 'Muslim' Ploy or Wider State Practice?

Despite unanimous support and statements to this effect, official records show that most states also jealously guarded their sovereignty and territory by demanding the ICC be a forum of last resort and work complementary to national courts. They believed that the ICC regime ought to intervene only in situations where domestic jurisdictions are unable or unwilling to prosecute. These concerns were shared by Muslim states as well and articulated by the Malaysian delegation stating: "the International Criminal Court should complement and not replace national courts. In setting up a court to judge those who had committed very serious crimes abhorred by the international community, the national sovereignty of all nations must be upheld".[27]

Alongside this, many states were uncomfortable with the role and powers of the Prosecutor to initiate proceedings, as it was feared that this would infringe on state sovereignty and the principle of complementarity. This again was a position adopted by Muslim states *as well as other states* in general. For example, Mr. Al Awadi (United Arab Emirates), supported by Mr. Khalid Bin Ali Abdullah Al-Khalifa (Bahrain) expressed their concerns with regard to an independent prosecutor with the power to initiate proceedings which would "give the Prosecutor the right to take certain

[26] *Ibid.*, p. 87, paras. 59–62. Similar statements in support of the Statute and the ICC were also made by the representatives of Oman, Egypt, Kazakhstan, Pakistan, Brunei Darussalam, United Arab Emirates, Morocco, Niger, Nigeria, Sudan, Turkey and Kuwait.

[27] *Ibid.*, p. 109, paras. 45–50. Similar statements about the importance of complementarity were made by Qatar, Afghanistan and Bosnia and Herzegovina.

measures without the approval of the State concerned, which was incompatible with the principle of complementarity".[28] In contrast, some nations including Jordan, were supportive of an independent prosecutor, with Prince Zeid Ra'ad Zeid Al Hussein stating: "in the interests of an effective and credible Court, the Prosecutor would have to be in a position to refer matters to it, in compliance with the principle of complementarity, and to initiate investigations on the basis of information analysed responsibly and in a manner unaffected by international media coverage".[29]

It would seem, therefore, that issues expressed by Muslim states were not motivated in particular by Islamic law or *Sharí'ah* rather these concerns in relation to complementarity and an independent prosecutor were shared by other non-Muslim nations protecting their sovereignty.

8.6. Political and Historical Factors Influencing Statements of Participants: Call to Look Beyond Western Legal Systems for Genuine Universality

Drafting processes of international treaties are narratives of peoples and nations, their struggles and aspirations on various aspects of national, regional and international governance. They also provide a forum for agreements, disagreement and compromises on standard-setting texts that all states – sometimes with reservations – accept as guidelines for their actions. During the Rome Conference, many national delegates recalled their national experiences when making interventions, as is reflected in the observations below. It is quite telling that here, too, no mention of Islam, Muslim or Islamic law is made, although some Muslim states mentioned the importance of looking beyond Western legal systems to ensure genuine universality of principles in the Rome Statute. For example, Mr. Milo (Albania) stated:[30]

> that public opinion was increasingly concerned about the failure of the international community to prevent the continuing serious violations of international humanitarian law and punish those who committed them and the political leaders who were directly responsible for them. The perpetrators of the Serbian massacres in Bosnia were still unpunished, and

[28] *Ibid.*, p. 349, para. 9.

[29] *Ibid.*, p. 199, paras. 89–91.

[30] *Ibid.*, p. 82, paras. 11–14.

> the same crimes were being repeated in Kosovo, where the genocidal massacres by the Serbian authorities were a consequence of an institutionalized policy of genocide and State terrorism carried out through the military, paramilitary and police machinery against Albanians. The Albanian people of Kosovo were prey to a policy of ethnic cleansing, and their resistance to that policy in self-defense could never be identified with terrorism. The international community's slow or inadequate response to such crimes tended to cast doubt on the effectiveness of international institutions. Security Council recommendations had not only failed to prevent the violence and terror in Kosovo but had even won time for the Serbian authorities to launch large-scale ethnic cleansing operations. For those reasons, Albania strongly advocated investing the International Criminal Court with universal jurisdiction over such crimes as genocide and ethnic cleansing, war crimes, whether international or domestic, aggression and other crimes against humanity.

The representative of Libyan Arab Jamahiriya, Mr. Al-Maghur, recalled that his country had submitted five issues to the International Court of Justice ('ICJ') and had complied with its decisions in all those cases. A similar conduct had regrettably not been adopted by certain other States, some of which were permanent members of the Security Council and were represented in the ICJ.[31] He also observed that "Western values and legal systems should not be the only source of international instruments. Other systems were followed by a large proportion of the world's population".[32] The Libyan representative's intervention was arguably one of the most politically 'loaded' statements and expressed his disaffection with 'Western' states. He referred to the need to include other sources of law and not confine the discussion to Western values and legal systems.

Delegates from Afghanistan also spoke to their country's devastation at the hands of aggression, war and devastation thus:[33]

> [H]is country had been a victim of aggression and the theatre of violations of humanitarian law, first by the former Soviet Union and more recently by the Taliban mercenaries with the

31 *Ibid.*, pp. 101–02, paras. 80–84.

32 *Ibid.*

33 *Ibid.*, p. 87, paras. 59–62.

> direct participation of foreign militia and military personnel. The acts committed by the former constituted war crimes or crimes against humanity, while the latter continued to perpetrate war crimes, crimes against humanity and genocide. United Nations resolutions had gone unheeded. Those tragic events were evidence of the need for an independent, credible and impartial court which should not be hostage to a political body. Political considerations and the geo-strategic and geo-economics interests of Security Council veto-holders should not prevent the International Criminal Court from condemning aggressors. The world needed to establish a historical record of major international crimes, if only to establish the truth and to educate future generations, in order to deter potential criminals and avoid the repetition of such crimes […] He warned against the danger of the selectivity and double standards that prevailed in the assessment of human rights in the world.

Ensuring inclusivity of diverse legal systems was voiced by delegates from Afghanistan, Lebanon, Libya and Malaysia in various statements emphasising the importance of a court that was "truly independent, fair, effective and efficient, so that it could dispense justice in accordance with principles acceptable to the international community, bearing in mind diverse legal systems and cultures".[34] In addition, the Moroccan delegate stressed inclusivity by stating that "the Court must address the rights of all peoples. It must be permanent, universal, effective, credible, impartial, and independent of any political approach".[35]

Groupings on the basis of region, political and ideological leanings were also visible during the Rome Conference as demonstrated by the text of the interventions. Most prominent among these were the Arab Group, the African Group and the Non-Aligned Movement, although states also tended to be in more than one group. Thus, Indonesia as one of the founders of the non-aligned movement made the following statement; Mr. Effendi (Indonesia) said that "his delegation fully endorsed the position of the Movement of Non-Aligned Countries concerning the crime of aggression and nuclear weapons".[36] Countries in such groups convened individ-

[34] *Ibid.*, p. 109, paras. 45–50.

[35] *Ibid.*, p. 103, paras. 105–09.

[36] *Ibid.*, pp. 337–38, paras. 33–36.

ual meetings and relayed their respective position during the Rome Conference; hence Mr. Alhadi (Sudan), speaking on behalf of the Group of Arab States, stated:[37]

> The Conference had created a historic document, the signing of which would be a moment of dignity for all humanity [...] While the Arab States would not stand in the way of the adoption of the Statute of the Court, he felt bound to place on record that they were not convinced by what had been agreed upon [...] The Arab States were afraid that the inclusion of non-international conflicts within the Statute would allow interference in the internal affairs of States on flimsy pretexts [...] The Statute gave the Prosecutor, acting *proprio motu*, a role beyond the control of the Pre-Trial Chamber [...] The Group of Arab States had expressed their fear that the Security Council might be granted powers that could affect the role of the Court concerning any war criminal, regardless of country, religion, or nationality.

Even at this point, none of the concerns put forward by the Group of Arab States focused on an incompatibility with Islamic law or *S̲harīʿah*; rather they were centred on the possibility of interfering with sovereignty of nations.

8.7. Limiting the International Criminal Law Menu? The Internal/External Conflict Debate

Discussions regarding inclusion of internal conflicts within the jurisdiction of the ICC led to different positions being taken by Muslim states. Bahrain, Pakistan, Turkey, Saudi Arabia, United Arab Emirates, Syria, Algeria, and Tunisia did not agree with the proposal of extending jurisdiction to internal conflicts within a state, stating quite strongly:[38]

> The future Court should have nothing to do with internal troubles, including measures designed to maintain national security or root out terrorism. Conferring a *proprio motu* role on the Prosecutor risked submerging him with information concerning charges of a political, rather than a juridical nature. To make the Statute universal and effective, reservations should at least have been permitted on certain articles

[37] *Ibid.*, pp. 126–27, paras. 74–78.

[38] *Ibid.*, p. 124, paras. 41–44.

> on which the Conference was deeply divided. For those reasons, Turkey had been unable to approve the Statute and had found itself obliged to abstain.

Mr. Dhanbri (Tunisia) agreed with the inclusion of genocide but was keen to emphasise that "his delegation interpreted crimes against humanity as taking place only in international armed conflicts; otherwise intervention by the Court would amount to interference in internal affairs contrary to the principles of the United Nations".[39] Jordan, Uganda, Brunei Darussalam and others approved of the Court having jurisdiction over internal as well as external conflicts. In support of the proposal, Mr. Sadi (Jordan) said: "the goal was to create a credible juridical deterrent to those who intended to commit grave breaches of international humanitarian law. Grave crimes should be prosecuted, whether they occurred in internal or external conflicts, and whoever committed them".[40] And later, joining the consensus on the inclusion of genocide in the Statute, he stated: "with respect to crimes against humanity, no distinction should be made between international and internal conflicts; that would introduce double standards, which his country could not accept".[41]

Other areas Muslim states were concerned about the inclusion of 'enforced pregnancy' as a crime against humanity and the 'death penalty' in sentencing. With regard to 'enforced pregnancy', Libya,[42] United Arab Emirates,[43] Egypt,[44] Iran,[45] and Jordan[46] were worried this could impact upon their national laws against abortion. However, this concern was not voiced in relation to Islamic law or *Sharīʿah*; the Arab states, alongside the Holy See delegation and other Catholic countries (including Ireland and several Latin American countries), during the Preparatory Committee stage put forward a proposal to replace the term 'enforced pregnancy'

[39] *Ibid.*, p. 144, paras. 33–34.

[40] *Ibid.*, p. 114, paras. 6–9.

[41] *Ibid.*, p. 147, para. 28. The delegates of Senegal and Mali also concurred with this viewpoint.

[42] *Ibid.*, p. 160, para. 63.

[43] *Ibid.*, p. 160, para. 66.

[44] *Ibid.*, p. 164, paras. 30–33.

[45] *Ibid.*, p. 166, paras. 71–72.

[46] *Ibid.*, p. 332, paras. 72–80.

with 'forcible impregnation'.[47] During the Rome Conference, a compromise was reached to ensure that the crime of 'enforced pregnancy' did not conflict with national laws regarding abortion. Article 7(2)(f)[48] containing the crime, stipulates non-interference with national law relating to pregnancy. Similarly, states including Lebanon,[49] United Arab Emirates,[50] Jordan,[51] and Saudi Arabia[52] discussed the inclusion of the death penalty in sentencing; however, it was decided that while the Court would not impose the death penalty, it would not interfere with countries that did. Mr. Sadi from Jordan noted that "on the vexed issue of the death penalty […] while international human rights instruments called for the phasing out of capital punishment, they did not yet prohibit it altogether". Neither of these issues were articulated citing Islamic law or *Sharí'ah*, and they were also not unique to Muslim states; as discussed above, Catholic countries were similarly concerned about the wording of 'enforced pregnancy' and American states as well as China also impose the death penalty. What drove the interventions from Muslim states therefore, was incompatibility with national legislation.

8.8. Claiming Universality through Inclusivity: Some Concluding Remarks

A close reading of the official records leading to the establishment of the ICC confirms the active participation of Muslim states during the negotiation process – although not always supporting some of its provisions. In this, they were not alone but in the company of the United States of America, India and Israel, who, according to commentaries on the process, gave negotiators a difficult time. Muslim states voiced general support to the treaty with varying degrees of warmth. They voiced concern at the role and powers of the Prosecutor, and also made interventions guarding the

47 Cate Steaines, "Gender Issues", in Roy S.K. Lee (ed.), *The International Criminal Court: The Making of the Rome Statute – Issues, Negotiators and Results*, Kluwer Publishers, The Hague, 1999, p. 367-90.

48 Statute of the International Criminal Court, 17 July 1998, in force 1 July 2001 ('Rome Statute'), Article 7(2)(f) (http://www.legal-tools.org/doc/7b9af9/).

49 Rome Conference, p. 357, paras. 8–9, see *supra* note 18 (http://www.legal-tools.org/doc/253396/).

50 *Ibid.*, p. 357, para. 11.

51 *Ibid.*, p. 114, paras. 6–9.

52 *Ibid.*, p. 357, para. 9.

principle of complementarity and national jurisdiction. They were divided in their position on whether internal conflicts also ought to fall within the remit of the ICC – a position informed by their fear of intrusion in their domestic affairs.

Some commonalities, however, were evident in their approach towards an international criminal court. By arguing for complementarity principle to be upheld and for the ICC to be the institution of last resort, these states were perhaps conscious of the inadequacies in their legal and judicial systems. Hence, it would be a more plausible critique of the role of Muslim states in the drafting process of the Rome Statute to argue that they shied away from ratification as it meant incurring legal obligations. States would be open to inspections and monitoring of their internal laws, both substantive as well as procedural. The political elite of most of these states would be extremely uncomfortable at this state of affairs as harsh punishments, summary disposal of cases and weak and ineffective access to justice reinforce their power and hegemony over the population. This approach has nothing to do with religion, least of all with Islamic law and *S̲harí῾ah*.

Coming to the issue of incompatible provisions between Islamic criminal law and the Rome Statute, this is a fact and one can point to a few here. As mentioned above, the death penalty, amputation of limbs, flogging and similar harsh punishments for sexual relations outside of marriage, blasphemy, and apostasy are areas for serious and honest debate across the religious, political and cultural divides. But this dialogue must have as its primary aim the urge to deepen understandings of diverse criminal law regimes with a view to evolving some core common principles inclusive of these regimes. From the perspective of Islamic legal traditions, employing the concept of justice rather than law would be more fruitful. *'Adl* (justice) is the opposite of *ẓulm* (injustice) and it is these opposites that lay the foundation of its criminal law regime. So what is unjust cannot be acceptable law. Jurists and judges applied *'adl*-based law on a case by case basis as this was the essence of Islamic criminal law. But these concepts get lost in translation; hence, inclusivity might be fruitful were there a sincere effort to understand concepts in different legal traditions. It is therefore appropriate to use the word justice rather than law when discussing Islamic criminal regimes and distinguish between Islamic criminal justice in theory as opposed to whether and how it is applied in Muslim states today. In arriving at universal core principles as a number of writers on the subject have suggested, justice appears more amenable to universality as legal formulations tend to vary across diverse legal systems.

A number of misconceptions and half-truths also require correction. Private vengeance for murder and the Qur'ánic injunctions on retribution are seen as the rationale for continued acceptance of *diyát* (compensation) in some Muslim communities. But this is only a partial truth, for its continued acceptance is not only due to these factors which are not fixed categories. Penal codes of some Muslim countries have legal provisions where the judge is required to also continue prosecution and apply a penalty for the murder. That this does not happen also implies lack of state will and a weak criminal justice system in these states rather than the absence of evolutionary and dynamic essence in the Islamic legal traditions.

Records of the drafting processes of the Rome Statute, in the same way as those relating to the CEDAW drafting narrative, de-stabilise the existing binaries in describing Muslim state practice in international law – Muslim/non-Muslim, Western/non-Western. The picture that emerges is more complex, richer and more nuanced, and this is evident in alliances beyond those based on religion. For instance, the like-minded group of countries, which Bassiouni describes, as well as the African group and non-aligned group of states. Therefore, applying a linear and simplistic analysis by attributing all actions of Muslim states to their religion is unhelpful for developing a genuinely universality of criminal justice norms. Arguments linking non-ratification of the Rome Statute by Muslim states to Islamic law and *Sharí'ah* implies uncritical evaluation of Muslim state practice in international law as well as within their countries. To be taken seriously by Muslim states in particular, and the international community more generally, scholarship on the ICC, the Rome Statute and international criminal law must be informed by credible and deep knowledge of Muslim state practice, how Muslims actually live Islam. Most importantly, there is no single monolithic Islam; neither is there one single homogenous body of *Sharí'ah* or Islamic law. Dropping everything vaguely 'Islamic' into one basket is probably the most serious correction the world community will have to reflect upon to arrive upon universality of norms. That respectful inclusivity of diversity will be the measure of universality.

9

Is There a Place for Islamic Law within the Applicable Law of the International Criminal Court?

Mohamed Elewa Badar*

9.1. Introduction[1]

In the *Al Mahdi* case, the International Criminal Court ('ICC') came eye to eye with the question of Islamic injunctions. The Defence in the case sought to present the destruction of ancient shrines in Timbuktu as a reflection of the defendant's interpretation of the divine. It claimed that Mahdi believed he was doing the right thing and was merely "seeking the means to allow his conception of good over evil to prevail".[2] By taking this approach, the Defence sought to frame the Defendant's version of Islam as a worldview fundamentally incompatible with that of the ICC.[3] Numerous scholars have debated and critiqued the formation, functioning and practice of the ICC. One of the most contentious of these debates is on the issue of the general principles of law that can be applied by the Court in various cases. During the Rome negotiations, the participating Muslim-majority states supported the existence of an international crimi-

---

* **Mohamed Elewa Badar** is a Professor of Comparative and International Criminal Law and Islamic Law at Northumbria University, Newcastle, United Kingdom. He is the author of *The Concept of Mens Rea in International Criminal Law* (Hart, 2013) and *Islamist Militants and their Challenges to Sharia and International Criminal Law* (Hart, 2019 forthcoming), and has published 25 articles in refereed journals as well as 15 chapters in prominent books, such as the *Commentary on the Rome Statute of the International Criminal Court*. He served as senior prosecutor and judge at the Ministry of Justice, Egypt.

1 An earlier and slightly different version of this Chapter appears in *Leiden Journal of International Law*, 2011, vol. 24, pp. 411–33 under the title "Islamic Law (*Sharí'ah*) and the Jurisdiction of the International Criminal Court".

2 ICC, Situation in the Republic of Mali, *Prosecutor v. Ahmad Al Faqi Al Mahdi*, Pre-Trial Chamber, Confirmation of Charges, Transcript, ICC-01/12-01/15-T-2-Red-ENG, 3 March 2016, p. 98 (http://www.legal-tools.org/doc/410498/).

3 Mohamed Elewa Badar and Noelle Higgins, "Discussion Interrupted: The Destruction and Protection of Cultural Property under International Law and Islamic Law – Prosecutor v. Al Mahdi", in *International Criminal Law Review*, 2017, vol. 17, pp. 486–516.

nal justice institution. However, they also viewed it with suspicion and showed reluctance in ratifying the statute, with only five Arab states to date being States Parties to the Statute of the ICC ('Rome Statute').[4]

There is a tendency for Islamic law to be viewed as a static or non-progressive legal system.[5] However, most Western scholarly debates center on Islamic criminal law on a basic level without an in-depth grasp of the subject. This has been thought to be due to a *lacuna* in the available English literature on Islamic criminal law that "cries to be filled".[6] It has also been argued that it is almost impossible for Islamic law to be compared to the Western legal system, making the path for the creation of a dialogue between Islamic law and international institutions virtually non-progressive.[7]

The aim of this chapter is to find out whether the basic principles of Islamic criminal law are indeed incompatible with the Western legal systems and if not, what can Islamic law bring to the international criminal law table in order to enrich it and make it a true reflection of the legal systems of the world. To enable a basic understanding of Islamic law and its non-monolithic nature, this chapter begins with an examination of the sources of Islamic law, the leading schools of Islamic jurisprudence (*madhāhib*) and the application of Islamic law in Muslim-majority states. It then looks at the categories of crimes as found in the Islamic legal tradition to identify potential conflicts and convergence with international

[4] See Mohamed Elewa Badar and Noelle Higgins, "General Principles of Law in the Early Jurisprudence of the ICC", in Triestino Mariniello (ed.), *The International Criminal Court in Search of Its Purpose and Identity*, Routledge, Oxford, 2014; Juan Carlos Ochoa, "The Settlement of Disputes Concerning States Arising From the Application of the Statute of the International Criminal Court: Balancing Sovereignty and the Need for an Effective and Independent ICC", in *International Criminal Law Review*, 2007, vol. 7, p. 3.

[5] Adel Maged, "Status of Ratification and Implementation of the ICC Statute in the Arab States", in Claus Claus Kreß *et al.* (eds.), *The Rome Statute and Domestic Legal Orders*, vol. 2, Nomos Verlag, Baden-Baden, 2005, pp. 469–78.

[6] Mohammad Hashim Kamali, "Legal Maxims and Other Genres of Literature in Islamic Jurisprudence", in *Arab Law Quarterly*, 2006, vol. 20, p. 77; Gamal Moursi Badr, "Islamic Law: Its Relationship to Other Legal Systems", in *American Journal of Comparative Law*, 1978, vol. 26, p. 187.

[7] Mahdi Zahrá, "Characteristic Features of Islamic Law: Perceptions and Misconceptions", in *Arab Law Quarterly*, 2000, vol. 15, p. 168. See also David Westbrook, "Islamic International Law and Public International Law: Separate Expressions of World Order", in *Virginia Journal of International Law*, 1993, vol. 33, p. 819.

criminal law. The chapter then turns to legal maxims and conducts a comparative study between Islamic law and Western legal systems on some of the fundamental principles of criminal law such as the principle of legality, the presumption of innocence, the concept of *mens rea*, and the standards used by Muslim jurists for determining intention in murder cases as well as other general defences such as duress and superior orders. It concludes that the Islamic legal system is not fundamentally in conflict with Western legal traditions and that the flexibility of Islamic law and especially the abstract nature of its legal maxims put it in a position where it could play an important role in the potential codification of new crimes at the ICC.

9.2. *Sharíʿah* Introduction to Islamic Law (*Sharíʿah*)

Islamic law (*Sharíʿah*) has its roots deeply embedded in the political, legal and social aspects of all Islamic states and it is the governing factor of all Islamic nations.[8] It is often described by both Muslims and Orientalists as the most typical manifestation of the Islamic way of life – the core and kernel of Islam itself.[9] Other commentators deem this an exaggeration and do not believe Islam was meant to be as much of a law-based religion as it has often been made out to be.[10] In any case, Islamic law (*Sharíʿah*), one of the recognised legal systems of the world,[11] is a particularly instructive example of a 'sacred law' and differs from other systems so significantly that its study is indispensable in order to appreciate adequately its full range of possible legal phenomena.[12]

Islamic law, like Roman law, used to be a 'jurist law', in the sense that it was a product neither of legislative authority nor case law, but a

---

[8] Hamid Enayat, *Modern Islamic Political Thought*, University of Texas Press, Austin, 1982; Albert Hourani, *Arabic Thought in the Liberal Age: 1798–1939*, Cambridge, University Press, Cambridge 1983; Wael B. Hallaq, *A History of Islamic Legal Theories: An Introduction to Sunni Usul Al-Fiqh*, Cambridge University Press, Cambridge, 1997.

[9] Joseph Schacht, *An Introduction to Islamic Law*, Oxford University Press, Oxford, 1964, p. 1.

[10] Mohammad Hashim Kamali, *Shari'ah Law: An Introduction*, Oneworld Publication, Oxford, 2008, p. 1.

[11] See Rene David and John Brierly, *Major Legal Systems in the World Today*, Stevens & Sons, London, 1978, p. 421.

[12] Schacht, 1964, p. 2, see *supra* note 9.

creation of the classical jurists, who elaborated on the sacred texts.[13] However, with the first formal codifications in the mid-nineteenth century, Islamic law became 'statutory law', promulgated by a national territorial legislature.[14]

It is no secret that most Islamic nations are viewed as being non-progressive, especially with respect to their national legal systems and implementation of criminal laws.[15] On the other hand, the Islamic states view the West and East as being unethical, immoral and unduly biased towards the religious, cultural and political aspects of Islam itself.[16]

9.2.1. The Application of Islamic Law in Muslim-Majority States Today

The modern Muslim world is divided into sovereign nation-states. Today there are 57 Member States of the Organisation of Islamic Cooperation ('OIC'), which is considered the second largest inter-governmental organisation after the United Nations ('UN').[17] The OIC claims to be the collective voice of the Muslim world and aims to safeguard and protect its interests.[18] Most states who joined the OIC are predominantly *Sunní*, with

---

13 Aharon Layish, "The Transformation of the Shariah from Jurists Law to Statutory Law", in *Die Welt des Islams*, 2004, p. 86. See also Farooq Hassan, "The Sources of Islamic Law", in *American Society of International Law Proceedings*, 1982, vol. 76, p. 65.

14 *Ibid.*

15 John Esposito, "The Islamic Threat: Myth or Reality?", in Javaid Rehman *et al.* (eds.), *Religion, Human Rights and International Law: A Critical Examination of Islamic State Practices*, Martinus Nijhoff Publishers, Leiden, 2007, p. 5. See also Javaid Rehman, *Islamic State Practices, International Law and the Threat from Terrorism: A Critique of the 'Clash of Civilizations' in the New World Order*, Hart Publishing, Oxford, 2005.

16 James Gathii, "The Contribution of Research and Scholarship on Developing Countries to International Legal Theory", in *Harvard International Law Journal*, 2000, no. 41, p. 263; Shaheen Sardar Ali and Javaid Rehman, "The Concept of Jihad in Islamic International Law", in *Journal of Conflict & Security Law*, 2005, no. 10, pp. 321–43; Marcel A. Boisard, "On the Probable Influence of Islam on Western Public and International Law", in *International Journal of Middle East Studies*, 1980, vol. 11, p. 429.

17 This number includes the State of Palestine. For more information, see the web site of the OIC.

18 In 2004, the OIC has made submissions on behalf of Muslim states regarding proposed reforms of the UN Security Council to the effect that "any reform proposal, which neglects the adequate representation of the Islamic *ummah* in any category of members in an expanded Security Council will not be acceptable to the Islamic countries". See UN Doc. A/59/425/S/2004/808 (11 October 2004), para. 56, quoted in Mashood A. Baderin (ed.), *International Law and Islamic Law*, Ashgate Publishing, Aldershot, 2008, p. xv.

only Iran, Iraq, Azerbaijan, Bahrain, and Lebanon having a predominantly *Shí'ah* population. Apart from Lebanon and Syria, all Arab states consider Islam as the state religion and source of law constitutionally.[19]

Bassiouni divides Muslim-majority states into three categories. The first category comprises secular states, like Turkey or Tunisia, who despite their moral or cultural connection with Islam do not directly subject their laws to the *Sharí'ah*. Countries from the second category such as Iraq and Egypt, expressly state in their constitutions that their laws are to be subject to the *Sharí'ah*, therefore, their constitutional courts decide on whether or not a given law is in conformity with the *Sharí'ah* and can also review the manner in which other national courts interpret and apply the laws to ensure conformity.[20] The third category of states comprises Saudi Arabia and Iran as they proclaim the direct applicability of the *Sharí'ah* to civil, commercial, family, criminal, and all legal matters. According to one commentator, a significant number of Muslim-majority states fall between the two poles of 'purist' Saudi Arabia and 'secular' Turkey.[21] Most states have been selective in determining which *Sharí'ah* rules apply to their national legislations.[22] As a consequence of colonialism and the adoption of Western codes, *Sharí'ah* was abolished in the criminal law of some Muslim-majority countries in the nineteenth and twentieth centuries, but has made a comeback in recent years with countries like Iran, Libya, Pakistan, Sudan, and Muslim-dominated northern states of Nigeria reintroducing it in place of, or operating side by side with, Western criminal codes.[23]

19 Clark. B. Lombardi, "Islamic Law as a Source of Constitutional Law in Egypt: The Constitutionalization of the Sharíah in a Modern Arab State", in *Columbia Journal of Transnational Law*, 1998, vol. 37, p. 81.

20 M. Cherif Bassiouni, *The Shari'a and Post-Conflict Justice*, 2010 (on file with the author). See also M. Cherif Bassiouni, *The Shari'a and Islamic Criminal Justice in Time of War and Peace*, Cambridge University Press, Cambridge, 2014.

21 John L. Esposito, "Contemporary Islam: Reformation or Revolution?", in John L. Esposito (ed.), *The Oxford History of Islam*, Oxford University Press, Oxford, 1999, p. 643.

22 Haider Hamoudi, "The Death of Islamic Law", in *Georgia Journal of International and Comparative Law*, 2009, vol. 38, p. 325.

23 Rudolph Peters, *Crime and Punishment in Islamic Law: Theory and Practice from the Sixteenth to the Twenty-first Century*, Cambridge University Press, Cambridge, 2005, p. 124.

9.2.2. Sources of Islamic Law: *Sharí'ah* and *Fiqh*

Islam is a way of life akin to a system that regulates the believer's life and thoughts in line with a certain set of rules.[24] The term 'Islamic law' covers the entire system of law and jurisprudence associated with the religion of Islam. It can be divided into two parts, namely, the primary sources of law (*Sharí'ah* in the strict legal sense) and the subordinate sources of law with the methodology used to deduce and apply the law (Islamic jurisprudence or *fiqh*).[25]

Sharí'ah is derived directly from the *Qur'án* and the *Sunnah*, which are considered by Muslims to be of divine revelation and thus create the immutable part of Islamic law, while *fiqh* is mainly the product of human reason.

9.2.2.1. The *Qur'án* and *Sunnah*

The *Qur'án* is considered by Muslims to be the embodiment of the words of God as revealed to the Prophet Muḥammad through the Angel Gabriel. It is the chief source of Islamic law and the root of all other sources. However, it is far from being a textbook of jurisprudence and is rather a book of guidance on all aspects of the life of every Muslim.[26] The *Qur'án* consists of more than 6,000 verses (*áyát*).[27] Jurists differ on the number of verses, which are of legal subject matter, as they use different methods of classification for determining what constitutes a legal verse – estimates range from eighty up to eight hundred verses.[28]

---

24 Majid Khadduri, "The Modern Law of Nations", in *American Journal of International Law*, 1956, vol. 50, p. 358.

25 Mashood A. Baderin, *International Human Rights and Islamic Law*, Oxford University Press, Oxford, 2005, pp. 32–34. Some scholars use the terms Islamic law, *Sharí'ah* and *fiqh* interchangeably. For example, Kamali consideres *Sharí'ah* to also include *fiqh*, see Kamali, 2008, *supra* note 9.

26 The *Qur'án* (translation by Arthur J. Arberry), 16:89; Mohamed Selim El-Awa, "Approaches to *Sharí'a*: A Response to N.J. Coulson's A History of Islamic Law", in *Journal of Islamic Studies*, 1991, vol. 2. pp. 143–46.

27 6,239 verses (Bassiouni, 2010, see *supra* note 19); 6,235 verses (Kamali, 2008, see *supra* note 9); and 6,666 verses (Irshad Abdal-Haqq, "Islamic Law: An Overview of Its Origin and Elements", in *Islamic Law and Culture*, 2002, vol. 7, p. 27).

28 There are 80 legal verses according to Coulson, 120 according to Bassiouni, 350 according to Kamali, 500 according to Ghazali, and 800 according to Ibn Al-Arabi. Shawkani opines that any calculation can only amount to a rough estimate.

To properly understand its legislation, one has to take into consideration the *Sunnah* as well as the circumstances and the context of the time of the revelation. According to the common understanding of Muslims, the sayings and practices of the Prophet Muḥammad or the *Sunnah*, collected in *ḥadíṯhs,* are the second source of Islamic law.[29] While the *Qur'án* is believed to be of manifest revelation – that is, that the very words of God were conveyed to the Prophet Muḥammad by the Angel Gabriel – the *Sunnah* falls into the category of internal revelation – that is, it is believed that God inspired Muḥammad and the latter conveyed the concepts in his own words.[30] The *Qur'án* and *Sunnah* therefore do not only provide specific rules and answers to particular real life situations but mostly give guidance and examples from which general principles can be derived that have a universal applicability.

9.2.2.2. *Fiqh*

Since the *Qur'án* and *Sunnah* many times do not address specific issues, the Prophet mandated the use of sound reasoning in reaching a judgement.[31] When appointing a judge to Yemen, the Prophet asked him:[32]

> According to what shalt thou judge? He replied: According to the Book of Allah. And if thou findest nought therein? According to the *Sunnah* of the Prophet of Allah. And if thou findest nought therein? Then I will exert myself to form my own judgement. [The Prophet replied] Praise be to God Who had guided the messenger of His Prophet to that which pleases His Prophet.

This concept of exerting one's reasoning in determining a matter of law is called *ijtihád* and it is the essence of *úṣúl al-fiqh,* a legal method of ranking the sources of law, their interaction, interpretation and application.[33] The result of this method is *fiqh*, which literally means human understanding and knowledge on deducing and applying the prescriptions of

29 El-Awa, 1991, p. 153, see *supra* note 26.

30 Kamali, 2008, p. 18, see *supra* note 10.

31 Abdal-Haqq, 2002, p. 35, see *supra* note 27.

32 Said Rammadan, *Islamic Law: Its Scope and Equity*, Macmillan, London, 1970, p. 75.

33 Mohammad Hashim Kamali, *Principles of Islamic Jurisprudence*, 3rd rev., The Islamic Texts Society, Cambridge, 2006, p. 469.

the *Sharí'ah* in real or hypothetical cases.[34] As such it does not command the same authority as that of the *Sharí'ah* and it is the subject of different *Sunní* and *Shí'ah* scholarly and methodological approaches.[35]

When a rule is discerned from the *Qur'án* and *Sunnah* based on analogy from an existing rule, this is referred to as *qiyás*.[36] An example of *qiyás* is the extension of the prohibition of wine to a prohibition of any drug that causes intoxication, because the prevention of the latter is the effective cause of the original prohibition.[37] When learned jurists reach a consensus of opinion on a legal matter (*ijmá'*), a practice established by the companions of the Prophet (*ṣaḥábah*),[38] this is considered a rational proof of *Sharí'ah*.[39] Other methods of determining legal rules within Islamic law include *istiḥsán* (equity in Islamic law), *maṣlaḥah mursalah* (unrestricted considerations of public interest), *'urf* (custom) and *istiṣḥáb* (presumption of continuity).[40]

9.2.3. The Leading Schools of Islamic Jurisprudence (*Madháhib*)

Early interest in law evolved where men learned in the *Qur'án* began discussions of legal issues and assumed the role of teachers.[41] At first students rarely restricted themselves to one teacher and it only became the normative practice in the second half of the ninth century for jurists to adopt a single doctrine.[42] When prominent jurists[43] began to have loyal

---

34 *Ibid.*, pp. 40–41.

35 Bassiouni, 2010, p. 10, see *supra* note 20.

36 See Robert M. Gleave, "Imami Shi'i Refutations of Qiyas", in Bernard G. Weiss (ed.), *Studies in Islamic Legal Theory*, Brill, Leiden, 2002, p. 267: "Refutations of the validity of *qiyás* are to be found in Imámi *Shi'i* collections of reports, all available *Shi'i* works of *úṣúl al-fiqh*, polemics against *Sunní* thought and not infrequently in works of *furú' al-fiqh*". See also Kamali, 2006, p. 264, *supra* note 33. The *'ulama'* (Muslim jurists) are in unanimous agreement that the *Qur'án* and the *Sunnah* constitute the sources of the original case, but there is some disagreement as to whether *ijmá'* constitutes a valid source for *qiyás*, see Kamali, 2008, p. 268, see *supra* note 10.

37 Kamali, 2006, p. 267, see *supra* note 33.

38 Abdal-Haqq, 2002, p. 25, see *supra* note 27.

39 *Ibid.*, pp. 28–29.

40 Kamali, 2006, see *supra* note 33.

41 Wael B. Hallaq, *The Origins and Evolution of Islamic Law*, Cambridge University Press, Cambridge, 2005, p. 153.

42 *Ibid.*

followers which would exclusively apply their doctrine in courts of law, the so-called 'personal schools' emerged and only a few of these leaders were raised to the level of founder of a 'doctrinal school', what is referred to in Islamic law as the *madhhab*.[44] When they emerged, the doctrinal schools did not remain limited to the individual doctrine of a single jurist but possessed a cumulative doctrine in which the legal opinions of the leading jurists were, at best, *primi inter pares.*[45]

The surviving four *Sunní* schools are the *Ḥanafí*, named after Imám Abú Ḥanífah, the *Máliki*, named after Imám Málik, the *Sháfi'í*, named after Imám Al Sháfi'í and the *Ḥanbalí* named after Imám Ibn Ḥanbal. Out of these schools, the *Ḥanafí* school was geographically the most widespread and, for much of Islamic history, the most politically puissant. The *Shí'ah* schools are the Twelvers, the *Ismá'ílí* and the *Zaydí.*[46] Out of these, the Twelvers are the best known and have the largest percentage in Iran and Iraq.[47]

It is hard to find consensus among the various schools and sub-schools; however, some consensus can be found among the four *Sunní* schools and some consensus among the *Shí'ah* schools. This proves that Islamic law is not a monolithic set of rules but rather an evolving body of legislation, depending on several factors at any given time. While the main schools have been dominant in the Islamic legal thought, this does not imply their monopoly on *ijtihád*, nor has it prevented interpretations and deductions from the *Sharí'ah*, which correspond to modern times and the new challenges faced by the Muslim community as well as humanity as a whole.

9.2.4. Categories of Crimes in Islamic Criminal Law

In Islamic law offences have been divided into three categories according to complex criteria which combine the gravity of the penalty prescribed,

43 *Ibid.* Those jurists are Abú Ḥanífah, Ibn Abí Layla, Abú Yúsuf, Shaybání, Málik, Awza'i, Thawri and Sháfi'í.

44 *Ibid.*, p. 157.

45 *Ibid.*, p. 156.

46 *Ibid.*

47 Bassiouni, 2010, see *supra* note 20.

the manner and the method used in incriminating and punishing and the nature of the interest affected by the prohibited act.[48]

The first category is *ḥudúd* crimes. These crimes are penalised by the community and punishable by fixed penalties as required in the *Qur'án* and the *Sunnah*.[49] Both crime and punishment are precisely determined with some flexibility for the judge depending upon the intent of the accused and the quality of the evidence.[50] Mostly there are seven recognised *ḥudúd* crimes: *riddah* (apostasy); *bagh̲í* (transgression); *sariqah* (theft); *ḥirábah* (highway robbery or banditry); *ziná'* (illicit sexual relationship); *qad̲hf* (slander); and *s̲harb al-k̲hamr* (drinking alcohol).[51] It has been argued that these matters cover the most vital areas of collective life (in the following order of priority: religion, life, family, intellect, wealth)[52] and require collective commitment to these values as law.[53] In these offences it is the notion of man's obligation to God rather than to his fellow man that predominates.[54] The state owes the right to Allah to implement the *ḥudúd*.[55]

Opinions vary on which crimes are to be considered *ḥudúd*. Mawardi (of the *S̲háfi'í* school) claims there are four *ḥudúd* offences: adultery, theft, drunkenness, and defamation, while Ibn Rushid and Al Gazali (also of the *S̲háfi'í* school) claim there are seven: apostasy, rebellion, adultery, theft, highway robbery, drunkenness, and defamation.[56] Some of these offences, such as apostasy, adultery, drunkenness, and defamation of religion are clearly in conflict with modern Western legal sys-

---

48 Nagaty Sanad, *The Theory of Crime and Criminal Responsibility in Islamic Law: S̲harí'ah*, University of Illinois, Chicago, 1991, p. 50.

49 Aly Mansour, "Hudud Crimes", in M. Cherif Bassiouni (ed.), *The Islamic Criminal Justice System*, Oceana Publications, New York, 1982, pp. 195–209.

50 Kamali, 2008, p. 161, see *supra* note 10.

51 M. Cherif Bassiouni, "Crimes and the Criminal Process", in *Arab Law Quarterly*, 1997, vol. 12, p. 269.

52 Imran Ahsan Khan Nyazee, *General Principles of Criminal Law: Islamic and Western*, Advanced Legal Studies Institute, Islamabad, 2000, p. 28.

53 El-Awa, 1991, p. 157, see *supra* note 26.

54 Noel Coulson, *A History of Islamic Law*, Edinburgh University Press, Edinburgh, 1964, p. 124.

55 Nyazee, 2000, p. 18, see *supra* note 52.

56 Butti Sultan Al-Muhairi, "The Islamisation of Laws in the UAE: The Case of the Penal Code", in *Arab Law Quarterly*, 1996, vol. 11, p. 363.

tem and a secular international law. It is not surprising, therefore, that based on these categorisations of *ḥudúd* crimes, many believe that there exists an essential incompatibility between Islamic law and international criminal law. However, one has to acknowledge that based on Qur'ánic principles, such as 'no compulsion in religion', some have started to doubt that there is a basis in the primary sources to characterise apostasy or blasphemy as *ḥudúd* offences in the first place. Regardless of an actual or perceived lack of uniformity between Islamic law and international criminal law when it comes to the category of *ḥudúd* crimes, there is no need to criminalise said conduct on an international level and therefore there is no practical conflict between the two systems.

The *Qur'án* unequivocally considers that apostasy amounts to a religious sin. This position can be understood from a number of verses, such as verse 4:137, which refers to "those who have believed, then disbelieved, then believed, then disbelieved". Ibn Kathir says that this verse is characteristic of hypocrites, noting that they "believe, then disbelieve, and this is why their hearts become sealed". However, this verse is notable as it clearly illustrates that apostates could not have been killed for their (un)belief, because had this been the case, they could not have "believed" again. It implicitly proves that the apostate was not to be punished by death, since it mentions a recurrence of apostasy. If the *Qur'án* had prescribed the death penalty for the first instance of apostasy, then such repetition of the 'offence' would not be possible. As former Chief Justice of Pakistan S.A. Raḥmán observed: "The verse visualises repeated apostasies and reversions to the faith, without mention of any punishment for any of these defections on this earth. The act of apostasy must, therefore, be a sin and not a crime".[57] Perhaps a more pertinent conflict presents itself in the context of the second category of crimes in Islamic law, which consists of *qiṣáṣ* and *diyya* crimes. In Islamic law, the punishment prescribed for murder and the infliction of injury is named *qiṣáṣ*, that is, inflicting on the culprit an injury exactly equal to the injury he or she inflicted upon his or her victim. The right to demand retribution or compensation lies with the victim or in cases of homicide the victim's next of kin. Sometimes the relationship between this person and the offender can prevent retaliation.[58]

[57] See Mohamed Elewa Badar *et al.*, "The Radical Application of the Islamist Concept of Takfir", in *Arab Law Quarterly*, 2017, vol. 31, pp. 137–38.

[58] *Ibid.*, p. 48.

Qiṣáṣ and *diyya* crimes fall into two categories: homicide and battery.[59] International criminal law, as it stands, does not allow for the imposition of the death penalty or any other corporal punishment based on the crimes of the offender. In other words, war criminals can only get prison sentences. This may be problematic from the point of view of Muslim societies, who may perceive it as unfair, especially in cases of the worst international crimes.

The third category of crimes in Islamic law is called *ta'zír* crimes. These crimes are punishable by penalties left to the discretion of the ruler or the judge (*qáḍí*). They are not specified by the *Qur'án* or *Sunnah*; any act which infringes private or community interests of the public order can be subject to *ta'zír*.[60] It is the duty of public authorities to lay down rules penalizing such conduct. These rules must however draw their inspiration from the *Sharí'ah*.[61] An example of a *ta'zír* crime is the trafficking of persons. It is not defined in the *Qur'án* or the *Sunnah* but it constitutes a clear violation of the right to personal security, one of the five essentials of Islam.[62]

Ta'zír is used for three types of cases:

1. Criminal acts which must by their very nature be sanctioned by penalties which relate to *ḥudúd*, for example attempted adultery, illicit cohabitation or simple robbery;
2. Criminal acts normally punished by *ḥudúd*, but where by reason of doubt, for procedural reasons or because of the situation of the accused, the *ḥudúd* punishment is replaced by *ta'zír*; and
3. All acts under the provisions of the law, which are not punished by *ḥudúd or qiṣáṣ*.[63]

---

59 M. Cherif Bassiouni, "Quesas Crimes", in M. Cherif Bassiouni (ed.), *The Islamic Criminal Justice System*, Oceana Publications, New York, 1982, p. 203.

60 Ghaouti Benmelha, "Ta'azir Crimes", in M. Cherif Bassiouni (ed.), *The Islamic Criminal Justice System*, Oceana Publications, New York, 1982, p. 213.

61 *Ibid.*

62 United Nations Office on Drugs and Crime, "Combating Trafficking in Persons in Accordance with the Principles of Islamic Law", 13 October 2016, p. 45 (http://www.legal-tools.org/doc/0056b6/).

63 Benmelha, 1982, pp. 213–14, see *supra* note 60.

9.3. Core Principles of Islamic Law Corresponding to Core Principles of International Law

Despite the potential conflicts between the two systems, there are many convergences when it comes to core principles as recognised by both. Some of these are described below.

9.3.1. Islamic Legal Maxims (*Al-Qawá'id Al-Fiqhíyyah*)

An example of the flexibilities which can be found in the Islamic legal traditions and which may prove particularly useful for international criminal law in the future are legal maxims. In public international law, 'maxims of law' are viewed as synonymous with 'general principles of law'.[64] Similarly, in Western legal traditions, maxims play a vital role in the process of judgment. According to a Latin proverb, a general principle is called a maxim because its dignity is the greatest and its authority the most certain, and because it is universally approved by all.[65] For instance, by the time of Coke,[66] the maxim *actus non facit reum nisi mens sit rea*[67] (an act does not make a person guilty unless his mind is guilty) had become well ingrained in common law.

Islamic legal maxims (*al-qawá'id al-fiqhíyyah*), similar to their Western counterparts, are theoretical abstractions in the form usually of

[64] As noted by the English jurist Lord Phillimore in the Proceedings of the Advisory Committee of Jurists, 16 June to 24 July 1920, in *Proces-verbaux* 335, quoted in Frances Freeman Jalet, "The Quest for the General Principles of Law Recognized by Civilized Nations – A Study", in *Los Angeles Law Review*, 1963, no. 10, p. 1046.

[65] "Maxime ita dicta quia maxima est ejus dignitas et certissima auctoritas atque quod maxime omnibus probetur", see Earl Jowitt and Clifford Walsh, *Jowitt's Dictionary of English Law*, 2nd ed., Sweet and Maxwell, London, 1977, p. 1164, quoted in Luqman Zakariyah, *Legal Maxims in Islamic Criminal Law: Theory and Applications*, Brill Nijhoff, Leiden, 2015, p. 55, fn. 154.

[66] See Edwardo Coke, *The Third Part of the Institutes of the Laws of England*, W. Clarke and Sons, London, 1817 ('Coke's Third Institute'), p. 6. The Latin maxim appears in Chapter 1.

[67] James Stephen notes that the authority for this maxim is Coke's Third Institute, where it is cited with a marginal note ('Regula') in the course of his account of the Statute of Treasons. Stephen admits that he does not know where Coke quotes it from, see James F. Stephen, *A History of the Criminal Law of England*, Macmillan, London, 1883, p. 94. Pollock & Maitland traced it correctly back to St. Augustine where the maxim reads "Reum non facit nisi mens rea" and certainly contained no reference to an *actus*; see Frederick Pollock and Frederic William Maitland, *The History of English Law Before the Time of Edward I*, 2nd ed., Cambridge University Press, London, 1923, p. 476.

short epithetic statement that are expressive of the nature and sources of Islamic law and encompassing general rules in cases that fall under their subject.[68] They are different from *úṣúl al-fiqh* (fundamental guiding principles of Islamic jurisprudence) in that the maxims are based on the *fiqh* itself and represent rules and principles that are derived from the reading of the detailed rules of *fiqh* on various themes.[69] One of the main functions of Islamic legal maxims is to depict the general picture of goals and objectives of Islamic law (*maqáṣid al-Sharí'ah*).[70] Today, legal maxims have become "*sine qua non* for any Islamic jurist and judge to master a certain level of rules (*al-qawá'id al-fiqhíyyah*) in order to be able to dispense Islamic verdicts and to pass accurate judgment".[71] As Imám Al-Qarrafi affirms:[72]

> These maxims are significant in Islamic jurisprudence […] By it, the value of a jurist is measured. Through it, the beauty of *Fiqh* [Islamic jurisprudence] is shown and known. With it, the methods of *Fatwá* [legal verdict or opinion] are clearly understood […] Whoever knows *Fiqh* with its maxims (*al-qawá'id al-fiqhíyyah*) shall be in no need of memorizing most of the subordinate parts [of *Fiqh*] because of their inclusion under the general maxims.

Legal maxims aid judges in comprehending the basic doctrines of Islamic law on any contentious issue. For instance, the Islamic legal maxim which calls upon judges to avoid imposing *ḥudúd* and other sanctions when beset by doubts as to the scope of the law or the sufficiency of the evidence is frequently referenced and applied by judges of the Abu Dhabi Supreme Court of the United Arab Emirates.[73] It has been noted that "ex-

68 Mustafa A. Al-Zarqá, *Al-Madkhal al-Fiqhí al-'Amm*, vol. 2, 1983, p. 933.

69 Kamali, 2008, p. 143, see *supra* note 10.

70 Kamali, 2006, p. 78, see *supra* note 6.

71 Zakariyah, 2015, pp. 57–58, see *supra* note 65.

72 A. Al-Qarafi, *Al-Furúq*, vol. 1, p. 3, quoted in Zakariyah, 2015, p. 59, see *supra* note 65.

73 Supreme Court of the United Arab Emirates ('UAE'), Appeal No. 36, Penal Judicial Year 5, Session 9 January 1984; Supreme Court of the UAE, Appeal No. 40, Penal Judicial Year 6, Session 18 January 1985; Supreme Court of the UAE, Appeal No. 32, Penal Judicial Year 13, Session 15 January 1992; Supreme Court of the UAE, Appeal No. 42, Penal Judicial Year 8, Session 1986; Supreme Court of the UAE, Appeal No. 43, Penal/*Sharí'ah* Judicial Year 18, Session 4 May 1996.

ploring this opportunity would also give scholars, judges and jurists of Islamic law the ability to deliver sound and just legal judgments".[74]

It is difficult to trace the precise dates for the emergence of Islamic legal maxims (*al-qawá'id al-fiqhíyyah*) as a distinctive genre of roots of Islamic jurisprudence (*úṣúl al-fiqh*). Suffice to say that *al-qawá'id al-fiqhíyyah* has gone through three stages of development.[75] The first stage (the primitive stage) can be traced back to the seventh century (around 610–632) as the Prophet of Islam was endowed with the use of precise yet comprehensive and inclusive expressions (*jawámi' al-kalim*).[76] Despite the fact that the term *qawá'id* (plural of *qa'idah*) was not explicitly mentioned in the expressions of the Prophet, the prophetic *ḥadí<u>th</u>* are full of expressions of legal maxims. For instance, the *ḥadí<u>th</u>* of '*lá ḍarar wá-lá dirár*' (let there be no infliction of harm nor its reciprocation); '*innamá al-a'mál bil-niyyát*' (acts are valued in accordance with their underlying intentions); and '*al-bayyinah 'alá al-mudda'í wa al-yamín 'alá man ankar*' (the burden of proof is on the claimant and the oath is on the one who denies) are few of those prophetic *ḥadí<u>th</u>s* that emerged as Islamic legal maxims.

The second stage (the florescence stage) where *al-qawá'id al-fiqhíyyah* began to gain popularity was in the middle of the fourth century of *Hijrah* and beyond when the idea of imitation (*al-taqlíd*) emerged and the spirit of independent reasoning (*ijtihád*)[77] was on the edge of extinction.[78] At this stage, legal maxims became recognised as a distinct subject from *úṣúl al-fiqh*.[79] The first visible work on Islamic legal maxims, *úṣúl al-Kar<u>kh</u>í*, was written by the *Ḥanafí* jurist, Ibn Al-Hassan Al-Kar<u>kh</u>í.[80] This was followed by other significant contributions by jurists from other

74 Zakariyah, 2015, pp. 56–59, see *supra* note 65.

75 *Ibid.*, pp. 25–35.

76 *Ibid.*, p. 25.

77 *Ijtihád* (independent reasoning) literally means legal methods of interpretation and reasoning by which a *mujtahid* derives or rationalizes law on the basis of the *Qur'án*, the *Sunnah* or consensus.

78 Zakariyah, 2015, pp. 28–32, see *supra* note 65, pp. 28–32.

79 *Ibid.*

80 <u>Kh</u>aleel Mohammed, "The Islamic Law Maxims", in *Islamic Studies*, 2005, vol. 44, no. 2, pp. 191–96; Wolfhart Heinriches, "Qawa'id as a Genre of Legal Literature", in Bernard Weiss (ed.), *Studies in Islamic Legal Theory*, Brill, Leiden, 2002, p. 369.

madháhib (legal schools), namely the *Sháfi'í*, *Ḥanbalí* and *Máliki* schools.[81]

The Islamic legal maxims reached the stage of maturity (the third stage) around the thirteenth century AH (eighteenth century AD). According to one commentator, "one of the distinctive features of this stage is the establishment of maxims as a separate science in Islamic jurisprudence, while at the same time the formula of their codification was standardized".[82] The *Mejell-i Ahkam Adliyye*, an Islamic law code written by a group of Turkish scholars, in the late nineteenth century, is said to present the most advanced stage in the compilation of Islamic legal maxims.

Islamic legal maxims are divided into two types. The first are those which reiterate the *Qur'án* and the *Sunnah*, whereas the second are those formulated by jurists.[83] The former carry greater authority than the latter. The most expansive collection of legal maxims is known as '*al-qawá'id al-fiqhíyyah al-aslíyah*' (the original legal maxims) or '*al-qawá'id al-fiqhíyyah al-kulíyah*' (the overall legal maxims). These types of maxims stand as the pillars of *úṣúl al-fiqh*; they could be applied broadly to the entire corpus of Islamic jurisprudence; each of these maxims has supplementary maxims of a more specified scope and; there is a consensus among the legal schools over them.[84] The five generally agreed upon maxims are as follows:

1. '*Al-umúr bi-maqáṣidhá*' (acts are judged by their goals and purposes);
2. '*Al-yaqín lá yazálu bi'l-shak*' (certainty is not overruled by doubt);
3. '*Al-mashaqqatu tajlib al-taysír*' (hardship begets facility);
4. '*Al-ḍararu yuzál*' (harm must be removed); and
5. '*Al-'áda muḥakkamah*' (cultural usage shall have the weight of law).

The maxim 'certainty is not overruled by doubt', has several submaxims, one of which reads: 'Knowledge that is based on mere probabil-

81 Kamali, 2006, pp. 142–44, see *supra* note 33.

82 Zakariyah, 2015, pp. 32–35, see *supra* note 65.

83 Heinriches, 2002, pp. 364, 385, see *supra* note 80; Mohammed, 2005, pp. 191–209, see *supra* note 80; Mohammad Hashim, "Sharia and the Challenge of Modernity", in *Journal of the Institute of Islamic Understanding Malaysia*, 1994, vol. 1, reprinted in *Islamic University Quarterly*, 1995, vol. 2.

84 Zakariyah, 2015, p. 55, see *supra* note 65.

ity is to be differentiated from knowledge that is based on certainty' ('*yufarraqu bayn al-'ilmi baynahu idhá thabata yaqínan*'). Two examples are illustrative in this regard: "When the judge adjudicates on the basis of *certainty*, but later it appears that he *might have* erred in his judgment, if his initial decision is based on clear text and consensus, it would not be subjected to review on the basis of a mere probability".[85] This maxim also applies for a "missing person whereabouts is presumed to be alive, as this is the certainty that is known about him before his disappearance. The certainty here shall prevail and no claim of his death would validate distribution of his assets among his heirs until his death is proven by clear evidence. A doubtful claim of his death is thus not allowed to overrule what is deemed to be certain".[86]

It has been observed that "[t]he abstract and synoptic stance of the Islamic Legal maxims gives them elevated level of elasticity and agelessness; and thus makes them related to all current global issues".[87] For example, the legal maxim 'no harming and no counter-harming' derived from the common principles of several *ḥadíths* and Qur'ánic verses, can be taken as a basis for environmental law and also for filling the *lacuna* that exists in international criminal law in terms of environmental crimes.

The provisions from the *Qur'án* and the *Sunnah* on which this maxim is based provide guidelines for elimination of damages caused to environment and also demonstrate the versatility of *Sharí'ah* and its applicability to all matters at any imminent era.[88]

9.3.2. Principle of Legality and Non-Retroactivity

One of the rare provisions set out as a non-derogable norm in all of the major human rights instruments is the *nullum crimen sine lege* rule.[89] Ar-

85 M.A. Barikati, *Qawá'id al-Fiqh*, 1961, pp. 142–43, quoted in Kamali, 2008, p. 145, see *supra* note 10.

86 S.M. Zarqá, *Sharh al-Qawá'id al-Fiqhiyyah*, 1993, p. 382, in Kamali, 2008, p. 145, see *supra* note 10.

87 Muḥammad Shettima, "Effects of the Legal Maxim: 'No Harming and no Counter-Harming' on the Enforcement of Environmental Protection", in *International Islamic University Malaysia Law Journal*, 2011, vol. 19, p. 308.

88 *Ibid.*

89 William A. Schabas, *The International Criminal Court: A Commentary on the Rome Statute*, Oxford University Press, Oxford, 2010, p. 403 with reference to universal and regional human rights instruments. See also Geneva Convention (III) relative to the Treatment of

ticle 22 of the Rome Statute confirms the core prohibition of the retroactive application of criminal law together with other two major corollaries of this prohibition, namely, the rule of strict construction and the requirement of *in dubio pro reo*.[90] The prohibitions of retroactive offences together with the prohibition of retroactive penalties, *nulla poena sine lege*,[91] form the 'principle of legality'.

In Islamic law, there is no place for an arbitrary rule by a single individual or a group.[92] In fact, long before the Declaration of the Rights of Man, which in 1789 first proclaimed the legality principle in Western law, the Islamic system of criminal justice operated on an implicit principle of legality.[93] Evidence of this principle can be found in the following Qur'ánic verses: "We never chastise, until We send forth a Messenger (to give warning)";[94] and "[We sent] Messengers who bear good tidings, and warning, so that mankind might have no argument against God, after the Messengers; God is All-mighty, All-wise".[95]

Islamic law includes a number of legal maxims which complement this principle, for example: "the conduct of reasonable men (or the dictate of reason) alone is of no consequence without the support of a legal text", which means that no conduct can be declared forbidden (*ḥarám*) on grounds of reason alone or on the ground of the act of reasonable men;

Prisoners of War, 12 August 1949, in force 21 October 1950, Article 99 (http://www.legal-tools.org/doc/365095/); Protocol (I) Additional to the Geneva Conventions of 12 August 1949, and Relating to the Protection of Victims of International Armed Conflicts, 8 June 1977, in force 7 December 1978, Article 2(c) (http://www.legal-tools.org/doc/d9328a/); Protocol (II) Additional to the Geneva Conventions of 12 August 1949, and Relating to the Protection of Victims of Non-International Armed Conflicts, 8 June 1977, in force 7 December 1978, Article 6(c) (http://www.legal-tools.org/doc/fd14c4/).

90 See Bruce Broomhall, "Article 22 – *Nullum crimen sine lege*", in Otto Triffterer and Kai Ambos (eds.), *Commentary on the Rome Statute of the International Criminal Court*, 2nd ed., Nomos, Baden-Baden, 2008, p. 714.

91 Statute of the International Criminal Court, 17 July 1998, in force 1 July 2001 ('Rome Statute'), Article 23 (http://www.legal-tools.org/doc/7b9af9/).

92 Kamali, 2008, p. 180, see *supra* note 10.

93 Taymour Kamel, "The Principle of Legality and its Application in Islamic Criminal Justice", in M. Cherif Bassiouni (ed.), *Islamic Criminal Justice System*, Oceana Publications, New York, 1982, pp. 149–50.

94 The *Qur'án*, 17:15, see *supra* note 26.

95 *Ibid.*, 4:165.

rather, a legal text is necessary.[96] Another maxim declares that 'permissibility is the original norm' (*al-aṣl fi'l-ashyáh al-ibáhah*) which implies that all things are permissible unless the law has declared them otherwise.[97] *Sharí'ah* also establishes the rule of non-retroactivity, unless it is in favour of the accused:[98]

> Say to the unbelievers, if they give over He will forgive them what is past; but if they return, the wont of the ancients is already gone![99]

This principle is also mirrored in the tradition of the Prophet. When 'Amr Ibn Al-'Ass embraced Islam, he pledged allegiance to the Prophet and asked if he would be held accountable for his previous transgressions. To this the Prophet replied: "Did you not know, O 'Amr, that Islam obliterates that which took place before it?".[100] Similarly, the Prophet refrained from punishing crimes of blood or acts of usury which had taken place prior to Islam: "Any blood-guilt traced back to the period of ignorance should be disregarded, and I begin with that of Al-Harith Ibn 'Abd Al-Muttalib; the usury practised during that period has also been erased starting with that of my uncle, Al-'Abbás Ibn 'Abd Al-Muttalib".[101]

Ḥudúd crimes are firmly based on the principle of legality as the crimes themselves, as well as the punishments, are precisely determined in the *Qur'án* or the *Sunnah*. *Qiṣáṣ* crimes are bound to specific procedures and appropriate penalties in the process of retribution and compensation and thus also show their basis in the principle of legality.[102] More problematic are *ta'zír* crimes, which according to some schools of thought give very broad discretionary powers to the *Caliph* (ruler) and to the *qáḍí* (judge) with regard to the applicable punishment for particular conduct.[103]

---

96 Kamali, 2008, p. 186, see *supra* note 10.

97 Al-Ghazálí, a-Mustasfá, I, 63; Al-Āmidí, Al-Ihkám, I, 130, in Kamali, 2008, see *supra* note 10.

98 Kamali, 2008, p. 188, see *supra* note 10.

99 The *Qur'án*, 8:38, see *supra* note 26.

100 Muslim, Sahíh Muslim, Kitáb Al-Imán, Báb al-Islam yahdim má qablah wa kadhá al-hijrah wa al-ḥajj; Abú Zahrah, Al-Jarímah, 343 in, Kamali, 2008, p. 186, see *supra* note 10.

101 Taymour Kamel, 1982, p. 151, see *supra* note 93.

102 *Ibid.*, p. 161.

103 Silvia Tellenbach, "Fair Trial Guarantees in Criminal Proceedings Under Islamic, Afghan Constitutional and International Law", in *Zeitschrift für ausländisches öffentliches Recht und Völkerrecht (ZaöRV)*, 2004, vol. 64, pp. 929–41.

While *ta'zír* crimes are for that reason viewed by Western scholars as clearly violating the principle of legality,[104] Muslim scholars have mostly defended the wide discretion given to judges, claiming that this is merely a safeguard which serves to balance the principle of legality and thus avoid the problem of its potential inflexibility.[105]

One might argue that the application of *ta'zír* crimes runs contrary to the principle of legality as the jurisprudence of the UN Human Rights Committee and the European Court of Human Rights expressly states that the law must be adequately accessible and that "a norm cannot be regarded as a law unless it is formulated with the sufficient precision".[106]

9.3.3. Presumption of Innocence

The provision on the presumption of innocence as enshrined in Article 66 of the ICC Statute[107] is threefold and its mechanics are best illustrated by the European Court of Human Rights in *Barberà v. Spain*. It requires, *inter alia*, that when carrying out their duties: (1) the members of a court should not start with the preconceived idea that the accused has committed the offence charged; (2) the burden of proof is on the prosecution; and (3) any doubt should benefit the accused.[108]

Under Islamic law, no one is guilty of a crime unless his guilt is proved through lawful evidence.[109] One of the sub-maxims of the maxim, 'certainty is not overruled by doubt', is the maxim, which reads: 'The norm [of Sharí'ah] is that of non-liability' (*al-aṣlu bará'al-dh-dhimmah*). The prophet is reported to have said "everyone is born inherently pure".[110]

---

104 Taymour Kamel, 1982, p. 157, see *supra* note 93.

105 *Ibid*., p. 151; Mohamed Selim El-Awa, 1991, see *supra* note 26; Ghaouti Benmelha, 1982, see *supra* note 60.

106 European Court of Human Rights, *Case of the Sunday Times v. the United Kingdom*, Judgment, Application no. 6538/74, 6 November 1980, para. 49. (http://www.legal-tools.org/doc/46e326/).

107 Rome Statute, Article 66, see *supra* note 91 (http://www.legal-tools.org/doc/7b9af9/).

108 European Court of Human Rights, *Case of Barberà, Messegué and Jabardo v. Spain*, Judgment, Application no. 10590/83, 6 December 1988, para. 77 (http://www.legal-tools.org/doc/a84e3a/), quoted in William Schabas, "Presumption of Innocence", in Otto Triffterer and Kai Ambos (eds.), *Commentary on the Rome Statute of the International Criminal Court*, 2nd ed., Nomos, Baden-Baden, 2008, p. 1236.

109 Abú Yúsuf, *Kitáb al-Kharáj*, p. 152, quoted in Kamali, 2008, p. 181, see *supra* note 10.

110 Baderin, 2008, p. 103, see *supra* note 18.

According to the legal principle of *istiṣḥáb*, recognised by the *Sháfi'í* and *Ḥanbalí* schools, there is a presumption of continuation of a certain state, until the contrary is established by evidence.[111] Therefore, an accused person is considered innocent until the contrary is proven. In the words of Kamali: "to attribute guilt to anyone is treated as doubtful. Certainty can [...] only be overruled by certainty, not by doubt".[112] The Prophet is reported to have said:

> The burden of proof is on him who makes the claim, whereas the oath [denying the charge] is on him who denies.[113]
>
> Had Men been believed only according to their allegations, some persons would have claimed the blood and properties belonging to others, but the accuser is bound to present positive proof.[114]
>
> Avoid condemning the Muslim to *ḥudúd* whenever you can, and when you can find a way out for the Muslim then release him for it. If the Imám errs, it is better that he errs in favour of innocence (pardon) than in favour of guilt (punishment).[115]

From the latter *ḥadíth*, jurists have derived the general principle and it is agreed by the four major *Sunní* schools that doubt (*shubhah*) also fends off *qiṣáṣ*.[116] The following case is illustrative in this regard:[117]

> During the time of the Muslim polity's fourth *Caliph* 'Alí, Medina's patrol found a man in the town ruins with a blood-stained knife in hand, standing over the corpse of a man who had recently been stabbed to death. When they arrested him, he immediately confessed: "I killed him." He was brought

[111] Kamali, 2006, p. 384, see *supra* note 33.

[112] Kamali, 2008, pp. 145–46, see *supra* note 10.

[113] Al-Bayhaqí, "As-Sunan Al-Kubrá, Kitáb Ad-Da'wá wa Al-Bayyinát, Báb Al-Bayyinah 'alá al-Mudda'á wa al-Yam n 'alá al-Mudda'á 'alayh", in Kamali, 2008, p. 182, see *supra* note 10.

[114] Al Baihagi, *The 40 Hadith of Imam al Nawawi*, No. 33 in Bassiouni, 2010, p. 40, see *supra* note 20.

[115] *Ibid.*; Al Turmuzy, no. 1424; Al Baihagi, No. 8/338; Al Hakim, no. 4384.

[116] Sayed Sikander Shah Haneef, *Homicide in Islam: Legal Structure and the Evidence Requirements*, A.S. Noordeen, Kuala Lumpur, 2000, p. 120.

[117] Quoted in Intisar A. Rabb, "Islamic Legal Maxims as Substantive Canons of Construction: Hudud – Avoidance in Cases of Doubt", in *Arab Law Quarterly*, 2010, vol. 17, pp. 64–65.

> before ‘Alí, who sentenced him to death for the deed. Before the sentence was carried out, another man hurried forward, telling the executioners not to be hast. “Do not kill him. *I* did it,” he announced. ‘Alí turned to the condemned man, incredulously. “What made you confess to a murder that you did not commit?!” he asked. The man explained that he thought that ‘Alí would never take his word over that of the patrolmen who had witnessed a crime scene, he was a butcher who had just finished slaughtering a cow. Immediately afterward, he needed to relieve himself, so entered into the area of the ruins, bloody knife still in hand. Upon return, he came across the dead man, and stood over him in concern. It was then that the patrol arrested him. He figured that he could not plausibly deny having committed the crime of murder. He surrendered himself and confessed to the “obvious”, deciding to leave the truth of the matter in God’s hands. The second man offered a corroborating story. He explained that *he* was the one who had murdered for money and fled when he heard the sounds of the patrol approaching. On his way out, he passed the butcher on the way in and watched the events previously described unfold. But once the first man was condemned to death, the second man said that he had to step forward, because he did not want the blood of *two* men on his hands.

Having realised that the facts surrounding the above case had become doubtful without a fail-safe means to validate one story over the other, the fourth *Caliph* released the first man and pardoned the second.[118]

The system of proof applicable for *ḥudúd* and *qiṣáṣ* makes it very difficult and sometimes almost impossible to prove a crime.[119] On this matter the *Qur’án* states:[120]

> And those who cast it up on women in wedlock, and then bring not four witnesses [to support their allegation], scourge them with eighty stripes, and do not accept any testimony of theirs ever; those – they are the ungodly […].

---

[118] *Ibid.*, p. 66.

[119] Tellenbach, 2004, p. 930, see *supra* note 102.

[120] The *Qur’án*, 24:4, see *supra* note 26.

9.3.4. *Mens Rea*

For the first time in the sphere of international criminal law, and unlike the Nuremberg and Tokyo Charters or the Statutes of the ex-Yugoslavia and Rwanda Tribunals, Article 30 of the Rome Statute[121] provides a general definition for the mental element required to trigger the criminal responsibility of individuals for serious violations of international humanitarian law. This provision is in line with the Latin maxim '*actus non facit reum nisi mens sit rea*', that is, an act does not make a person guilty unless there is a guilty mind. But Article 30 goes still further, assuring that the mental element consists of two components: a volitional component of intent and a cognitive element of knowledge.[122]

In *Sharí'ah*, one of the basic legal maxims agreed upon by Muslim scholars is '*al-umúr bi-maqáṣidhá*', which implies that any action, whether physical or verbal should be considered and judged according to the intention of the doer.[123] The first element of the maxim, *umúr* (plural of *amr*), is literally translated as a matter, issue, act, physical or verbal.[124] The second word is *al-maqáṣid* (plural of *maqaṣad*), which literally means willing, the determination to do something for a purpose.[125] Thus, for an act to be punishable the intention of the perpetrator has to be established. Evidence of this maxim can be found in the *Qur'án* and the *Sunnah*: "[A] man shall have to his account only as he has laboured";[126] "[T]here is no fault in you if you make mistakes, but only in what your hearts pre-meditate. God is All-forgiving, All-compassionate".[127] This stand is further affirmed by the *Sunnah* of the Prophet:

---

121 Rome Statute, Article 30, see *supra* note 91 (http://www.legal-tools.org/doc/7b9af9/).

122 See Mohamed Elewa Badar, "The Mental Element in the Rome Statute of the International Criminal Court: A Commentary from a Comparative Criminal Law Perspective", in *Criminal Law Forum*, 2008, vol. 19, pp. 473–518.

123 Zakariyah, 2015, pp. 60–64, see *supra* note 64. For more details on the concept of intention in Islamic criminal law, see Mohamed Elewa Badar, *The Concept of Mens Rea in International Criminal Law: The Case for a Unified Approach*, Hart Publishing, Oxford, 2013, pp. 208–19.

124 Zakariyah, 2015, p. 64, see *supra* note 65.

125 *Ibid.*, p. 65.

126 The *Qur'án*, 53:39, see *supra* note 26.

127 *Ibid.*, 33:5.

> Actions are to be judged by the intention behind them and everybody shall have what he intends.[128]
>
> Verily, Allah has for my Sake overlooked the unintentional mistakes and forgetfulness of my *ummah* (community) and what they are forced to do.[129]
>
> Unintentional mistakes and forgetfulness of my *ummah* (community) are overlooked.[130]

Yet, the general rule in Sharí'ah is that a man cannot be held responsible for a mere thought. In Islam, a good thought is recorded as an act of piety and a bad thought is not recorded at all until it is acted upon.[131] According to Imám Abou Zahra, an eminent scholar, the criminal intent is the intent to act wilfully, premeditatedly and deliberately with complete consent as to its intended results.[132] Intentional crimes must meet three conditions: premeditation, a free will to choose a certain course of action, and the knowledge of the unlawfulness of the act.[133] The difference between intentional and unintentional results is in the degree of punishment.

The established jurisprudence of the Supreme Federal Court of the United Arab Emirates recognises different degrees of mental states other than the one of actual intent. Most notably, the United Arab Emirates adheres to Málik's school of thought, according to which, in murder cases, it is not a condition *sine qua non* to prove the intent of murder on the part of the defendant; it is sufficient, however, to prove (presumably on grounds of recklessness) that the act was carried out with the purpose of assault and not for the purpose of amusement or discipline. A practical example is set forth in one of Al-Máliki's jurisprudencial sources: "if two people

---

128 Al-Bukhari, *Sahih, ḥadíth* 1; Muslim, *Sahih, ḥadíth* 1599.

129 Sahih Al-Bukhari, vol. 9, p. 65, quoted in Yahaya, Y. Bambale, *Crimes and Punishment in Islamic Law*, Malthouse Press, Ibadan, Nigeria, 2003, p. 7.

130 *Ibid.*

131 Abdullah O. Naseef, *Encyclopedia of Seerah*, The Muslims Schools Trust, London, 1982, p. 741, in Bambale, 2003, p. 6, see *supra* note 129.

132 Muḥammad Abú-Zahra, *Al-Jarima Wal-Uqubа fil Islam*, Dar al Fiqr al 'Araby, Cairo, 1998, p. 396.

133 *Ibid.*, p. 106.

fought intentionally and one of them was killed, retaliation (*qiṣáṣ*) should be imposed on the person who survived".[134]

9.3.5. Standards Used for Determining Intention in Murder Cases

Because the intention of a person is difficult to determine, Muslim jurists do not envisage an exploration of the psyche of the killer, or any extensive examination of behaviour patterns or the gradation of the relationship between the killer and the victim.[135] Instead, they consider the objects used in the crimes described by the relative *ḥadíth* as external standards that are likely to convey the inner working of the offender's mind and thus distinguish between *'amd* (intentional) and *shíbh 'amd* (quasi-intentional).[136]

In drawing analogies from relevant *ḥadíths*, the majority of Muslim scholars concluded that the *mens rea* of murder is found when the offender uses an instrument that is most likely to cause death or is prepared for killing, such as a sword, a spear, a flint or fire.[137] Abú Ḥanífah excluded all blunt instruments, such as a wooden club, from the list of lethal weapons, and claimed they testify to quasi intention, irrespective of the size of the instrument or the force applied.[138] However, he does not exclude an iron rod, relying on the words of the *Qur'án*: "We sent down Iron, wherein is great might, and many uses for men".[139] However, Ḥanífah's disciples, Imám Abú Yúsuf and Imám Muḥammad Al-Shaybání, rebutted his arguments saying that the stone and stick mentioned in the *ḥadíth* refer to a stone and stick which in the ordinary course do not cause death, not just any stone or stick.[140] This is also the opinion of the majority of jurists.[141]

---

134 Supreme Federal Court of the United Arab Emirates, Appeal 52, Judicial Year 14, Hearing, 30 January 1993.

135 Paul. R. Powers, "Offending Heaven and Earth: Sin and Expiation in Islamic Homicide Law", in *Islamic Law and Society*, 2007, vol. 14, p. 42.

136 Badar, 2008, pp. 215–19, see *supra* note 122; Nyazee, 2000, p. 98, see *supra* note 52.

137 The *Qur'án*, 57:25, see *supra* note 26; Haneef, 2000, p. 1, see *supra* note 116.

138 Nyazee, 2000, p. 99, see *supra* note 52; Haneef, 2000, p. 35, see *supra* note 116.

139 The *Qur'án*, 57:25, see *supra* note 26; Nyazee, 2000, p. 99, see *supra* note 52.

140 Imram Abú Jafar Ahmed Ibn Muḥammad Al-Tahawi, *Sharih Ma'ani al-Athar*, Dár Al Kotob Al-Ilmiyah, Beirut, 2013, vol. 3, p. 186, quoted in Haneef, 2000, p. 36, see *supra* note 116.

141 Haneef, 2000, p. 36, see *supra* note 116.

The overall balance between using subjective and objective criteria in determining intent thus tips decidedly in favour of reliance on objective evidence,[142] which seemingly becomes a constituent element of the crime in itself, replacing the actual intent. Accordingly, *Ḥanafí* Ibn Mawdud Al-Musili defines intentional killing as "deliberately striking with that which splits into parts, such as a sword, a spear, a flint, and fire",[143] and *Ḥanbalí* Ibn Qudáma deems intentional any homicide committed with an instrument "thought likely to cause death when used in its usual manner".[144]

9.3.6. Duress and Superior Orders

The Rome Statute recognises two forms of duress as grounds for excluding criminal responsibility, namely duress[145] and duress of circumstances.[146] The latter form is treated by English courts as a defence of necessity.[147] The elements of the two forms are almost identical. Unlike the jurisprudence of the International Criminal Tribunal for the former Yugoslavia, the ICC allows the defence of duress to murder which runs contrary to Islamic law (*Sharí ʿah*) as will be discussed later in this section.

In international criminal law, the defence of superior orders is often confounded with that of duress, but the two are quite distinct. For superior orders to be a valid defence before the ICC three conditions have to be established: the defendant must be under a legal obligation to obey orders of a government or a superior; the defendant must not know that the order was unlawful; and the order must not be manifestly unlawful.[148]

In Islamic law, duress (*ikráh*) is a situation in which a person is forced to do something against his will.[149] The *Qur ʾán* acknowledges such a situation and prescribes: "excepting him who has been compelled, and

---

142 Powers, 2007, p. 48, see supra note 135; Peters, 2007, p. 43, see *supra* note 23.

143 Powers, 2007, pp. 42, 48, see *supra* note 135.

144 *Ibid.*, p. 49.

145 Rome Statute, Article 31(1)(d)(i), see *supra* note 91 (http://www.legal-tools.org/doc/7b9af9/).

146 *Ibid.*

147 See Court of Appeal (Criminal Division) of England and Wales, *R. v. Conway*, Judgement, 28 July 1988, [1988] 3 All ER 1025; Court of Appeal (Criminal Division) of England and Wales, *R. v. Martin*, Judgement, 29 November 1988, [1989] 1 All ER 652.

148 Rome Statute, Article 33, see *supra* note 91 (http://www.legal-tools.org/doc/7b9af9/).

149 Nyazee, 2000, p. 144, see *supra* note 51.

his heart is still at rest in his belief".[150] The Prophet is reported to have said: "My *ummah* will be forgiven for crimes it commits under duress, in error, or as a result of forgetfulness".[151]

Under duress, the person commits a criminal act not as an end in itself but as a means to save himself from being injured. If the threat concerns persons other than the person under compulsion, the *Máliki* consider it duress, some *Ḥanafís* do not, while the *Sháfi'í* and other *Ḥanafís* believe it to be duress only if the threat relates to the father, son or other close relative.[152]

Islamic law recognises two kinds of duress:

1. '*Duress imperfect*' is a kind of duress that does not pose a threat to the life of the agent. For example, the (threat of) confinement for a certain period or subjecting the agent to physical violence which does not pose a threat to his life. This kind of duress has no force in crimes.[153]
2. '*Duress proper*' is a kind of duress where the life of the agent is threatened. Both the consent and the choice of the agent are neutralised. Under duress proper, certain forbidden acts will not only cease to be punishable but will become permissible. These relate to forbidden edibles and drinks. Other acts, such as false accusation, vituperation, larceny and destroying the property of another will remain unlawful, but punishment will be invalidated.[154] However, murder or any fatal offence are unaffected by duress and will become neither permissible acts, nor subject to lenient penalty.[155]

In the situation of duress, *Sharí'ah* disapproves of both courses of action the person under duress can choose from. It prohibits doing harm to others as well as endangering one's own safety. In this situation, two legal maxims apply: 'one harm should not be warded off by its like (another

[150] The *Qur'án*, 16:106, see *supra* note 26.

[151] *Ibid.*; Ibn Majah, *As-Sunan*, *ḥadíths* 2045, in Zakariyah, 2015, p. 72, see *supra* note 65.

[152] Peters, 2007, p. 23, see *supra* note 23.

[153] Abdul Qader Oudah, *Criminal Law of Islam*, vol. 2, Kitábbhavan, New Delhi, 2005, p. 293.

[154] *Ibid.*, pp. 300–03.

[155] *Ibid.*, p. 298.

harm)' and when this is inevitable one should 'prefer the lesser evil'.[156] Therefore, if a person has to choose between causing mild physical harm or being killed, and he chooses the former, his action is justified.[157] In the case of murder, however, both evils are equal, as no person's life is more precious than another's.[158]

The issue of punishment in the case of murder is disputed. Most Islamic scholars agree that there must be retribution (*qiṣáṣ*), however, some prescribe only blood money (*diyát*) on the ground that duress introduces an element of doubt.[159] Within Ḥanífah's school there are three different opinions:

1. Qiṣáṣ must be borne by the forced person, for it is he who actually carried out the criminal act;
3. Neither the person who inflicts duress nor the person under duress shall be punished by qiṣáṣ, as the person who inflicts duress is merely an inciter, while the person under duress, neither has the criminal intent, nor is he satisfied with the result of the act, and blood money should only be paid by the person who compels;[160]
4. Qiṣáṣ should be borne by the person who inflicts, as the person under duress is just a puppet or a tool of murder at the hands of the one who threatens him. For a person it is a lesser evil to choose the death of another than his own. This does not mean however that he will be blameless in the next world, because his sin shall be forgiven by God on the day of judgement.[161]

Insofar as the defence of superior orders is concerned, "Islam confers on every citizen the right to refuse to commit a crime, should any government or administrator order him to do so".[162] The Prophet is reported to have said: "There is no obedience in transgression; obedience is

156 Zakariyah, 2015, pp. 158–72, see *supra* note 65.
157 Abú-Zahra, 1998, p. 379, see *supra* note 132.
158 Zakariyah, 2015, p. 73, see *supra* note 65; Oudah, 2005, p. 306, see *supra* note 153.
159 Peters, 2007, p. 24, see *supra* note 23; Zakariyah, 2015, pp. 151–52, see *supra* note 65.
160 Abú-Zahra, 1998, p. 382, see *supra* note 132; Oudah, 2005, p. 299, see *supra* note 153.
161 Abú-Zahra, 1998, p. 382, see *supra* note 132.
162 Abul A'la Mawdúdí, *Human Rights in Islam*, Islamic Foundation, London, 1980, p. 33.

in lawful conduct only";[163] and "There is no obedience to a creature when it involves the disobedience of the Creator".[164] The order of a competent authority, which implies punishment of death, grievous injury, or imprisonment for the disobedient, will be treated as duress.[165] However, if the order is given by an official who does not have the necessary powers, it will only be treated as duress if the person under his command is sure that if he fails to carry out the order, the means of duress will be applied to him or that the official in question is in the habit of applying such measures when his orders are defied.[166] In other cases, no offender may seek to escape punishment by saying that the offence was committed on the orders of a superior; if such a situation arises, the person who commits the offence and the person who orders it are equally liable.[167]

9.3.7. Rulers are Not Above the Law: Irrelevance of Official Capacity-Immunity

Similar to Article 27 of the ICC Statute (irrelevance of official capacity),[168] in Islamic law there is no recognition of special privileges for anyone and rulers are not above the law. Muslim jurists have unanimously held the view that the head of state and government officials are accountable for their conduct like everyone else.[169] Equality before the law and before the courts of justice is clearly recognised for all citizens alike, from the most humble citizen to the highest executive in the land.[170] A tradition was reported by *Caliph* Umar showing how the Prophet himself did not expect any special treatment: "On the occasion of the battle of Badr, when the Prophet was straightening the rows of the Muslim army, he hit the stomach of a soldier in an attempt to push him back in line. The soldier complained: 'O Prophet, you have hurt me with your stick.' The Prophet

163 Sahíh Muslim, *Kitáb al-Amánah*, Báb Wujúb Tá'at Al-Umará' fí Ghayr Al-Ma'siyah wa Tahrímuhá fi'l-Ma'siyah, *hadíth* 39. This *hadíth* is reported in both Bukhári and Muslim.

164 Abú Dáwúd Al-Sijistání, *Sunan Abú Dáwúd*, *hadíth* no. 2285.

165 Oudah, 2005, p. 295, see *supra* note 153.

166 Hasia Ibn Abideen, vol. 5, p. 112 in Oudah, see *supra* note 153.

167 Mawdúdí, 1980, p. 33, see *supra* note 162.

168 Rome Statute, Article 27, see *supra* note 91 (http://www.legal-tools.org/doc/7b9af9/).

169 Kamali, 2008, p. 180, see *supra* note 10.

170 Mawdúdí, 1980, p. 33, see *supra* note 162.

immediately bared his stomach and said, 'I am very sorry, you can revenge by doing the same to me'".[171]

When a woman from a noble family was brought before the Prophet in connection with a theft and it was recommended that she be spared punishment, the Prophet made his stance on the equality of everyone before the law even clearer: "The nations that lived before you were destroyed by God, because they punished the common man for their offences and let their dignitaries go unpunished for their crimes; I swear by Him (God) who holds my life in His hand that even if Fatima, the daughter of Muḥammad, had committed this crime, then I would have amputated her hand".[172]

9.4. General Remarks and Conclusion

Islamic law has developed over many centuries of juristic effort into a complex reality. The differences between the jurists and schools of Islamic jurisprudence represent "different manifestations of the same divine will" and are considered as "diversity within unity".[173] As noted by Picken:[174]

> Islamic law, like any other, has its 'sources' (*al-maṣádir*); it also has its 'guiding principles' (*al-úṣúl*) that dictate the nature of its 'evidence' (*al-adillah*); it equally employs the use of 'legal maxims' (*al-qawá'id*) and utilises a number of underlying 'objectives' (*al-maqáṣid*) to underpin the structure of its legal theory.

This study shows that Islamic legal maxims, the majority of which are universal, play a vital role in the process of judgment. Thus, the presumption of innocence, the most fundamental right of the accused as enshrined in Article 66 of the ICC Statute, finds its counterpart in the Islamic legal maxim 'certainty is not overruled by doubt' and its sub-maxim 'the norm of [*Sharí'ah*] is that of non liability', a very explicit rule, which obligates judges not to start the trial with the preconceived idea that the accused has committed the offence charged. The second paragraph of Article 66, which stipulates that the burden of proof is on the Prosecution, is

[171] *Ibid.*

[172] *Ibid.*

[173] Kamali, 2006, p. 196, see *supra* note 33.

[174] Gavin Picken, *Islamic Law: Volume 1*, Routledge, 2011, p. 1.

equivalent to the *ḥadíth* which states: "The burden of proof [is] on him who makes the claim, whereas the oath [denying the charge] is on him who denies". But the practice of the ICC says otherwise. Our examination of the law of *mens rea* reveals that there are exceptions regarding the application of the default rule of intent and knowledge to the crimes within the *ratione materiae* of the ICC. The *Lubanga* Pre-Trial Chamber has affirmed that the ICC Elements of Crimes can by themselves "provide otherwise". The Pre-Trial Chamber considered that the fault element of negligence, as set out in the Elements of Crimes for particular offences, can be an exception to the intent and knowledge standard provided in Article 30(1) of the ICC Statute.[175] In such situations, where conviction depends upon proof that the perpetrator had 'reasonable cause' to believe or suspect some relevant fact, the prosecution has not much to do and the burden of proof, arguably, will lie upon the defendant – a practice which apparently conflicts with the above mentioned *ḥadíth*.

As far as the *mens rea* is concerned, the exclusion of recklessness as a culpable mental element within the meaning of Article 30 of the ICC runs in harmony with the basic principles of Islamic law that no one shall be held criminal responsible for *ḥudúd* crimes (offences with fixed mandatory punishments) or *qiṣáṣ* crimes (retaliation), unless he or she has wilfully or intentionally (*'amdan*) committed the crime at issue. The approach followed by Muslim jurists in determining the existence of *mens rea* in murder cases warrants further consideration. They consider the objects used in committing the crime in question as an external factor that are likely to convey the defendant's mental state.

The two systems collide regarding the validity of duress as a general defence to murder. Unlike the ICC Statute, which allows such defence, Islamic jurisprudence has a firm stand on this point as no person's life is more precious than another's. This position is based on the Islamic legal maxim 'one harm should not be warded off by its like (another)'.

Based on this preliminary study and other scholarly works,[176] there is no reason for the Islamic legal system, which is recognised by such a

---

175 ICC, Situation in the Democratic Republic of the Congo, *Prosecutor v. Thomas Lubanga Dyilo*, Pre-Trial Chamber I, Decision on the Confirmation of Charges, ICC-01/04-01/06-803, 29 January 2007, paras. 356–59 (http://www.legal-tools.org/doc/b7ac4f/).

176 Bassiouni, 1982, see *supra* note 59; M. Cherif Bassiouni, "Protection of Diplomats under Islamic Law", in *American Journal of International Law*, 1980, vol. 74, p. 609; Mohamed

considerable part of the world, to be completely disregarded in international criminal law, leading to an unnecessary alienation of the Muslim world. The Islamic legal maxims particularly offer enough flexibility for a wide application, which could be used in the future development of international criminal law. As Rudolph Schlesinger put it:

> The time has come, perhaps, to discard or limit the visionary goal of 'one law' or 'one code' for the whole world and to substitute for it the more realistic aim of crystallizing a common core of legal principles.[177]

M. El Zeidy and Ray Murphy, "Islamic Law on Prisoners of War and Its Relationship with International Humanitarian Law", in *Italian Yearbook of International Law*, 2004, vol. 14, p. 53; Farhad Malekian, "The Homogenity of ICC with Islamic Jurisprudence", in *International Criminal Law Review*, 2009, vol. 9, p. 595; Adel Maged, "Arab and Islamic *Sharí'ah* Perspectives on the Current System of International Criminal Justice", in *International Criminal Law Review*, 2008, vol. 8, p. 477; Steven C. Roach, "Arab States and the Role of Islam in the International Criminal Court", in *Political Studies*, 2005, vol. 53, p. 143.

177 Rudolf B. Schlesinger, "Research on the General Principles of Law Recognized by Civilized Nations", in *American Journal of International Law*, 1951, vol. 51, p. 741. Ambos has noted that a purely Western approach must be complemented by non-Western concepts of crime and punishment, such as Islamic law, to establish and develop a universal system. See Kai Ambos, "International Criminal Law at the Crossroads: From Ad Hoc Imposition to a Treaty-Based Universal System", in Carsten Stahn and Larissa Van den Herik (eds.), *Future Perspective on International Criminal Justice*, T.M.C. Asser, The Hague, 2010, p. 177.

INDEX

‘

‘Abd Al-Salam Ibn Sa‘id Ibn Habib Al-Tanukhi, 87
‘Alá Al-Dín Al-Kásání, 140
‘Alí Ibn Abí Ṭálib, 123
‘Amr Ibn Al-‘Ass, 219
‘Ata’ Ibn Abi Rabah, 89, 98
‘Umar Ibn ‘Abd Al-‘Aziz, 85
‘Umar Ibn Al-Khaṭṭab, 88, 107

A

Abd Al-Rahman Ibn Al-Qasim Al-‘Ataki, 87
Abdelrahman Afifi, 9, 11, 101
Abdullahi Ahmed An-Na’im, 5
Abou El Fadl, 133
Abú Al-Hasan Al-Mawardi, 86
Abú Bakr, 58, 113, 117
Abú Bakr Al-Baghdádí, 136
Abú Bakr Al-Sarakhsi, 90
Abú Ḥanífah, 24, 38, 127, 225, 228
Abú Hurayrah, 115
Abú Isháq Al-Shátibí, 52
Abú Jafar Muḥammad Al-Baqir, 38
Abú Muṣ‘ab Al-Zarqáwí, 136
Abú Zahra, 90
Additional Protocol II to the Geneva Conventions, 121, 130
Afghanistan, 1, 138, 156, 184, 186, 190, 191, 193
African Court of Human and Peoples’ Rights, 147
African Union, 160
Ahmad Nassar, 183
Ahmed Al-Dawoody, 6, 9, 12, 121
Ahmed Ibn Ḥanbal, 38
Al Gazali, 210
Albania, 186, 192
Al-Bayḍáwí, 71
Al-Bukhari, 29
Alexander Boldizar, 73
Alfred Guillame, 29
Alfred P. Rubin, 63
Algeria, 138, 150, 195
Al-Ghazálí, 40
Ali Khashan, 163
Al-Málikí, 224
Al-Mawardi, 99, 210
Al-Qaeda, 6, 136
Al-Qarafi, 33
Al-Ramlí, 140
Al-Shabáb, 59, 80, 155
Al-Shaybání, 40, 57, 80, 117
Al-Shirbíní, 140
Al-Suyuti, 94
Al-Tabari, 99
Al-Zuhayli, 90
Amanda Alexander, 56
Amnesty International, 129
Andrew Novak, 65
Anwar Sadat, 94
Arab League, 163
Arab Spring, 129, 161, 164, 182
Asma Afsaruddin, 8, 11, 83
Ayatullah Khomeini, 182
Azar Gat, 69
Azerbaijan, 184, 205

B

Bahrain, 150, 184, 191, 195, 205
Bangladesh, 184, 186, 190
Barack Obama, 137
Benin, 186
Bernard G. Weiss, 34
Boko Ḥarám, 59, 80
Bosnia and Herzegovina, 2, 62, 191, 192
Brunei Darussalam, 184, 191, 196
Burkina-Faso, 186

C

Cairo Declaration on Human Rights in Islam, 62
Cambodia, 2
Charles C. Hyde, 64

Charles Dukes, 171
Charles Habib Malik, 171
Chechnya, 138
China, 56, 197
Christianity, 88, 98, 126, 139, 170
colonialism, 41, 169, 182, 205
Comoros, 186
Convention on Combating International Terrorism, 169
core international crimes, 2
Cote D'Ivoire, 186
crime of aggression, 2, 64, 74, 194
crimes against humanity, 2, 64, 74, 159, 167, 196

D

Dagestan, 138
David A. Schwartz, 119
David Kennedy, 68
democracy, 4, 181
Djibouti, 186
domestic criminal law, 79
domestic law
  repugnancy clauses, 156
  Sharí'ah law clause, 154
domestic legal systems, 78
due process, 78, 142, 183

E

Edwardo Coke, 213
Egypt, 23, 94, 129, 138, 150, 158, 171, 184, 191, 196, 205
Ethiopia, 171
European Court of Human Rights, 147
  Barberà v. Spain, 220
  The Sunday Times v. the United Kingdom, 220
Extraordinary Chambers in the Courts of Cambodia, 2

F

fair trial, 78, 130, 165, 168, 183
Fakhr Al-Din Al-Razi, 86, 98
Farhad Malekian, 6, 66, 67
First World War, 151

G

Gaafar Muḥammad An-Nimeiri, 182
Gabon, 187
Gambia, 187
Geneva Conventions, 56, 121, 130
genocide, 1, 2, 11, 54, 63, 64, 69, 74, 99, 167, 196
Ghassame Ghani, 171
Ghulam Ahmad Parwez, 29
Gideon Boas, 47, 70
Guinea, 187
Guyana, 187

H

Hague Convention (II), 56
Hague Convention (III), 56
Hersch Lauterpacht, 171
Hosni Mubarak, 158
human rights, 4, 8, 42, 70, 81, 142, 171, 182

I

Ibn Al-Hassan Al-Karkhí, 215
Ibn Kathir, 211
Ibn Mawdud Al-Musili, 226
Ibn Qudama, 90, 112, 226
Ibn Rushid, 210
Ibn Taymiyyah, 40, 123
Idris Al-Sháfi'í, 28, 38, 99
Ignác Goldziher, 29
Ilias Bantekas, 69
Imám Abou Zahra, 224
Imám Al-Qarrafi, 214
Imám Muḥammad Al-Shaybání, 225
India, 21, 56, 197
Indonesia, 184, 186, 194
Inter-American Court of Human Rights, 147
International Committee of the Red Cross, 121
International Court of Justice, 148
  Statute, 46
International Covenant on Civil and Political Rights, 61
International Criminal Court, 9, 63

complementarity, 167, 172, 188, 191, 198
drafting of the Statute, 175
Elements of Crimes, 231
legitimacy, 14
Muslim state practice, 158, 175, 199
Office of the Prosecutor, 160, 172, 191
participation of Muslim states, 4, 13
Prosecutor v. Al Mahdi, 201
Prosecutor v. Bosco Ntaganda, 161
Prosecutor v. Thomas Lubanga Dyilo, 160, 231
Prosecutor v. William Samoei Ruto and Joseph Arap Sang, 161
Rome Conference, 175, 184, 201
Statute, 1, 13, 46, 65, 135, 150, 157, 202, 218, 220, 229
international criminal justice
holistic perspective, 10, 55, 67
legal dimension, 78
moral dimension, 73
political dimension, 75
social dimension, 68
international criminal law, 1, 54, 63
complementarity, 152
death penalty, 196
diplomatic immunity, 229
duress, 226
enforced pregnancy, 196
mens rea, 223
non-international armed conflict, 195
nulla poena sine lege, 218
nullum crimen sine lege, 217
presumption of innocence, 220
superior orders, 226
universality, 4, 11, 13, 47
International Criminal Tribunal for Rwanda, 65
Statute, 223
International Criminal Tribunal for the former Yugoslavia, 1, 65, 226
Statute, 223
international human rights law, 54, 60, 162, 176, 188, 217
international humanitarian law, 54, 55, 103, 151, 168, 176
universality, 11
international law
'object and purpose' principle, 11, 48
state practice, 13
International Military Tribunal, 65
Charter, 223
International Military Tribunal for the Far East, 65
Charter, 223
Iran, 23, 150, 155, 171, 182, 184, 190, 196, 205, 209
Iraq, 1, 10, 23, 45, 59, 136, 150, 171, 184, 205
Islamic law
al-siyar, 80
criteria for consideration as *bugháh*, 124
development of, 84
distinction between rebels and armed criminals, 126
diyya offences, 211
fatwá, 139
interpretation of the *Qur'án*, 84, 101, 107
judicial discretion, 220
jurisdiction, 141, 151
legal maxims, 105
madhhab (doctrinal school), 209
maxims, 213
mujtahid (jurist), 5, 11, 20, 24, 28, 33, 34, 36, 50, 84, 89, 90, 98, 103, 111, 123, 172, 203
of war, 11, 103, 107, 111
on defence of superior orders, 228
on diplomatic immunity, 229
on legality, 218
on *mens rea*, 224
on non-international armed conflicts, 6, 12, 122
on non-retroactivity, 218
on treatment of *bugháh* (armed rebels, separatists), 12, 122, 123
on treatment of *khawárij*, 12, 122, 130
on treatment of *muḥáribún*, 12, 122, 133
on treatment of *murtaddún* (apostates), 12, 122
on treatment of *mushrikún* (polytheists), 85, 87, 94
on use of force, 42, 127
on war, 83
penalties, 228

perspective on amnesty, 110
perspective on justice, 13, 109, 173
perspective on prisoners of war, 116
plurality of, 177, 199, 202
presumption of innocence, 220
principle of non-combatant immunity, 87, 88, 90
prohibition against destruction of property, 88, 115
prohibition of mutilation, 114
qáḍí (judge), 219
relation to domestic legal systems, 154, 205
relation to international criminal justice, 46
relation to international criminal law, 2, 4, 6, 13, 63, 145, 169, 175, 198, 202
relation to international human rights law, 5, 60
relation to international humanitarian law, 6, 11, 55, 97, 101, 118, 125
relation to international law generally, 146
relation to *Qur'ánic* principle of non-aggression, 11, 84, 88, 107
relation to *Qur'ánic* principle of non-coercion, 90
relation to ratification of ICC Statute, 13, 150
rules of engagement with rebels, 128
siyar (Islamic international law), 7, 12, 57, 83, 122
socio-legal norms, 10, 45, 46, 53, 60
ta'zír offences, 212
treatment of *mus̲h̲rikún* (polytheists), 92

Islamic law perspective on justice, 179

Islamic law, categories of offences in, 180
ḥudúd, 60, 79, 123, 133, 142, 156, 180, 181, 210, 219
qiṣáṣ, 79, 180, 211, 219
ta'zír, 60, 79, 180, 219

Islamic law, concepts of
'adl (justice), 179, 198
al-ma'rúf (common good), 60
al-maṣlaḥah (interest), 104, 112
al-moṣalaḥah (well-being), 52
amán (quarter), 135
combative *jihád*, 88, 91
diyát (blood money), 180, 199
fasád, 66
fasád fí al-'arḍ (corruption in the land), 133
fatwá (expert legal opinion), 104
ikráh (duress), 226
iṣmat al-anbiyá (Prophetic infallibility), 26
jihád, 11, 12, 83, 103, 108, 122
k̲h̲urúj, 123, 126, 131
maqáṣid (purposes, objectives), 11, 12, 48, 104, 106, 119, 149, 214
maṣlaḥah mursalah (unrestricted considerations of public interest), 208
munáẓarah (debate), 127
non-combatant immunity, 11, 84, 109, 111
proportionality, 109
s̲h̲awkah, man'ah, fay'ah, 124, 137
siyásah al-S̲h̲arí'ah (*S̲h̲arí'ah*-oriented policy), 12, 104, 106, 119
ta'áwwun (co-operation), 61
takfír (excommunication), 139
tawḥíd (unity of God), 22
ta'wíl, 126, 134, 138
ẓulm (injustice), 179

Islamic law, development of, 15, 23

Islamic law, juristic techniques of, 24, 32, 179
ijmá' (consensus of opinion), 16, 36, 105, 208
ijtihád (independendent legal reasoning), 215
ijtihád (independent legal reasoning), 16, 34, 40, 53, 102, 207
istiḥsán, 25, 208
istiṣḥáb (presumption of continuity), 208
qiyás (analogy), 105, 208
takhsis, 93
taqlíd (imitation), 12, 35, 39, 102, 119, 215
uṣúl al-fiqh, 215
úṣúl al-fiqh, 22, 158

Islamic law, primary sources of, 16, 22, 104, 206
the *ḥadít̲h̲*, 27, 207

the *Qur'án*, 16, 22, 51, 83, 101, 105, 179, 206
the *Sunnah*, 25, 51, 57, 83, 101, 105, 179, 207
Islamic law, secondary sources of, 32
fiqh (jurisprudence), 4, 22, 104, 206
Islamic law, *Shí'ah* schools of
Ja'farí, 38
Islamic law, sources of, 10, 15
Islamic law, specific offences in
baghi (transgression), 180, 210
ḥirábah, 125, 133, 140, 180, 210
qadhf, 210
riddah (apostasy), 180, 210
sariqah (theft), 180, 210
sharb al-khamr (drinking alcohol), 180, 210
ziná' (sexual relations outside marriage), 180, 181, 210
Islamic law, *Sunní* schools of, 130, 158
Ḥanafí, 38, 125, 141, 156, 209, 215, 227
Ḥanbalí, 38, 123, 125, 132, 133, 142, 209, 216, 221
Málikí, 38, 86, 123, 133, 136, 140, 142, 209, 216, 224, 227
Sháfi'í, 38, 86, 123, 126, 209, 210, 216, 221, 227
Islamic legal traditions
plurality of, 3
Islamic State of Iraq and Syria, 1, 6, 14, 59, 80, 122, 136
grounds for prosecution, 122, 136
Islamic State of Iraq and the Levant. *See* Islamic State of Iraq and Syria
Israel, 163, 197

J

Jafar Sadiq, 38
Jamil Baroody, 172
Japan, 56
John L. Esposito, 26, 37, 41
Jordan, 150, 185, 192, 196
Joseph Schacht, 21, 29
Judaism, 88, 95
jus ad bellum, 9, 11, 84, 103
jus cogens, 7
jus in bello, 9, 11, 88, 101, 110

K

Kazakhstan, 185, 191
Kenya, 59
Kofi Annan, 62, 68
Kuwait, 150, 185, 191
Kyrgyzstan, 185

L

League of Nations, 151
Lebanon, 1, 151, 170, 184, 194, 197, 205
Liberia, 171
Libya, 1, 10, 45, 138, 151, 155, 173, 185, 193, 196, 205
Louise Arbour, 76
Luis Moreno-Ocampo, 163

M

M. Cherif Bassiouni, 6, 55, 57, 186, 189, 199, 205
Malaysia, 181, 185, 191, 194
Maldives, 164
Mali, 187
Málik Ibn Anas, 38, 86
Martti Koskenniemi, 73
Mashood A. Baderin, 8, 10, 45
Mauritania, 150
Max H. Hulme, 49
Mohamed Elewa Badar, 9, 13, 201
Mohammad Hashim Kamali, 36, 221
Mohammed Morsi, 159
Morocco, 150, 185, 191, 194
Mu'tazila, 29
Muadh Ibn Jabal, 35
Muḥammad 'Imara, 90
Muḥammad Abduh, 90
Muḥammad Al-Sháfi'í, 88
Muḥammad Hamidullah, 58, 77
Muḥammad Zia-ul-haq, 182
Muhammed Abú Zahrah, 102
Mujahid Ibn Jabr, 84, 98
Muqatil Ibn Sulayman, 85, 98
Muslim Brotherhood, 159
Muslim Ibn Al-Hajjaj, 29
Muslim minority groups, 1
Bosniaks, 2
Cham, 2

Rohingya, 1, 14
Myanmar, 1

N

Niger, 185, 187, 191
Nigeria, 1, 59, 138, 150, 155, 181, 187, 191, 205
Noel J. Coulson, 31
Non-Aligned Movement, 194
non-international armed conflict, 121

O

Oman, 150, 185, 191
Omar Al-Bashir, 162
Omar Ibn Abdul Aziz, 110
Omar Ibn al Khittab, 179
Onder Bakircioglu, 8, 10, 15
Organisation of Islamic Cooperation, 66, 175, 204
Organisation of the Islamic Conference, 169
Osman Ebeid, 171
Outi Korhonen, 73

P

Pakistan, 138, 150, 156, 181, 185, 186, 191, 195, 205
Palestine, 162, 187
Philippines, 150
Prince Zeid Ra'ad Zeid Al Hussein, 186, 192
Prophet Muḥammad, 16, 25, 35, 36, 51, 52, 57, 72, 74, 83, 104, 207, 219, 227, 229

Q

Qatar, 98, 151, 156, 185, 191

R

Ramesh Thakur, 76
reformist movements, 41
Republic of Ireland, 196
Rome Statute. *See* International Criminal Court:Statute
Rudolph Peters, 177, 181
Rudolph Schlesinger, 232
rule of law, 10, 42, 62, 68, 76, 105
Rwanda, 62, 65, 173, 223

S

Satwant Kaur Heer, 13, 175
Saudi Arabia, 138, 151, 156, 170, 181, 185, 195, 205
Sayyid Abul A'lá Mawdúdí, 72
Sayyid Ahmad Khan, 29
Sayyid Qutb, 71
Second World War, 151
Senegal, 187
Shaheen Sardar Ali, 9, 13, 175
Sharí'ah. *See* Islamic law
Shí'ah denomination of Islam, 205
Shí'ah denomination, branches of
  Ismá'ílí, 209
  Twelvers, 209
  Zaydí, 209
Sierra Leone, 187
Siraj Khan, 9, 13, 145
Sohail S. Hashmi, 40
Somalia, 59, 150, 155
South Africa, 171
Steven Roach, 183
Sudan, 150, 155, 156, 166, 181, 191, 195, 205
Sunní denomination, 204
Surinam, 187
Syria, 1, 10, 14, 23, 45, 59, 80, 136, 150, 171, 185, 195, 205

T

Tafsir Al-Tabari, 85, 86, 87, 99
Tajikistan, 185
Tallyn Gray, 1
Tariq Ramadan, 22, 179
transitional justice, 1, 14, 62, 173
Tunisia, 150, 163, 185, 195, 205
Turkey, 185, 191, 195, 205

U

Uganda, 187, 196
Umar Ibn Al-Khaṭṭáb, 114
ummah (Muslim community), 2, 5, 14, 52, 204
United Arab Emirates, 150, 155, 185, 191, 195, 214, 224
United Kingdom
- *R. v. Conway*, 226
- *R. v. Martin*, 226

United Nations, 204
- Charter, 153
- Commission on Human Rights, 171
- Convention on the Elimination of All Forms of Discrimination Against Women, 188
- Convention on the Rights of the Child, 149, 188
- Development Programme, 165
- High Commissioner for Human Rights, 76
- Human Rights Committee, 220
- Peacekeeping, 121
- Secretary-General, 62, 68, 166
- Security Council, 66, 76, 153, 167

United States of America, 137, 153, 176, 183, 197
Universal Declaration of Human Rights, 60, 163, 170
Usmani Sháfi', 72
uti possidetis, 170
Uzbekistan, 184

V

Vienna Convention on the Law of Treaties, 49, 168

W

Wahhábi denomination of Islam, 124
wahy (divine revelations), 17
war crimes, 2, 46, 54, 62, 69, 74, 135, 138, 167
Werner Menski, 5

Y

Yasser Arafat, 162
Yazid Ibn Abi Sufyan, 117
Yazid Ibn Sufyan, 113
Yazidi, 139
Yemen, 10, 35, 45, 114, 138, 150, 156, 185, 207
Yusuf Al-Qaradawi, 98

Z

Zaid Ibn Thábit, 18

TOAEP TEAM

OTHER VOLUME IN THE NUREMBERG ACADEMY SERIES

Linda Carter and Jennifer Schense (editors):
Two Steps Forward, One Step Back: The Deterrent Effect of International Criminal Tribunals
Torkel Opsahl Academic EPublisher
Brussels, 2017
Nuremberg Academy Series No. 1 (2017)
ISBN: 978-82-8348-186-0

All volumes are freely available online at http://www.toaep.org/nas/. For printed copies, see http://toaep.org/about/distribution/. For reviews of earlier books in this Series in academic journals and yearbooks, see http://toaep.org/reviews/.

CPSIA information can be obtained
at www.ICGtesting.com
Printed in the USA
BVHW092020131118
533032BV00005B/32/P

9 788283 481884